Robert Harley is a
uate of the Royal C
high technology products received a string of awards throughout the 1980s including a Design Council Award for a revolutionary telephone and *The Sunday Times* Personal Computer of the Year. In 1989 he, together with a partner, set up a new company, Fresco Group, specializing in the development of new consumer products. He has always been fascinated with biorhythms and it was his own success with a biorhythmically controlled diet that inspired him to devise the *Bodyclock* Diet.

The BODYCLOCK Diet

ROBERT HARLEY

SPHERE BOOKS LIMITED

A *Sphere* Book

First published in Great Britain in 1991
by Sphere Books Ltd,

Typeset by Leaper & Gard Ltd, Bristol, England
Printed and bound in Great Britain by
Cox & Wyman Ltd, Reading

ISBN 0 7474 1030 5

Sphere Books Ltd
A Division of
Macdonald & Co (Publishers) Ltd
165 Great Dover Street
London SE1 4YA
A member of Maxwell Macmillan Publishing Corporation

Contents

Acknowledgements

Thanks to all the dieters, professionals and technicians who have helped to make the *Bodyclock* Diet possible. Your generosity and encouragement have been remarkable.

I am especially grateful to Jenny Lacey for her skill, enthusiasm and commitment throughout the project.

Preface

At the turn of the century two medical scientists, working independently, unwittingly made the same startling discovery – one that was to intrigue and baffle scientists around the world. Dr Hermann Swoboda in Vienna and Dr Wilhelm Fleiss in Berlin concluded that we are built not just of flesh and blood but also of *time*.

Using extensive collections of data, they were able to demonstrate that we all have an internal 'bodyclock' which regulates the rhythmical ebb and flow in our body energies – effectively making us different from one day to the next. These rhythmical biological forces became known as 'biorhythms'; they naturally create the 'highs' and 'lows' which impact the lives of the human species – invisibly influencing every aspect of our existence. We all know that we feel some days are 'up' and others are 'down' – but what we are not aware of is that these physical, emotional and intellectual variations are in regular sequence, which can be forecast.

Was this another crank scientific theory? Far from it. Such was the regard for their important discovery that Fleiss became President of the German Academy of Sciences, a member of the Berlin Board of Health and Sigmund Freud's own physician, whilst Swoboda was awarded a special medal and an honorary degree from the University of Vienna.

Over the last 90 years, major scientific organizations such as NASA and commercial interests such as large insurance companies in Japan and Switzerland have developed and augmented the observations of this phenomenon. Even electronics giants Olivetti and Casio have taken an active interest and produced special computers dedicated to predicting these fascinating rhythms.

The *Bodyclock* has been designed to monitor and forecast your individual daily rhythms, and show how you are likely to feel and perform in the future. Like all the best ideas, this is not new – in fact, the original biorhythm calculator was created by Dr Swoboda to accompany his book *The Critical Days of Man* in 1909 – the same year the aeroplane made history by flying across the English Channel and Hollywood produced its first film.

The Bodyclock Diet shows how knowledge of your daily rhythms can be used not only to enhance your life, but also to create a completely new and effective diet strategy.

CHAPTER ONE

What makes the *Bodyclock* Diet different?

We are surrounded today by a myriad range of diets and body-shaping programmes. Books, magazines, videos, television – they are everywhere. Some have now become household names because of the famous personality involved, the catchy title or some unusual food strategy. Some diet plans even have sequels.

What is the difference between all these plans? Dietary research has clearly established that there are no miracle foods – none, that is, until the food industry succeeds in developing a one-calorie chocolate cake! Neither are there any miracle solutions or quick fixes. The fact is that for sound reasons the best diets are very similar and based upon similar strategies.

Our bodies have evolved over many thousands of years to thrive on certain foods. In our modern world of plenty, the typical Western diet has become out of balance with the requirements of our health and, more obviously, our appearance. The symptoms of this imbalance are body fat, and the frightening and increasingly widespread number of diseases associated with overeating and a bad diet.

Most experts now agree that the typical Western diet generally contains:

Too much:

Saturated and other fats, sugar, salt, additives, processed foods, animal products, alcohol.

Too little:

Fresh fruit and vegetables, dietary fibre, balanced selection, pure drinks.

Armed with this simple information, almost any competent domestic science student could probably devise a diet as likely to be effective as the many famous-name diet programmes – which is precisely why there are so many diet plans around today.

But that is not the end of the story; in fact, it's just the beginning. The bad news is that only a tiny percentage of dieters have any real success with even the best conventional diets. The successful are the exception rather than the rule, and the overwhelming majority of dieters return to their original weight within one year. So in the face of all this sound dietary knowledge, why is there such a high failure rate?

Diet plans typically vary considerably from the good to the not-so-good – despite the fact that they are all invariably endorsed by medical, nutritional or fitness experts. The criteria by which all diets should be judged are:

- *How much excess fat (not weight) you lose*
- *How easy and how healthy the diet is*
- *How long the results last*

Horror stories of failure on the poor quality diet

plans are now fairly well known. Typically they include reports such as:

> 'All I seemed to lose was water and lean tissue instead of ugly fat.'
> 'My metabolism slowed down so much that it became impossible to lose fat.'
> 'I rebounded to my previous weight immediately the diet stopped.'

Most people fail on even the best diet plans, and there is one single reason for this. Talk to any failed dieter and, not surprisingly, you will invariably get the same explanation: *lack of willpower*.

Dieting is difficult – and there are many temptations and pitfalls. The best conventional diets need a lot of determination and discipline to make them work, which is why so many people fail on them.

What do we mean by willpower? It is certainly not the same experience for everybody; in fact, it tends to be used as a general description to cover a whole mix of changing physical and emotional sensations. But why should willpower have so much influence on such a basic issue as eating?

Willpower affects our eating simply because eating is not a straightforward 'Am I hungry?' decision. As babies, the sensation of sucking sweet warm milk is usually the first and most important pleasurable emotional experience. As children we learn that treats, rewards and times of celebration are invariably associated with sweets, chocolate or ice cream. Therefore, it is hardly surprising that we grow up eating and selecting foods for all kinds of reasons other than our basic physical needs – such as habit, comfort, taste, smell, appetite, visual appeal, reward, entertaining, being part of a group and so on.

How does lack of willpower ruin a diet? Typically, we embark on a conventional diet with good intentions and then lapse or give up soon afterwards. It is all too easy to abandon the resolve and determination we have several days earlier and decide to take a 'holiday' from our diet or a 'reward' for some small progress made. Sometimes we simply choose to forget momentarily that we are on a diet at all when in the face of temptation.

Failure on conventional diets is so often a process of positively deciding to reshape ourselves on a day when we are 'up' and then abandoning the plan on a day when we are 'down' – or sometimes deciding to lose weight for all the wrong reasons when we are 'down', and then simply letting go of our negative ideas when we are 'up'. These rhythmical ups and downs are precisely the same biorhythms as observed by Fleiss and Swoboda so long ago, and described briefly in the preface. They affect every aspect of our lives, and the physical and emotional components that make up our willpower are no exception. An even more surprising aspect of these rhythms is that we are more likely to successfully lose weight on some days rather than others.

'Everything is possible with time and effort', the saying goes, but conventional diets rely too much on effort and not enough time ... and timing. Just as nature has its seasons, so does your body. A good diet needs to go with the flow' and synchronize with your rhythmical body energies. Few dieters experience pleasant feelings or achieve satisfaction on diet programmes that cut across, or are out of step with, their 'body time'. Every part of your being is harmonized to these natural rhythms.

The *Bodyclock* itself can be set to show and accurately forecast your 'body time', so you can not only see how you are predisposed to feel and perform today, but also look ahead to see how you are likely to fare in the future. You can see the potential for good days and bad days in all aspects of your life, including dieting.

The *Bodyclock* Diet strategy

Body fat was vital to our prehistoric ancestors in dealing with the practicalities and dangers of day-to-day living in an uncivilized world. Fat provided a valuable energy store and thermal insulation. Females needed extra fat to provide protection for unborn babies and to create distinctive sexual shaping. Fat even served as a storage place for some toxins that could not be processed quickly by other organs.

Twentieth-century farming techniques, housing, supermarkets, clothing, central heating, transport and medical science, have gradually made superfluous most of the original functions of body fat, which has now become a major health threat rather than a health safeguard. What is more, in modern times when slim body shapes are generally regarded as attractive, the fully-rounded female figure which would have made our cave-man ancestors swoon with desire is frequently a major source of unhappiness, embarrassment and frustration.

That our bodies attempt to retain excess fat is a legacy of our prehistoric evolution. They are naturally programmed to conserve fat in times of plenty as a safeguard against possible future food shortages. We have to *trick* our bodies into naturally letting go of their fat stores, and the most effective tricks we can use are not only to implement a better way of eating and living, but also to make these changes in time with our natural rhythms.

A healthy body will naturally shed unwanted fat far more readily than an unhealthy one, so the *Bodyclock* Diet aims to improve all-round health as part of the process of losing weight and improving physical appearance. However, it should not be considered as a cure or as a substitute for advice from your doctor. As with all diet plans, you are strongly recommended to consult your medical adviser before starting the *Bodyclock* Diet, to ensure that any changes in diet and lifestyle are fully compatible with your individual medical profile.

There are no drugs, crank foods or man-made potions involved – only a basic understanding of our bodies' natural rhythms and the best unrefined natural foods, in accordance with the best medical advice on healthy dietary habits. The *Bodyclock* Diet aims to become part of a fulfilled lifestyle, not to be temporary 'punishment'. The diet includes recipes with the most effective food combinations, together with advice on simple exercise. The *Body-clock* Diet plan also works in conjunction with your *Bodyclock* to enable you to:

- *Start your diet at your best 'body time' for fat loss*
- *Deal effectively with the 'danger' days*
- *Rhythmically harmonize your diet in order to improve long-term weight loss*
- *Feel good and have fun during the diet*
- *Enjoy long-term benefits after the diet has finished*

By following the *Bodyclock* Diet, you should not only lose weight quickly and substantially improve your health, but also find dieting easier than ever before and a more effective long-term solution. It is possible to achieve good results quite quickly and healthily as long as you ask your body to do what comes naturally – *when* it comes naturally.

The importance of the diet as a long-term solution is underlined by recently published medical studies carried out in Framingham, Massachusetts. The doctors involved concluded that fluctuations in body weight associated with failed dieting, may have 'negative health consequences independent of obesity'. This research clearly indicates that while it is dangerous to be overweight, we appear to increase the risks to our health by *temporary* weight loss.

Many people will have their own preferred diet for reasons of familiarity, allergies, culture or simply taste. The good news is that the *Bodyclock* Diet can be used as an adjunct to assist any reputable diet plan to become more effective. The principles can also be employed to increase the effectiveness of any exercise plan or body-shaping regime.

Although the *Bodyclock* Diet is unique in the way it harmonizes the weight loss process with the natural rhythms of our 'body time', the rhythmical approach is not usual. Millions of women around the world, who want to avoid the pill and other contraceptive devices, use the 'rhythm method' as a more natural and less intrusive approach to birth control. The *Bodyclock* Diet is the only diet programme designed to work in an analogous way – in time with your body rhythms and without the long-term side effects usually associated with drugs.

Recognizing that some people will find it more difficult to lose weight, and some will want to lose more than others, the *Bodyclock* Diet proposes special routes accordingly. It is designed to enable dieters to make the safest maximum weight loss with the minimum effort and change in lifestyle.

You can establish and keep track of your life's 'body time' easily and simply by using the *Body-clock*. Try it – and make up your own mind! Tuning in to your 'body time' will in turn help you to gain more control of your body and its compulsions, which will pay dividends for the rest of your life – helping you not only to look good but also to rediscover your body and the flow of its natural energies. Getting to know the phenomenon of your own 'body time' is an experience which should help you to achieve greater self-understanding.

CHAPTER TWO

The *Bodyclock* Phenomenon

The idea of an internal 'bodyclock' should not be too surprising, since the lives of most living things are clearly dominated by the 24-hour night-and-day cycle. The most obvious feature of the one-day rhythm is the way we feel tired and fall sleep at night and become awake and alert during the day. We seem to release energy during half of the day and recharge during the other half. If the 24-hour rhythm is interrupted, most people experience unpleasant side effects. For example, international travellers are well used to the disruptions caused through travelling across time zones; they call this experience 'jet lag' and usually avoid strenuous demands for at least a day or two until they have started to adjust to a new rhythmical basis.

Other than the single daily rhythm of sleeping and wakefulness, we also have other rhythms which last longer than one day and influence wide areas of our lives – the female menstrual cycle is a very clear example of this phenomenon – but scientists have observed that a wide range of less regular events including accidents and illness are also more (or less) likely to happen to any individual on certain predictable days.

How do we experience these rhythms?

Most of us would agree that we feel good on some days, and not so good on others. Sometimes we are all fingers and thumbs, but on other days have excellent manual dexterity and coordination.

Have you ever made a terrible decision and wondered a few days later whatever induced you to make it? Perhaps you bought something and then afterwards regretted it? Do you notice times when you appear to be accident-prone, or when your temper seems to be on a short fuse? Have you noticed how on some days you can sail through a mental or physical challenge better than on others?

Have you observed how ideas seem to flow on some days but at other times are non-existent? Musicians, painters, sportspeople etc. frequently talk about 'dry spells'. Fortunately, most experienced artists and players know that these unproductive periods come and go in fairly regular sequences, therefore they make the most of opportunities when 'the creative muse is with them' or when 'the ball is running for them'. Have you found that some of your clothes seem to fit differently on different days? On some days you are quite naturally slimmer and lighter than on others.

Human experience is always individual, and one thing is for certain – we each have our own impression and interpretation for our own bio-rhythmic experience. Some people experience such enormous physical turbulence on their Physical critical days that they have to take to their beds. Accidents appear to happen so frequently during turbulent biorhythms that some car insurance companies in Japan have issued biorhythm forecasts to policyholders in order to cut down the number of costly incidents.

A good analogy of the biorhythmic experience is biological weather. Some days are stormy and others are fine. Some things are easier to do on a sunny day ... and sometimes it's better to stay in on a rainy day!

Typical cycle

Each biorhythmic cycle has a high energy period and a low energy period of equal length, the high period being the strong part of the cycle. The low part of the cycle is a period of recharging, possibly analogous to sleep, but it is not the weak part. The time of changeover from the high energy period to the low energy period, or vice versa, is a 'critical' period of instability. This 'critical' time usually lasts up to one day and is the weak part of the cycle.

All biorhythms can be represented by the following typical cycle:

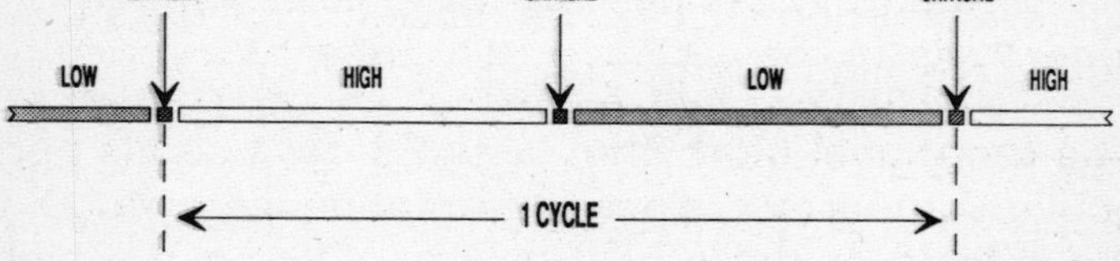

The major cycles

Of the many subtle and complex rhythms affecting our lives, researchers have identified the following three important and clearly defined biorhythmic cycles:

- *Physical*
- *Emotional*
- *Intellectual*

On any particular day your 'body time' – that is, the current status of your biorhythms – will predispose you to different intellectual, emotional and physical states.

The Physical biorhythm lasts 23 days and is the shortest major cycle. During the high energy period, we are more resistant to disease, better coordinated, stronger and better able to cope with hard physical work. During the low energy period, we are less resistant to disease, less well coordinated and tire more easily. The low period charges the energy batteries for the coming high energy period. During the critical days of the cycle – between the 11th and 12th days and the 23rd day – there is an increased potential for accident, illness and poor physical coordination. We are far less likely to achieve sporting success on these critical days than during the high energy period.

The Emotional biorhythm lasts 28 days and is particularly important, since it can influence or modify the effects of the other rhythms. During the high energy period, we are more positive, cooperative, relaxed and friendly. During the low energy period, we are typically less positive, less cooperative and less relaxed. The critical days are the 14th and 28th days of the cycle, on which days we are more likely to appear irrational, unduly emotional and vehemently disagreeable. Because the Emotional biorhythm is 28 days long, an Emotional critical day crops up every two weeks (14 days is half the 28-day cycle) from the day of your birth for the rest of your life. Consequently many people talk about their 'bad day of the week', when they are most frequently irritable or depressed – which is also the day of the week on which they were born!

The Intellectual biorhythm lasts 33 days and is probably the least studied so far. During the high energy period, our minds are more receptive, retentive, creative, adaptable and quick-thinking. During the low energy period, we find it less easy to accept new ideas, to remember, be creative, concentrate or think clearly. The critical days of the cycle – between the 16th and 17th days and the 33rd day – are typified by poor decisions and a lack of good ideas. Where possible, it is better to avoid making important decisions, taking examinations or dealing with difficult problems during this time.

Rhythms start at birth

All rhythms begin on the day we are born and, because of the different cycle lengths, do not repeat the identical rhythm picture for the first 58 years of our lives. The diagram overleaf shows the rhythm pattern during the first few weeks after birth:

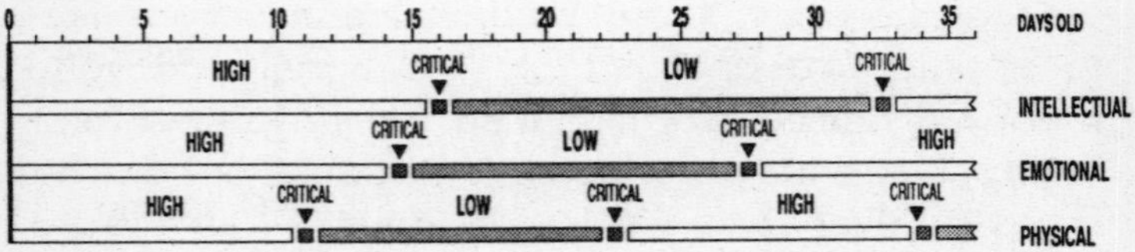

At the moment of birth, your natural body energies simultaneously sprang into a high energy mode to see you through the first critical week or so of your life. Since that day your body energies have ebbed and flowed according to regular patterns, helping to create the 'ups' and 'downs' which you have experienced periodically throughout your life.

The *Bodyclock* 'computer'

The *Bodyclock* has been designed to enable you to discover and keep an accurate track of your own individual body time with the minimum of effort. Before setting up your *Bodyclock* for your current body time, it is important to understand how information is displayed and what the characters signify.

The diagram on the adjacent page shows, in the same format as above, the three major cycles in a week when each has a critical day. Note that when a critical period falls in between two days (Friday and Saturday for the physical rhythm) it is shown as a critical for both days:

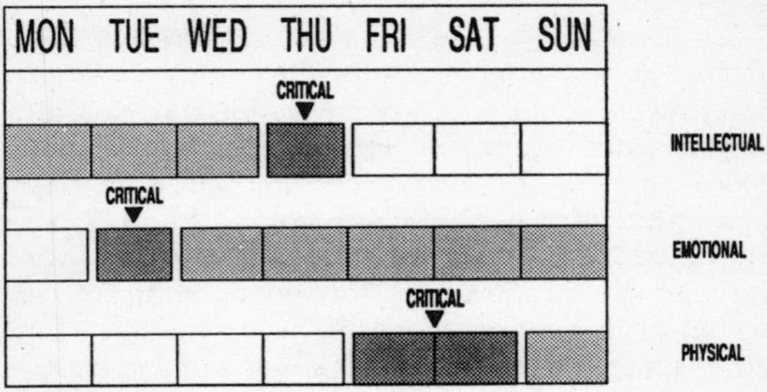

On the *Bodyclock*, this is shown as:

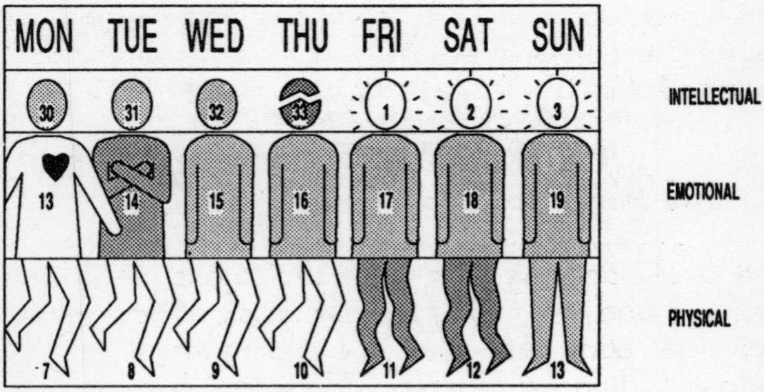

The biorhythms on each day are represented by picture people – where the major rhythms broadly correspond to the relevant parts of the human body. The 'head' shows the Intellectual rhythm, the body (heart) the Emotional rhythm and the legs the Physical rhythm. Each part of the figure has a number to indicate the number of days through the cycle. For instance, on the 10th day of the 23-day physical cycle the legs show the number 10. Normally we will only want to know whether we are high, low or critical for a particular day, but the numbers are useful for setting up and for quick reference as to our position on the cycle.

Green is the *Bodyclock* colour for the high energy periods (shown as white below). The intellectual high is shown by the head being 'lit up'. During an Emotional high, the heart is shown and the arms are held out from the sides of the body – ready for a hug. For a Physical high, the legs are running and jumping. High energy days for all three rhythms are displayed as follows:

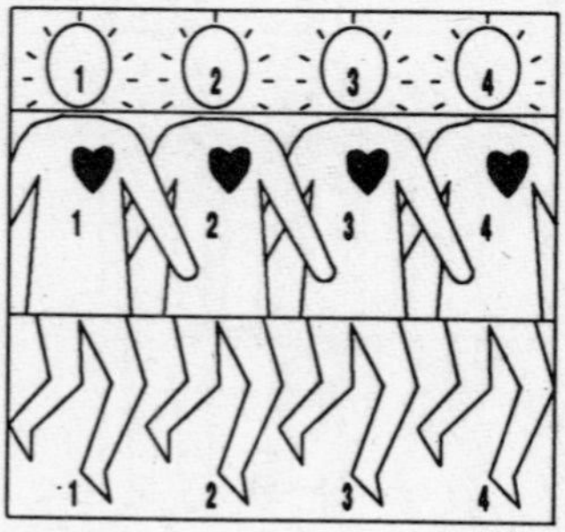

In the low energy periods, the body parts are shown in amber (the lightly shaded areas in the following diagrams). The head is empty for the Intellectual low and the arms straight by the sides for the Emotional low. During a Physical low the legs are straight. Low energy days for all three rhythms are as follows:

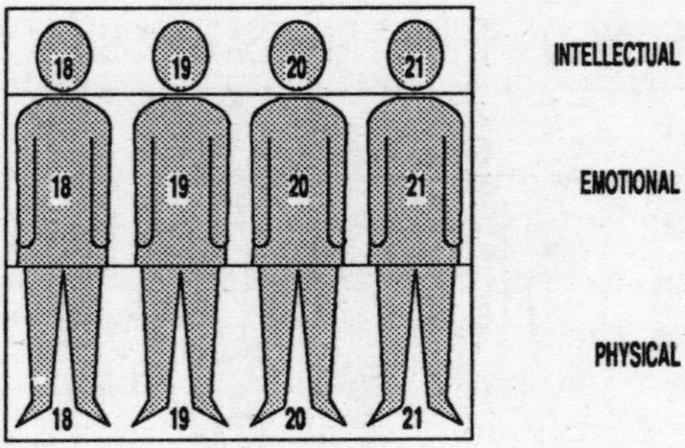

During the critical periods, the body parts are shown in red (the heavily shaded areas below). The Intellectual critical is shown by the head being broken or disconnected. For an Emotional critical, the hands are folded across the chest (heartache). During the Physical critical, the legs are 'wobbly'. Critical days for all three rhythms are as follows:

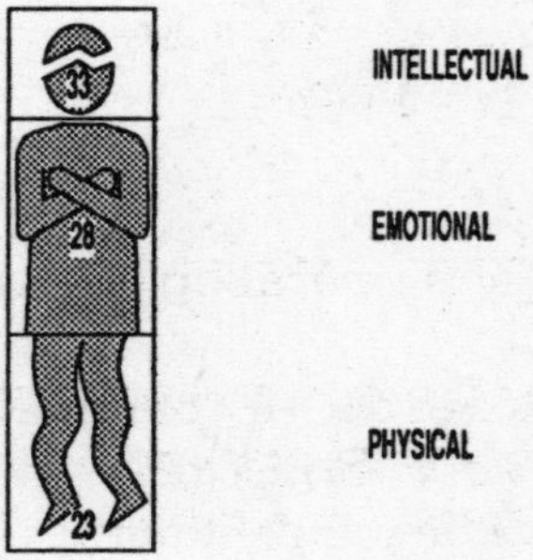

Let us look again at a typical week's *Bodyclock* and interpret the information it shows:

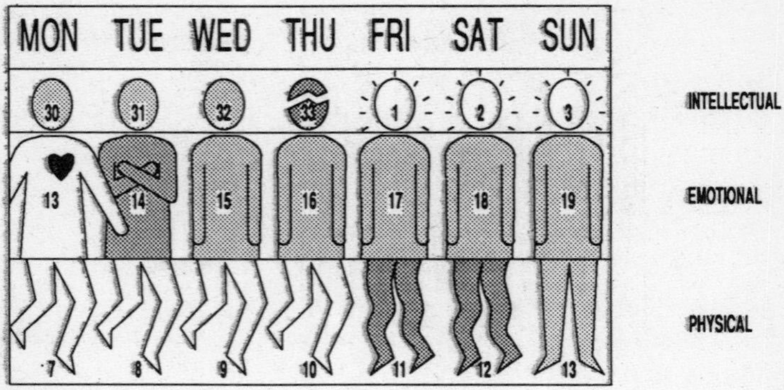

We can see that on Monday, the Intellectual rhythm is low and both the Emotional and Physical rhythms are high. Tuesday is an Emotional critical, and on Wednesday the Emotional rhythm enters the low part of the cycle. Thursday is an Intellectual critical, and on Friday the Intellectual rhythm enters a positive high phase. There is a Physical critical between Friday and Saturday, and the Physical rhythm then becomes low.

Setting up and operating your *Bodyclock*

Now turn to Appendix III (page 223) to find out how to set up your *Bodyclock* computer to show your own current biological time.

At the end of each week, you must remember to wind the *Bodyclock* forward to the next week as described in the Appendix. The current week number (1–52) is shown on the front bezel, and corresponding dates are shown on the back. If you forget whether you have wound forward or not, you can refer to the current week number and adjust accordingly. If at any time you are confused about its settings we recommend that you go through the setting-up procedure again as described in the Appendix. Do not be tempted to guess!

You may want to look forward to see what the future holds in store, and can find out how to do this in the setting-up instructions in the Appendix. Make a note of your biorhythms on any important dates, particularly criticals.

Common experiences

The *Bodyclock* is a very useful device, but biorhythms are not an exact science. Everybody's experience is unique to themselves and some find their 'body time' experience much more powerful and clearly discernible than others. The *Bodyclock* and its information cannot and will not **make** you feel one way or the other, but it can help you to understand what is naturally going on with your body energies and what is more likely to happen as a result.

Take the whole picture into account – the *Bodyclock* display has been specially designed to help you to do this. A single critical biorhythm may be compensated by high energy in the other two rhythms, especially with a high in the powerful Emotional cycle. However, a critical may be exacerbated by lows and changeable rhythms in other cycles. So remember to look at and interpret the whole body in the display.

Occasionally people find they are a day out in terms of what the forecast shows and what they experience – either early or late. Someone born very early in the morning is likely to have a slightly earlier experience than someone born late at night on the same day. Some people inexplicably appear to be consistently either early or late, but not usually by more than a day. Set your *Bodyclock* and compare your energy experiences with the forecasts. If you find after a few weeks that you feel early or late all the time, then adjust forward or backwards one day accordingly. Only personal observation can help here.

Another common experience is that the critical straddling the change from low to high is usually more severe than the critical between the change from the high to low phase of the cycle. However, you will have to experience this for yourself and see if it affects you.

Despite the fact that it is not an exact science – and there is a great deal we have yet to discover about this phenomenon – millions of people around the world currently monitor their 'body time' and use this knowledge to enhance their daily lives.

Is the *Bodyclock* anything to do with astrology?

In short, the answer is no. Astrology appears to be an elaborate and romantic prediction system based on the proposition that our lives are influenced by the position of the planets. Predictions frequently involve travel, money, career and romance. There is little scientific evidence to support astrology, although some scientists accept that gravitational fluctuations may have a discernible effect on individuals.

By comparison, biorhythms are very basic and their effects can be clearly monitored over large groups of people. They do not predict *when* events are going to happen; they simply help us to predict when things are *more likely* to happen as a direct result of our own actions and behaviour. We are more likely to feel better and perform physically and intellectually better on some days than on others – so the *Bodyclock* offers a kind of biological weather forecast.

Some people believe that the powerful 28-day Emotional cycle is associated with the phases of the moon, so this may be an area of overlap. Old wives' tales from many cultures often associate lunacy with the moon (luna = moon), and psychiatric hospitals frequently experience a larger number of admissions during the time of the new moon, so this idea may prove to have substance.

What is the origin of these rhythms?

Exactly why we have these rhythms is not known for certain. All living things are made up from a mass of tiny living cells. Each of these cells has a number of regular simple biological sequences which in highly complex creatures, such as humans, may interact to produce greater and more noticeable influential rhythms – in the same way, say, that many small forces combine to create large, powerful waves in the sea. But we seem to be not only internally rhythmical but also synchronized to fit into the rhythms of our external environment. This external environment may go much further than the immediately obvious night/day cycle of the turning earth. It may be that humans prove to be receptive to a wide range of rhythmic cosmic influences such as light, gravity and electromagnetism, all emanating from an infinite pulsating universe.

Scientific research has not proved conclusively whether our bodyclock is wholly internal or is partly reliant on external time clues. However, experiments have shown that test subjects isolated in subterranean caves for long periods of time, without clocks and watches, adjust naturally after initial disorientation to a regular daily rhythm of sleep and wakefulness.

CHAPTER THREE

Bodyclock Influences on Dieting

Most diet experts report that there are a number of danger points in any diet, especially after the first few days. As we considered in Chapter 1, the danger is always attributed to willpower and the desire to maintain new habits in the face of temptation, boredom or physical craving.

The dangers usually stem from emotional rather than simple physical needs, however. Looking at cakes in a baker's window, watching an advert for a chocolate bar, sitting in front of the TV, dining out with friends, feeling bored – these experiences can result in overeating to supply emotional not physical needs.

Let us consider in more detail what often happens.

Deciding to diet

'UP' dieters: Many dieters make the positive decision to diet and do something about their body shape on an 'up' day with plenty of high biorhythms. On an Intellectual 'high', we are more likely to recognize that we are in control of our lives, our health and our appearance. An Emotional 'high' naturally leads to a calmer, more confident approach and eagerness for the prospect of a new shape. We resist temptation more easily. A Physical 'high' can lead to higher energy, better health and experience of the body's natural desire to burn off unsightly and restricting fat.

'DOWN' dieters: Unfortunately some dieters choose to diet out of self-loathing and desperation – typically on a 'down' day with a mix of critical and low biorhythms. Dieting for self-punishment and other negative reasons is not only difficult and dangerous, but invariably unsuccessful. On an Intellectual critical, we are more likely to conclude that the world is against us and that our shape is all that stands between us and what we want – which of course is nonsense. An Emotional critical backs up the feeling of being unloved and a sense of emotional isolation from others. A Physical critical frequently leads to poor health and feeling in poor physical condition.

Staying on a diet

If the 'UP' dieters could stay up, then everything would be fine – or at least less difficult. But the problem comes some days later on a 'down' day with mixed or critical biorhythms; then we tend to forget that we are in control, we may feel physically sluggish or anxious, and possibly start to crave all the wrong foods. Our positive desire to improve our lives changes over this time, and the resolve and natural energies apparently evaporate.

It is just as well that 'DOWN' dieters shortly

encounter an 'up' day, with plenty of high biorhythms, when the world looks a much nicer place after all and body shape ceases to be the focus of all that is wrong. They abandon their self-punishment diet which otherwise could lead to serious health problems, unhappiness and frustration.

If changes in the biorhythms tend to lead to abandonment, how can we use this knowledge to maximize our chances of success?

Getting it right

The Physical and Emotional cycles appear to have the greater influence over the dieting process, while the Intellectual rhythm seems to be less influential – provided that sensible eating decisions are maintained during critical periods. Generally speaking, willpower is high when rhythms are high. Similarly, when rhythms are stable, so willpower should be fairly stable. But when either or both of the Physical and Emotional rhythms are critical, we will inevitably experience weakness and our behaviour over demands or stressful issues is more likely to be erratic. Also, at this time our body sensations are less comfortable and we are likely to get even more out of touch with our real physical needs.

Planning ahead is the way to succeed. Losing weight and becoming healthier is not easy and demands consistent willpower and motivation. By dieting in harmony with your biological 'weather' you will find the changes easier, more effective, longer lasting and, above all, more satisfying!

The best time to diet

Some days are simply better than others for losing weight and changing those life-long bad habits. The best time to begin dieting is when both the Physical and Emotional rhythms are high and stable – i.e. when they are both near the start of the high part of the cycle – although a stable Physical and Emotional period can work for those who don't find dieting too difficult.

A Physical high period is an ideal time for most people to absorb the physical changes of a diet with minimum side-effects and maximum weight loss because it is typified by strong resistance to disease, good strength and coordination, good energy and physical sensations. Similarly, an Emotional high period is an ideal time to go for maximum weight loss with the minimum effort, because it is characterized by a positive outlook, strong willpower and clearer aims.

All effective diet plans depend on some change in lifestyle. The changes required may involve different types of food, smaller amounts, less alcohol, more physical exercise – which could well include a number of things upon which you feel physically or emotionally dependent. For many people an effective diet will constitute a significant change to their body's expectations, so it is important to introduce the changes at a time of tranquillity and strength in the relevant biorhythms.

Nature equipped you with perfectly aligned 'highs' in every rhythm when you experienced the dramatic trauma of the first 10 days of your life; it gave you the best possible chance of getting through that difficult time successfully. Now you can mimic Mother Nature and use her techniques to get you through the 'rebirth' of your new self.

The diagram below shows a typical good time to start a diet. Both Emotional and Physical rhythms are high for the week shown on the *Body-clock*, and will remain high for part of the following week:

A TYPICALLY GOOD TIME TO START

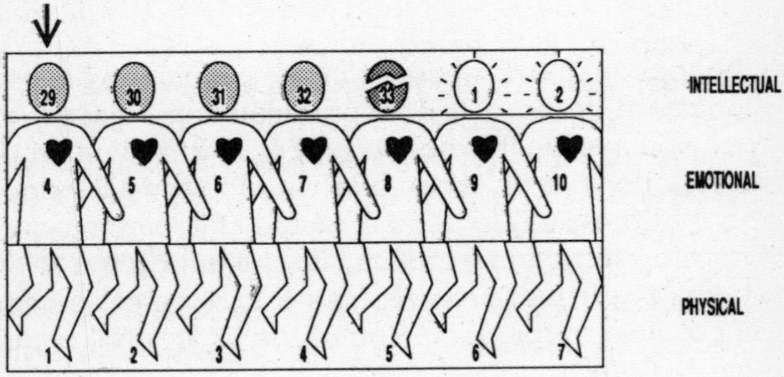

Remember that you can take less notice of the Intellectual critical because it is less important to the basic diet. However, you must take care to avoid making bad eating-related decisions around the critical period.

The diagram overleaf shows a typical bad time to start. Both the Emotional and Physical rhythms are unstable; i.e. they change between high and low, and have criticals during the week:

A TYPICALLY BAD TIME TO START

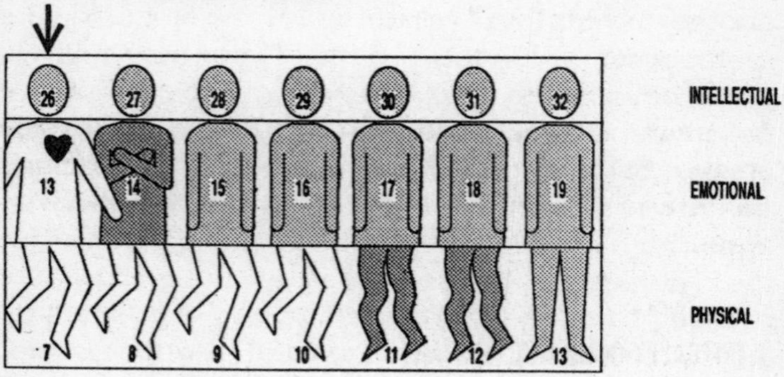

Changes in the Emotional cycle appear to have a significant effect on the physical experiences of many people, so it is not surprising that the onset of an Emotional critical can often lead to the abandonment of the diet plan – and, worse still, 'pigging-out'. Therefore emotional stability is vital during the early stages of the diet process, so start your diet as near as possible to the beginning of the Emotional cycle.

Rhythm dieting

Our actions are governed at any time by how we feel – and this is highly dependent on our body time. In order to be successful, we must plan to feel good during a diet – and therefore plan how we intend to cope with the critical days when we will not be feeling too good. Relaxing the diet during critical days effectively produces a rhythmical diet. Rhythm dieting not only helps you to stay on top during your Emotional and Physical 'storms', but also has another important benefit with regard to your metabolism.

Conventional dieting tends to lower the metabolic rate – that is, the rate at which we burn up energy: the energy supplied by food. It is precisely this lowering of the metabolic rate which encourages the human body to hold on to its store of fat, thus defeating the objectives of the diet. Often referred to as the 'famine reaction', it is a biological legacy from our prehistoric ancestors whose bodies would 'slow down' to store energy in the form of fat in times of natural famine.

The strategy behind the *Bodyclock* Diet is to use our body's naturally occurring opportunities to achieve the great weight loss. During critical periods the dieter reverts to a 'critical' programme in order to:

- *Avoid an undesirable slow-down in metabolic rate*
- *Avoid the diet 'blues' and casual abandonment on 'down' days*
- *Avoid dieting during naturally unproductive periods*
- *Maintain weight loss and positively orientate the body for further loss.*

Downtime

Many people decide to embark on diets or health routines at some point that is connected with events external to themselves. This may be preparing for a holiday, a wedding, summer clothes, a new job, or perhaps deciding to seek a new romance! Whatever the reasons and timescales involved, your body has its own fixed timetable which started at the time of your birth, and which your *Bodyclock* can show you. It is this timetable which you will have to consider alongside your other objectives to successfully achieve the body shape which you most desire.

As with most things in life, there is a downside to every good idea – you rarely get something good for nothing – and today may not be the best day to start your *Bodyclock* Diet.

However, a delay can be a blessing in disguise! Be careful about wanting to diet quickly and immediately, which is more than likely another facet of the compulsiveness that has landed you with body-shape problems in the first place. The decision to lose weight should be part of an overall lifestyle strategy; in this way the diet will be effective and not easily forgotten or pushed to one side. On average you should not have to wait longer than a week or so for a suitable Physical high period combined with a stable Emotional period. More importantly, any wait will give you a chance to ensure the essential preliminaries outlined in the next chapters are all understood, completed or arranged by the start of the diet.

Rhythm wreckers

The *Bodyclock* Diet will help you to utilize your body's natural best opportunities for dieting, but nothing will be gained unless you manage the day-to-day pressures from the outside world. Take into account any major social occasions which disrupt the diet plans of even the most determined. Give yourself the best chance for success: don't try to start a diet at Christmas! Don't try to lose weight at a time of great stress, e.g. exams, moving home, or during a period of grieving. However, do ensure that you have plenty to do while on the diet plan, rather than sitting with nothing to do all day except think of when the next meal is coming!

Some unlucky women experience the unpleasant rhythmical effects of Premenstrual Syndrome (PMS) – another, but less welcome, aspect of body time. Typical symptoms include anxiety, depression, water retention and food craving. Not all sufferers, of course, will experience just one symptom, but more likely a mixture of some or all of them in varying degrees of intensity. However, many women will find the strict adherence to the *Bodyclock* diet actually helps to relieve the symptoms and bring a new lease of life.

CHAPTER FOUR

Habits that make the Difference

Looking good is usually a matter of adopting the right habits. These are the habits which become second nature – not just an artificial regime adopted for a couple of days or weeks. The *occasional* chocolate bar is not usually the problem – it is what we do every day, hour by hour without thinking, that counts. Our daily habits need careful 'tuning' in order to ensure successful weight-loss. Get into the habit of using your *Bodyclock*, and watch out for the danger days – not only for the diet but also for other health, work and lifestyle issues.

The important habits that need to be adapted to help you lose weight and remain looking good are:

- *Food buying and cooking*
- *Eating and drinking*
- *High-energy living*

Food buying and cooking

Buy quality food

Really fresh unadulterated food is vital in any effective diet, which may mean that you have to rethink when, where and how to shop. Forget convenience food, if by 'convenience' you mean food that is processed, adulterated and laden with fats, sugar and additives – which includes most of the food you buy in tins, fancy packets and wrappers. Ask yourself if it is convenient to be overweight? Is it convenient not to fit into the fashionable clothes you want? Is it convenient not to do some of the things you would like to do because of embarrassment about your figure? Is it convenient to need to wear jumpers and loose fitting clothes to hide yourself?

The best food is inconvenient, meaning that it must be washed, prepared and eaten fresh. It will not keep long, and goes bad quickly. The best food also needs chewing and is difficult to overeat. The major drawback in the quest for fresh unprocessed food is that it isn't always easy to find because of the chemical pesticides and sprays in such widespread use. Meat such as beef and pork and other foods such as tomatoes, potatoes, oranges, apples and lettuce are all most likely to contain some toxic pesticides – unless they are organic. These kinds of pollutants can directly contribute to your fat.

If possible, buy organically grown produce, which a number of the big supermarket chains are now selling. Don't be concerned that such food may look less impressive than its cheaper counterparts – this is because it is not covered in anti-sprouting chemicals, cosmetic waxes and preservatives. The taste should convince you that it is far better, and the lower toxin content will help your body to shift some of the most troublesome fat deposits. Unfortunately, organic and free-range foods can cost a premium over conventionally farmed produce, but remember that natural and fresh is best, and the best sometimes costs more! Your body will look much better on 4oz of the best food than on 8oz of the worst costing the same money – and the taste will be a bonus.

Try buying less meat: it is generally expensive, full of fat and unnecessary in large quantities in the average diet. Try eating more vegetable dishes instead. Vegetarians usually have a better diet than meat-eaters – simply because they eat less fat and more fibre – and make up their protein intake from cheese, nuts, pulses and cereals. But this is not intended as an appeal to give up meat altogether!

Avoid tinned and packaged foods, or at any rate, be very careful about reading the labels. Most contain unnecessary sugar and salt, as well as chemicals. Also look for unsulphured dried fruits and tinned products without added salt, sugar and preservatives.

Food is a vital part of all our lives, but unfortunately the average person knows far too little about the important issues of food and nutrition. Take time to read Appendix II on page 199, which outlines the basic facts and the important issue of 'food combining'. Like biorhythms, food combining was pioneered in the last century. Its discoverer William Howard Hay, an American doctor, became well known for his ability to cure diseases through a 'natural' diet combining only certain types of foods. Since then a number of excellent books on Hay's principles have been published, including *Food Combining for Health* by Doris Grant and Jean Joice.

If you are part of a large family or group who

live together, decide how you are going to ensure that your meals are exactly right for you without causing the kind of disruption that will put pressure on you to abandon your plans. Talk openly to your living companions about what you are trying to achieve and endeavour to get them to support you from the outset. If you are the one who does the shopping, don't worry about buying more fresh food, since the other members of the family (even the skinny ones) will all benefit greatly from the extra vitamins and fibre and from a lower fat, salt and additive intake. Take care, though to introduce any changes to family food gradually over a period of time. The taste of fresh food will sell itself as long as you do not make it a confrontational issue.

Food preparation and cooking

If fruit and vegetables are organic, they should be well-washed or scrubbed, but not peeled. Unfortunately, if they are not organic they are better peeled because of the residues they may contain – although this is at the cost of some of their nutrients. Unless you can find the unsulphured variety, dried fruit should be soaked to remove the sulphur preservative and then the soaking water should be discarded.

As a general rule, food is better if it is eaten raw. Vegetables should be eaten raw or only lightly cooked, otherwise many of the vitamins and minerals will be lost. A microwave oven is recommended for cooking vegetables and some other foods; it is quick, convenient, inexpensive and, more importantly, keeps in all the vitamins and minerals that are usually cooked out during boiling. Alternatively, get an inexpensive steaming plate that fits on to a saucepan. The taste of steamed vegetables is equally delicious if slightly less convenient. And save the cooking liquid for vegetable stock!

Grill or bake food rather than frying in fat, but remember that most foods can be fried without fat as long as you use a heavy-based non-stick pan and also stir frequently to prevent sticking. Cooking with fat is a habit that should have died out when non-stick coatings were invented!

Never add salt when cooking – but take a tip from top chefs and add fresh herbs to complement and bring out the flavour of your food.

Eating and drinking

Eating

Do you remember how you were always told to chew your food properly as a child? Well, your mother was right! Chewing your food adequately is absolutely vital! Carbohydrates can only be digested if properly chewed, and efficient digestion is essential for good health and dieting. Chewing breaks down and neutralizes poisons which are sometimes present in modern foods, as well as helping enzymes in the mouth to combine with elements in the food to create health-giving properties that otherwise would pass through the body. Your body makes about two pints of saliva per day especially for this purpose – so use it.

Chewing also releases the full flavour of the

food and actually helps you to feel much fuller than you otherwise would. It gives you time to think as you eat! Get into the habit of always thinking about what you are eating: never swallow without thinking! You can actually get a bigger kick out of eating half your present consumption by holding it in the mouth longer and consciously experiencing the flavours and textures of each morsel.

Chew your food properly and the battle is half won! If you haven't the time to chew all your food, chew what you can thoroughly in the time available and leave the rest; you will feel equally satisfied and your weight will drop. And remember – good food is food that needs chewing. What's more, it takes about 20 minutes for the stomach to tell the brain it is full – another reason to eat slowly. More about chewing in relation to digestion can be found in Appendix II.

It is important to decide *when* you want to eat in relation to your daily activities and individual body demands, subject to the following provisos: NEVER starve and then binge the whole amount in one go. It is better for you physically and emotionally to have regular meal breaks, so spread your food intake across the day and if possible eat the last meal at least five hours before sleep. The issue of breakfast is quite emotive, with diet pundits divided as to its value. Nevertheless many people believe that breakfast is not strictly necessary after being in bed for eight hours. Even the Sherpas in Nepal, who carry colossal loads all day in the most arduous conditions – and for whom food is a vital energy source – do not eat breakfast but split their food intake between an early lunch and an evening meal.

The *Bodyclock* Diet includes light fruit-based breakfasts for those who want them. If you really don't like breakfast, eat the meal as a snack at some other time in the day when you feel hungry. Eat *only* if you are hungry. Remember to ask yourself if you are hungry before eating – if you are not, then don't be afraid to undereat or even skip a meal. But don't be afraid to eat either.

Nibbling between meals is a habit that can be both good and bad. Frequently we feel hungry when our blood sugar drops, so nibbling something sweet raises the blood sugar level and body temperature quickly and helps us to avoid getting ravenous and wolfing down food later. Nibbling is OK so long as:

- What you nibble is 'good' food
- You nibble a modest amount only when you are hungry
- Nibbling does not become just a routine habit

Sweets are generally bad. Refined sugar raises the blood sugar level so fast that there is a rebound effect leading on to lower blood sugar levels and false hunger fairly soon afterwards. So stick to nature's own sweets. Make sure you have a small bag of dried apricots or dried apples handy for moments when you feel very hungry. They are high in fibre and natural sugars, so they provide something substantial to chew as well as creating the essential rise in blood sugar levels. But be aware that you should not eat these without restraint; they are better than chocolate but still high in calories.

A major difficulty for many dieters is the television, which encourages them to sit passively for hours and nibble continuously. So, if you have this problem, decide whether you need to reduce the amount of television you watch in order to help reduce habitual nibbling.

Drinking
All too often, what we drink is a bigger problem than what we eat. We consume far too many drinks laden with calories, sugar and toxins, which have no nutritional benefit and don't result in the satisfied feeling that comes from a good meal. Conversely, we drink too little pure water. Over 50 per cent of our body weight is water – even our brains comprise 100 billion tiny neurons which are 85 per cent water. Not surprisingly, therefore, pure water is the liquid fuel on which our bodies depend.

Water is vital for the correct operation of the liver and kidneys – which flush away fat-creating toxins – as well as for a host of other important biological and cosmetic functions. Top photographic models frequently say that pure water is their secret weapon for maintaining healthy complexions and enviable looks – so take a tip from the professionals and drink plenty of it.

Tap water, however, is generally not as pure as we would like, and is best filtered before drinking to ensure that lead, pesticide traces and other unwanted contaminants are removed. Some of the most expensive spring waters, including those in fancy packages, can also provide a most unwelcome dose of sodium and nitrates, amongst other things – especially if you drink several litres. So choose carefully and ensure you buy the brands with low sodium and nitrate contents. Evian, for instance, is an excellent choice.

The *Bodyclock* Diet recommends drinking plenty of pure water.

Alcohol is forbidden on the *Bodyclock* Diet. It is high in calories, it stimulates artificial appetite and it dehydrates the body. The thought of an alcohol ban may strike terror into some hearts – but cutting out alcohol removes a source of useless calories as well as fat-creating toxins. If you really must have an alcoholic drink, then aim for damage limitation. A glass of good quality dry white wine, a 'spritzer' or a low-strength beer will not mean disaster, but remember that it will slow down your fat loss. If you like to be part of a 'drinking group' and not to stand out, then go for the low calorie mixer on the rocks, but without the spirit.

Beer dehydrates the body far less than spirits because of the high water content, but in any case try to drink water before, during and after any alcohol. Lord Hume, British Prime Minister in the 1960s, is now 88 and his tip is to drink a glass of water for every glass of wine – sound advice from living proof!

Humans are the only animals that drink **milk** after infancy – and then largely in the Western world. Most adults cannot physically digest milk properly because our bodies do not produce enough of the necessary enzyme after puberty and at 260 calories per pint (equivalent to a meal of baked potato and baked beans) it is a luxury that gives few feelings of satisfaction. A quarter of a pint of skimmed milk per day is allowed on the *Bodyclock* Diet for those who feel they cannot do without it, but otherwise try to cut it out.

Tea and **coffee** should become occasional rather than regular drinks, for times when you just cannot do without a caffeine fix. Coffee should always be filtered – never instant – and change to decaffeinated if possible. Tea is in fact a good source of some elements, but too much tea can interfere with iron absorption. Try herbal teas with all their wonderful flavours such as lemon, peppermint, rosehip, wild cherry, apple and cinammon, camomile etc. You can drink as much of these as you like and they have the added benefit of containing no caffeine or tannin. They may taste a bit strange to start with if you have not tried them before. Don't think of them as a substitute for ordinary tea, but as different drinks in their own right.

The *Bodyclock* Diet recommends drinking herbal tea and black decaffeinated filter coffee.

Fruit juices should be really pure and should not contain added sugar or flavour enhancers etc. Be careful with quantities, as it is easy to drink a lot of calories this way; if you eat the whole fruit instead, you will get the benefit of the fibre as well.

Artificial sweeteners should be used rather than sugar, but try to limit their use. If you really can't do without some form of sweetener, try a small amount of natural honey dissolved in warm water, but aim to cut down gradually. It is important to train your palate to accept and enjoy less sweet tastes – so do this and throw the chemical sweeteners in the dustbin.

High energy living

Energy

Energy is recognized as a positive thing, which we rightly associate with feeling good. Marketeers sell pills that supposedly give us energy; drink and chocolate companies frequently attempt to justify an unhealthy high sugar content as a high energy content. But what is energy?

Life is a continuous process of charging and discharging energy, twenty-four hours a day. This energy spans everything from breathing during sleep to running for a train. Dieticians frequently talk about the 'energy balance' i.e. the physics of energy output (exercise) being matched to energy intake (food). But on the *Bodyclock* Diet we are concerned with the whole energy experience, and getting in tune with this is vital to success. How does this experience work?

Energy creates energy

Take the phenomenon of travel. Apart from 'jet lag', travelling produces another interesting physical phenomenon: long journeys by road, rail or air tend to make us feel tired. But how can it be that sitting down for long periods actually makes us more exhausted than if we were enjoying a normal active day?

The fact is that we produce energy when we expend energy. This sounds illogical but it is true, and if we had an exercise break 'to stretch our legs' in the middle of the long journey, we would no doubt end up more refreshed and happy at the end of it. However, this doesn't mean that digging the garden vigorously all day will automatically make us feel like running five miles before dinner!

Consider the way in which the energy system is linked: at the end of a long and gruelling sports game, and often at the point of collapse, the winners invariably find sudden reserves of energy for celebrations or even a lap of honour. Why are they full of energy while the losers are exhausted and dejected?

Our energy experience appears to be emotionally and physically linked; it is possible to release physical energy through the emotions (e.g. jumping for joy). This is even more subtle the other way round – releasing emotional energy through the physical experience – but we all know the calm relaxation that comes from being totally exhausted after, say, a long walk in the country. If someone gives you an unexpected compliment or praise, or you have had a particularly successful meeting, see how it makes your energy level rise. Try complimenting other people and see the effect this has on them and their energy.

Are you a high energy or a low energy type?

We all have exactly the same high energy potential within us; the difference lies in what we do with it. Developing and releasing this energy is vital to happiness and successful slimming – and is the first necessary step in a positive lifestyle change.

Usually the slim people whom we envy are those who appear to be high energy types. Their energy does not in itself make them slim, but it supports and encourages the positive self-image and lifestyle which results in a better body shape. High energy individuals are healthier, more successful and much more attractive than low energy people.

Look at what makes your own personal energy go up. Typically this might involve: doing something physical, competitive games, participating in group activities, laughing, arguing, taking risks, getting yourself organized, good sexual relations, dancing, being with others with high energy, getting outstanding jobs finished, doing what you say you are going to do, being honest, being generous, giving a hug, tidying up.

Look also at what makes your energy levels go down. Typically this might involve: being on your own or around low energy people, being depressed, avoiding confrontations, avoiding risks, being embarrassed, being disorganized, being celibate, being sedentary, telling lies, procrastinating, feeling threatened, being jealous.

Make a list of your own activities and the resulting energy experiences. Now decide if you are hooked on low energy activities. Don't forget that eating, like everything else, is an energy experience. Digesting food uses energy, and digesting junk food saps energy. Eating large, rich meals and drinking alcohol tends to make most of us feel tired and drowsy; is this also part of your low energy lifestyle?

Notice how high energy always seem to revolve around these issues:

- *Doing something physical*
- *Being true to yourself*

- *Being successful*

These are the key issues in helping to create energy – which we can use to attack any situation when we feel our energy spiralling downwards.

Consider your habits and decide how you can raise your energy levels on a daily basis, and how you can fit exercise into your life. Attack temptation, boredom, unhappiness and just about anything else that is negative in your life – with energy. If it's legal and safe and it makes your energy rise, then do it; it's good for you and allows you to develop your own energy high naturally, without artificial stimulants.

High energy is infectious, which is one of the reasons why we find high energy people so attractive. In the same way, observe how low energy people drain you! In large groups, energy can multiply to become a 'sea of energy'. If you have ever been to an exciting major event, you will know that the live experience is completely different from watching it on film. Rather than relying totally on your own energy, consider getting together with a group of friends to join with you on the *Bodyclock* Diet. The *Bodyclock* will measure the ebb and flow of your natural energies, but it is essential to maximize those energies in the first place.

Exercise

Most people today know that some regular physical exercise is vital to good health, and without it life expectancy and resistance to disease is reduced. However, exercise also helps to create the right conditions to reduce body fat.

We are all too often experts in finding reasons

to avoid exercise: 'lack of time ... no equipment or facilities ... I'm not built for exercise ... it's too boring ... sudden exercise causes heart attacks ... it's too difficult ... I don't have an instructor or a friend to do it with ... I know plenty of slim people who never exercise ... I feel too self-conscious ... it's physically harmful ... I'm too old'. The list goes on and on!

However, the fact remains that the most successful and attractive people, with busy lifestyles, make time for exercise; they do this not only for pleasure but also to give them the energy to get through such a gruelling lifestyle while remaining slim and healthy.

Regular exercise helps to release endorphins into the brain – this is a substance which helps you to feel calm and relaxed and gives an overwhelming sense of well-being. Regular exercise naturally creates vitality and the desire and the energy for more exercise. Exercise also brings many cosmetic benefits – not only to muscle tone and body shape, but also to general appearance, posture, flexibility and strength – and the extra oxygen used helps skin tone and tissue regeneration. Over the age of 40, we tend to naturally lose about half a pound of lean tissue each year; exercise helps to prevent vital lean tissue loss and contributes to our looking younger for longer.

The Base Metabolic Rate (BMR) is the speed at which we burn up energy while resting, and this can be raised by exercise. Exercise not only helps maintain a higher metabolic rate, which can easily fall during any diet, but also produces adrenalin chemicals which help to depress the body's fat-making process.

Exercise in itself will not help you to lose weight! Many people who undertake vigorous exercise regimes while eating the same food find that although they do not lose weight their clothes become loose. This is simply because fat is lost and muscle is gained – and as muscle tissue is heavier and more compact than fat, weight can stay constant while clothes drop a size and appearance improves.

Many medical authorities agree that obesity is often more to do with lack of exercise than simply overeating or inherited body shaping. Inherited body shape does play a part in your current appearance, but it is very rare for obesity to be passed on as a genetic disorder. It is far more likely that fat parents encourage their children to accept their own fat self-image. As children, most of us were taught to eat by our mothers, who praised and loved us for eating everything on our plates at regular meal times. Our parents did not praise us for being energetic or noisy or forgetting to eat!

Exercise is part of a high energy lifestyle – not another punishment to be endured grudgingly. You can and must make time for exercise.

Many people in active occupations generally do not have the right kind of exercise even though they do a fair amount of very hard work each day. Vigorous housework for instance, provides a lot of valuable bending and stretching, but is of little aerobic exercise value.

The *Bodyclock* Diet rules on exercise are: *Do*

what works.... and what works for you.

What works is aerobic exercise – so be prepared to sweat a bit. This means continuous activities or sports – but definitely no burn-outs. The good news is that *duration* is generally far more important than *intensity* when it comes to aerobic exercise. It's about exercising gently for a reasonable period instead of fitting a herculean work-out into 10 minutes.

Typical aerobic activities are done with sufficient sustained speed and energy to get you slightly out of breath and raise the heart rate for 20–40 minutes. As a general guide only your heart rate will need to be raised to around 180 minus your age. If you are very fit, this can be raised up to 200 minus your age.

Why is aerobic activity useful in the shaping process? Our muscles can process energy in a number of different ways – one of these being the aerobic system, where the muscles utilize oxygen supplied by the respiratory system. This oxygen in the muscles allows stored foodstuffs (mainly glycogen but also protein and fat) to be converted into muscle energy. The conversion process can continue as long as the muscles continue to be supplied by the food store and the oxygen supply system.

Choose your exercise

There are all kinds of sports and exercise activities which each provide different levels of benefit. A typical selection might include for example:

Aerobics   Squash

Badminton	Swimming
Cycling	Tennis
Jogging	Walking
Skiing	Weight training

Tennis, badminton and, squash are 'stop and go sports and can provide some useful aerobic exercise provided you have the right level of competition. However, at an amateur level the pulse does not maintain the steady high rate required. Weight training is usually not aerobic, therefore not a good fat-reduction exercise. Swimming is non-stressful and a pleasurable activity exercising all parts of the body, but most people cannot sustain their heart rates at the desired level to make this aerobic. Skiing – and particularly cross-country skiing – can be very good exercise, but a week or two a year will not have a long-lasting effect.

By all means pursue any of these activities as they will help your overall fitness – but do them for fun as part of your high energy lifestyle, not as your main aerobic exercise activity. The activities that 'work' are those which raise the pulse *consistently* during the activity. From the list above only aerobics, cycling, jogging and walking are likely to do this. However, it is always better to do a less effective exercise that you really enjoy than a highly demanding activity that you willingly avoid at every opportunity.

If you are young, competitive and fairly fit, then squash or one of the other 'stop and go' sports will immediately appeal. However, do not consider this unless you have been fit for some time, and you have access to facilities and energetic partners on a regular basis. If you do not have the competitive spirit or the facilities at hand then jogging is another excellent aerobic activity for anyone who is fit. However, these activities are high impact exercises, in that they jar the frame and joints each time the feet hit the hard ground, and so can lead to injuries over time. These range from bad backs, joint problems and stress fractures, to retina detachment, in some rare cases.

Cycling is good for anyone who is unfit and overweight, simply because the body is supported and there is no danger of 'impact' damage. A good bicycle is not cheap, but after this initial outlay cycling is a fairly inexpensive and enjoyable exercise, particularly during the spring and summer months. Unlike jogging, fitness can be built up more gradually on a bicycle to the point where these two produce exactly the same benefits – except that you get to see more places on a bicycle! However, you need to consider the dangers associated with riding a bicycle on busy roads, if you do not have access to special cycle tracks.

Exercise bicycles and similar machines are a good alternative. But do not be tempted to dash out and buy the first exercise machine you see. Go to a gymnasium, try their equipment for a while, and ask the advice of the instructor about features and models which might be suited to you and your home.

Aerobics classes are an excellent method of exercise, particularly because you will usually be in an organized group, with a tutor, and with special classes for beginners. These classes are usually inexpensive, great fun, and you will have the added benefits of learning about stretching, and the importance of warming up and down before and after exercise. There are various types of aerobics sessions to try, and you can find out which technique or group you enjoy most.

Finally we come to the most simple, effective and underrated exercise of all – walking! Walking uses some of the biggest muscle sets in the body and burns energy at a high rate when compared with conscious effort. Walking at between 3.5 and 4.5 miles per hour delivers nearly the same aerobic benefits as running, but without the danger of impact damage normally associated with the latter. Most people normally walk at around 2.5 miles per hour (below the speed to create good aerobic effect) so you will need to consciously raise your pace above a stroll. You will know whether your walk is doing you any good without checking your pulse, as you will be sightly out of breath during the process – only *slightly* out of breath though, not gasping, and able to talk and walk!

Brisk walking is often a good option over other activities for a variety of reasons: if you are unfit, walking is the gentlest and safest exercise to start off with. No matter what your age, weight and condition, walking can easily be tailored to start producing the desired effect. Progress can be made gradually from, say, moving fairly slowly over short periods through to 'power walking' at a fast pace for long periods – and carrying small weights to enhance aerobic effect and add extra exercise for the upper body.

If you have a busy life and workstyle, walking can easily be fitted into your daily routine. No special clothes are necessary and you can do it at any opportunity. You could walk to work, walk the dog, walk to the shops, take a walk at lunchtime – the opportunities are endless. For those who are particularly self-conscious about exercising, walking is an ideal way to avoid embarrassment. It requires no special skills and is an 'invisible' exercise activity that attracts no attention. If you are on a tight financial budget, walking is ideal as it requires no special locations or special equipment, except a pair of comfortable shoes. If you have worries or problems a good walk is one of the best solutions; everything looks better after a long brisk walk.

Once you start to get fit extend your ideas as to how far a good walk might be – remember that as late as 1900 the average person walked about eight miles per day as part of their daily routine. So, unless you are already very fit, walking is the best 'duration exercise' to begin with, even if it does look unexciting at first. If you are over 35, have a picturesque walk nearby and own a dog, then you may well be easily persuaded. Otherwise remember that hiking forms an important part of most soldiers' physical training, and is the exercise which produces the bulk of their enviable fitness and firm physique. Clearly, if you live a very active life with plenty of genuine aerobic exercise you may not need to supplement this with any extra exercise at all. However, if this is genuinely the case then you are very unlikely to have any weight problem!

Try to make exercise part of your regular daily

routine and make sure you allocate around 30 to 40 minutes every day.

CHAPTER FIVE

The *Bodyclock* Diet

It is important to have a health check-up and seek advice from your physician before beginning any diet plan, to ensure that all changes to your diet and lifestyle are compatible with your individual medical condition.

Step 1 – Motivation

Achieving success on a diet is little different from any other human undertaking – it requires not only the right disciplines but also the right motivation to succeed. Without clear and positive motivation, a diet can easily become driven by the wrong kind of negative feelings.

However, motivation is not the sole prerogative of the 'thin' – despite the fact that fat people are often stereotyped as weak-willed. Surveys show that in general fat people are no less successful and adept at running their lives than thin people. In fact, some studies demonstrate that fat people frequently show fewer signs of stress than thin people and are far less likely to commit suicide!

If you are a 'go-getter' – that is, someone with cast-iron will and personal disciplines who always gets exactly what they want out of life – then you can skip this section and go on to Step 2. If you are not, then read on, because you need to develop some go-getting qualities to achieve the greatest diet success. 'Go-getters' clearly get what they want. Obviously they believe in themselves and that they can succeed – but how do they do it?

A key part of their secret is that they make clear decisions:

- *They decide what they want* *(objectives)*
- *They decide why they want it* *(rewards)*
- *They decide how to get it* *(actions)*

Notice also that 'go-getters' focus on long-term rather than short-term rewards. So, for example, they might focus on the long-term ongoing rewards of being slim rather than the momentary gratification of a chocolate bar. They focus all their energy on getting what they really want out of life.

Timing

The *Bodyclock* Diet provides you with the *Actions*, but you need to consider and clearly decide your *Objectives* and *Rewards*. It is important not to be over-optimistic – or over-pessimistic either. To ensure a balanced view, try to carry out the following exercises when your *Bodyclock* shows Emotional and Intellectual highs, with no criticals, such as:

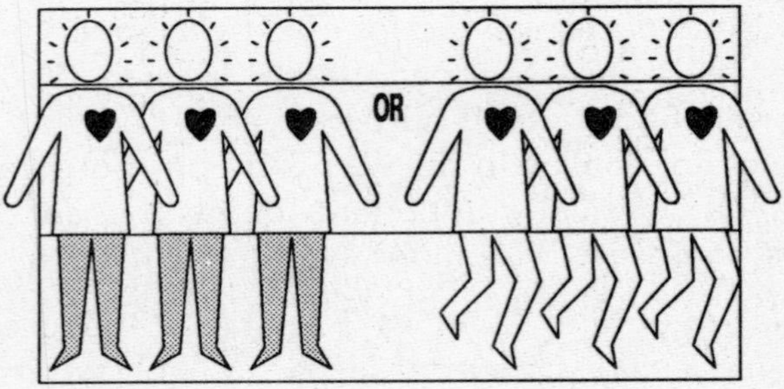

Ask yourself honestly: 'Why do I want to change my shape?'

Most people want to change shape in order to *look* and *feel* better. Feeling good about ourselves is the cornerstone of human happiness, and some medical experts believe this may also provide a measure of immunity against an increasing number of stress-related diseases and mental health problems.

The desire for self-improvement is no bad thing, but ultimate success depends on a very clear understanding of:

- *Your goals*
- *Why you want to achieve them*
- *What results can realistically be expected.*

Decide why you want to lose weight and improve your appearance. Be very clear and honest about your objectives, make a note of what you want to achieve, and decide not to settle for anything less than **total satisfaction.**

Be realistic

Bear in mind that the battle is not against weight in itself, it is against poor body shape in general and body fat in particular. Go for gold by all means – but avoid fantasies that cannot be fulfilled. Women generally find it much harder to shift body fat than men, simply because fat was a much more valued feminine physical component in the thousands of years before civilization began. Put this fact together with the total atypical female body shapes that Western culture perpetually promotes as 'desirable', and it is clear that the average woman has a harder job than a man to achieve satisfaction.

If you are short and dumpy, it is plainly unrealistic to expect to become tall and slender, though you could become better proportioned and more attractive. If you have a photo of yourself in younger, slimmer days or have saved some old clothes, these may help to indicate what sort of person lies underneath and what kind of shape you can realistically expect to achieve. Alternatively, if you have always been overweight, stand naked in front of a full-length mirror: take a long look at your height, bone structure and general build and try to see the 'thin person' within you who is trying to get out.

ACTION:

Write down your objectives:

I intend to become size .... by .... (date)

and include the dress/suit size or specific measurement (e.g. waist or hips) you would want to be by a particular date.

Write down your rewards:

When I am slim I will ....

....

and list all the benefits you hope to enjoy when you are slim.

Don't forget to enlist the help of friends and family – get them to take an interest, and support you. Those who encourage you will do so because they want you to be successful. Your success will be their reward. You never know – they may even decide to join you! Be wary of those people who try to persuade you to quit your diet and ask yourself what their reward will be?

Step 2 – Timing your diet

Good biorhythmic opportunities for maximum weight loss occur at frequent intervals, but timing your start is important. Make sure that your *Bodyclock* is set up correctly, according to the instructions in Appendix III. Begin the programme when Emotional and Physical rhythms are both at the start of a high stable period – with no criticals shown on your *Bodyclock*, in the illustration on page 29. Remember that the Intellectual biorhythm is less significant in your diet than the others, so that a critical does not matter. But beware of poor eating decisions on such days, especially if eating out.

The next best alternative is a high and low stable period with no criticals i.e. a high Emotional and low Physical or a high Physical and low Emotional.

Do not start your diet when your *Bodyclock* shows criticals in either your Emotional and/or Physical rhythms as in the illustration on page 30.

Step 3 – Selecting your diet plan

There are three variations of the *Bodyclock* Diet plan which have been designed to take account of different factors that will affect each individual. Turn to the questionnaire on the opposite page to find out your own *Body* and *Clock* factors. Your *Clock* factor is calculated from your age adjusted by your levels of daily physical activity; again, add the points together to find *your* Clock factor.

Now turn to the charts on page 64. Note that the top chart is for men and the bottom chart for women. Find your Body factor down the left-hand side of the chart, move your finger across to the right until it is above the number of your *Clock* factor shown at the bottom of your chart. Check which ever shaded area this is against the boxes at the bottom of the page, which will indicate whether you should follow diet plan A, B or C.

EXAMPLE

A 32-year-old sedentary woman of 5′5″, who is two stone overweight and takes some exercise, would have the following *Body* and *Clock* factors:

Height	**2**
Amount overweight	**2**
Total* Body *factor	**4**
Age	**2**
Work activity	**1**
Exercise	**2**
Total* Clock *factor	**5**

Bodyclock FACTORS

Basic *Body* factor: Height			***Points***
	for men	*for women*	
	under 5′6″	under 5′2″	**1**
	5′6″ to 5′10″	5′2″ to 5′6″	**2**
	over 5′10″	over 5′6″	**3**
Adjusting *Body* factor:			
Amount overweight	under $1\frac{1}{2}$ stone		**1**
	$1\frac{1}{2}$ stone to 3 stone		**2**
	over 3 stone		**3**
	Total *Body* factor		____
Basic *Clock* factor: Age			
	over 45		**1**
	25 to 45		**2**
	under 25		**3**
Adjusting *Clock* factors:			
Work activity	sedentary		**1**
	fairly active		**2**
	very active		**3**
Exercise	little		**1**
	some		**2**
	plenty		**3**
	Total *Clock* factor		____

CHOOSING YOUR DIET

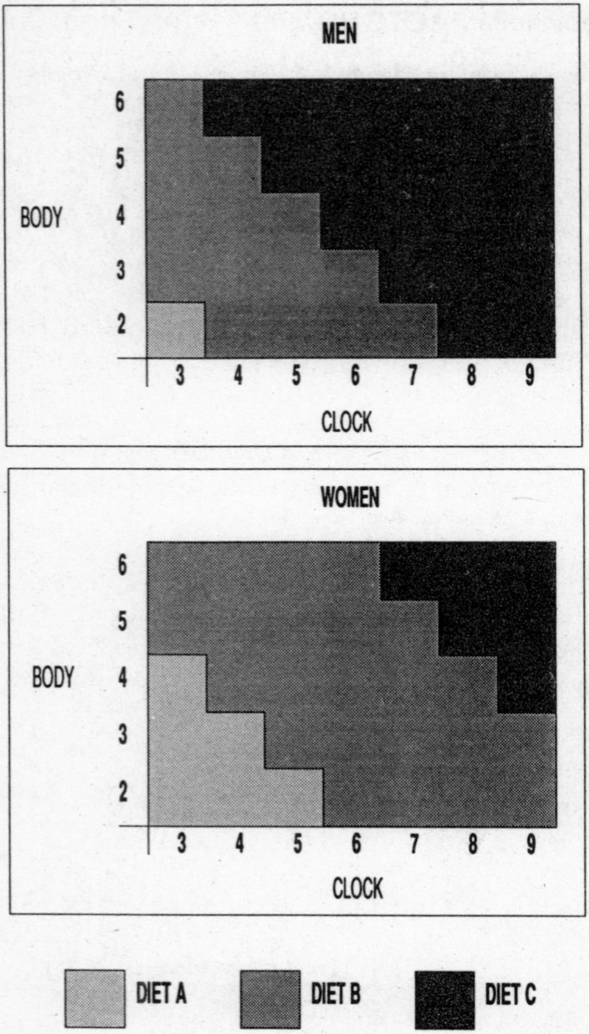

Turning to the chart for women on page 64, find *Body* factor 4 on the left and *Clock* factor 5 on the bottom. These meet in the dark shaded area representing Diet B.

Step 4 – Starting the diet

Twenty-day diet menus for each of the three plans follow on pages 81 to 95. You may pick a menu for the day in any order, but try to choose a variety of different day menus. The meals on one particular day may be eaten in a different order, but **don't swap** meals between different days, as each day's menu had been chosen to give you a balanced and combined intake of food.

Note: All calorific/nutritional information given in the Diet Menus is approximate.

On a critical Emotional or Physical day, you relax the diet restrictions, returning to your diet plan the following day. For example, if your *Bodyclock* display looks like this:

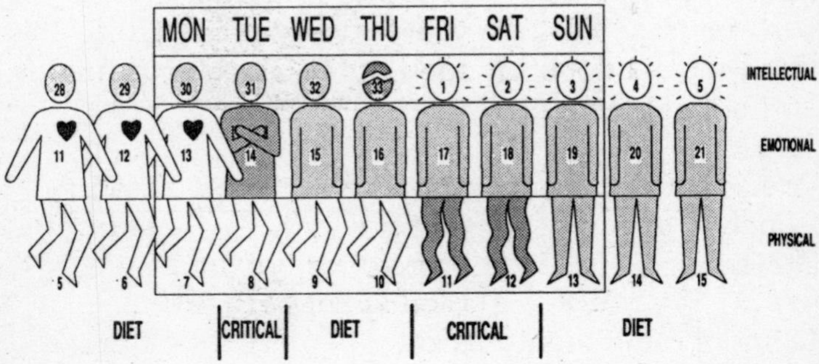

follow your diet plan on Monday, Wednesday, Thursday and Sunday. On Tuesday, Friday and Saturday you may relax the restrictions – either by following our special critical diet plans, if you are keen to see results as fast as possible, or if you want more freedom you may decide on your food for critical days yourself. Remember to eat healthy and balanced meals, but enjoy some (a sensible and modest portion) of your favourite food and drink. This planned break will help your diet, reinforce the routine and give you something to look forward to if you crave certain foods.

Eight special critical menus for each of the diet plans have been designed as 'treat' days. These are on pages 90 to 95. Choose any one day's menu for your critical day, but go back to the diet menus proper on the following day. The only additions to the menus are drinks: unlimited spring or filtered water (ideally 2 litres per day), or herbal tea. If you feel you must drink tea or filter coffee, do so with any milk to be taken from the daily allowances shown – but *no* instant coffee and *no* sugar.

Recipes for all the meals start on page 96. Each recipe is for four people, so that all the family can eat together. They are in order, split into the following sections for each of the *Bodyclock* menus and critical menus:

Breakfasts	protein	starch
Lunches snacks	protein	starch
Starters	protein for critical menus only	
Dinners main meal	protein	starch

Puddings	protein	starch
Side salads & dressings		

Step 5 – Exercise plan

If you do not take regular exercise already, then your heart may sink at this section. But don't panic, the *Bodyclock* Diet has a modest approach that you should find both easy and enjoyable!

The best exercise is one that feels good and fits naturally into your preferred daily routine. At the end of the day you will get out what you put in, but the *Bodyclock* can give you an advantage in your high energy programme. An exercise plan built around the *Bodyclock* Physical rhythm will be easier to carry out and more effective in terms of energy delivered. The technique is very simple:

Look at the Physical cycle and aim to start your exercise plan on day 2 of the new 'high' energy cycle. Why day 2 and not day 1? Because the low to high critical has more impact than the high to low critical, it is desirable to avoid physical stress until you are properly into the Physical high, having enjoyed a good two-day rest break. The Emotional and Intellectual rhythms are of no great significance for exercise except where they combine to create the occasional biorythmic 'storm', particularly when they are both critical, which does affect the Physical rhythm. In these circumstances, treat the day like a Physical critical and take a rest.

1. **Starting off:** You should initially take exercise with caution for the first 'high' period, but increase the pace and duration gently – ensuring that you do not overdo it.
2. **Rest:** You should rest during the 'critical period' spanning days 11 and 12 of the cycle.
3. **Maintain:** Maintain your new level of fitness at the same pace again for the 'low' period of the cycle between days 13 and 22. Do not increase the pace or duration during this time.
4. **Rest:** Rest again on the critical day of the end of the cycle and day 1 of the new cycle.
5. **Repeat:** Begin again on day 2 of the 'high' period, and gently increase the pace and duration of your exercise.

The following diagrams illustrate the pattern.

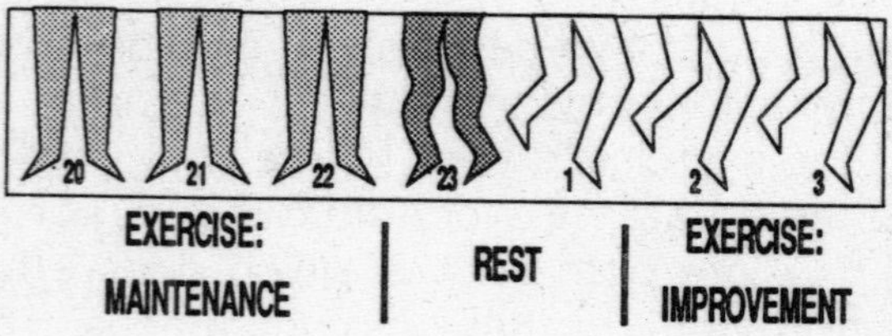

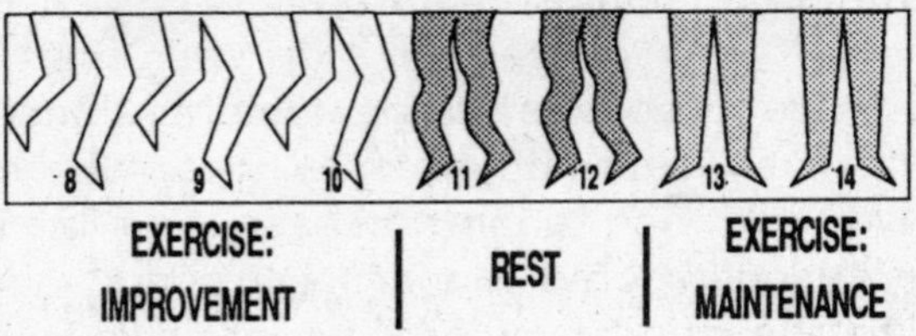

It is very important to take five minutes to warm up before exercising. Never leap straight into any vigorous physical activity, even walking. The warm-up will help to prevent injury and strains and the body to adjust to the required level of performance. Similarly, remember to warm down afterwards – don't just stop and fall into a chair. Towards the end of a session, start to ease the pace and gradually wind down: it is important to finish off with gentle bending and stretching exercises.

If you are ill – rest. Resume exercise with great care and well within your comfort level. Remember to improve only during the high period.

If you are totally unable to commit yourself to an exercise programme, then opt for the next best thing and make exercise as much a part of your daily life as possible. Walk or cycle to work. Forget the lift – take the stairs. Walk to the supermarket and leave the car behind. Forget the phone and walk over to see a friend. Tell the paper boy that you will fetch your own newspapers. When you go to parties, forget the food and drink and take a risk – get the dancing going. You will not only improve your health and your popularity, but also have great fun.

Step 6 – Positive imaging

If you have problems losing weight, there is an optional exercise that you may find relaxing and effective. This meditation process is similar to that which is used in some cancer treatments; it involves focusing the mind regularly on what you want to happen within your body in order to achieve successful results.

The human brain has two sides. The left side deals with issues such as language, logic and analysis, and is always in a hurry. The right side is much slower and more relaxed, and deals with subjective issues like spatial perceptions, development of ideas and appreciation of beauty. In order to focus our minds to help the reshaping process, we have to calm the 'little voice' that constantly chatters away to us – and we have to remove all left-side stimuli.

Try this exercise only when the Emotional and Intellectual rhythms are stable – *not* critical. The Physical rhythm is not very important for this exercise, so just look for one of the following patterns:

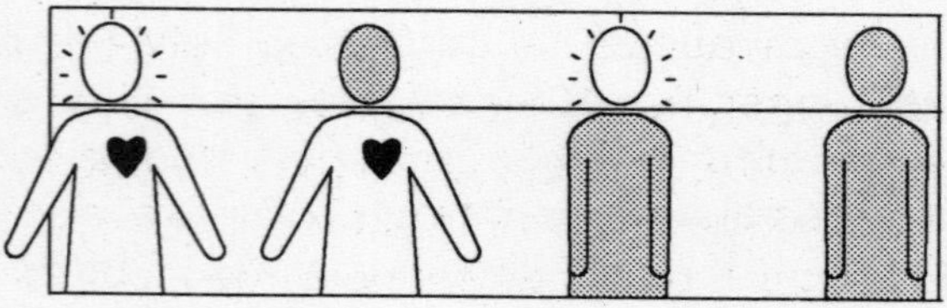

ACTION: Do the exercise in a quiet and darkened bedroom. Soft, calming music may help.

- *Kick off shoes, loosen clothes and lie on the bed* – relax totally and close eyes
- *Concentrate on each part of the body in turn, becoming more and more relaxed*
- *Relax the shoulders and breathe deeply from the diaphragm (stomach muscle) only. Note: your tummy should go out as you breathe in and in as you breathe out*
- *Once the whole body is relaxed, focus attention on your fat deposits*
- *Imagine the fat being dissolved in your body and gradually disappearing (or focus on a fire within you, burning the fat)*
- *Focus on different fat areas in turn and spend several minutes on each* – concentrate on how it looks and feels as the fat melts away.

Spend about 20 minutes actively doing this each day during the appropriate *Bodyclock* periods. Avoid falling asleep and ensure beforehand that you will not be disturbed.

Common problems

Appetite

Be very clear about the difference between appetite and hunger. Appetite is not hunger – it is simply your stomach's reaction to being fed meals at regular intervals over a number of years, and does not represent the true demands of your body. True hunger is normally experienced in the mouth, when saliva is produced in anticipation of food – any food. Appetite is usually recognized as a desire for certain specific foods, and a ravenous appetite is simply a symptom of eating too much too frequently.

False appetite is no more than a mild form of addiction, and can easily lead to wolfing down food. A small amount of initial self-control during the strong part of the Physical and Emotional cycles may be necessary to rid yourself of this. The false craving for food ceases quite quickly. Try drinking water if a false appetite starts up – this can help to control it.

Appetite can also be affected by the emotions as when people say that they have suddenly lost their appetite after some kind of shock or unexpected emotional reaction. So be very aware of your appetite in relation to your Emotional cycle.

If you are eating out of boredom, stress, loneliness or even just general unhappiness, remember that the antidote to stress and unhappiness is releasing energy – not in taking energy from more food. It you are bored, remember to release some energy! *A long walk will solve more problems than a packet of chocolate biscuits. An aerobic exercise session will get rid of more anger and stress than a chocolate bar.*

Food addiction

Some people appear to behave in an addictive way towards certain specific products – particularly chocolate – although food addiction is not an issue that is as widely discussed as drug or alcohol addiction. The issues that lie behind such addictions are complex, and may go much further than simply the texture, taste and ingredients of the food. The

Bodyclock Diet and exercise plan can help to beat addiction – especially if the diet rules and habits are rigorously observed, and habit is 'kicked' at the start of a long 'high' period in all biorhythms.

Willpower problems

Willpower covers a wide range of mental and physical disciplines that we use quite often. The *Bodyclock* Diet aims to help you maximize these. We learn that our actions can positively influence the results we want, even though some things may be a little hard to do at the time. A system of mental contracts and rewards is a harmless and useful device employed by many people to help them get through the day i.e. 'I'll get those boxes shifted first, and then I'll have a break!'

However, many people confuse *intention* with *manipulated willpower* – and they are two entirely different things. If, on the diet, you find that you are:

- *Just going through the motions*
- *Being constantly tempted to cheat*
- *Feeling slightly deprived and concentrating on what you are missing*

then you are almost certainly just manipulating your willpower to achieve results and this is bound to lead to failure and unhappiness.

Willpower manipulation tends to lead to:

- *Lack of motivation*
- *Stress and unhappiness*
- *Negativity and low energy.*

Intention is where you understand fully why you want something and take responsibility for its achievement. Where the intention is right, actions follow naturally, positively and almost as second nature. Intention springs from acknowledging yourself and channelling your natural positive energy towards your choice. Modern drug addiction treatments usually recognize the difference between willpower and intention. They support the addict without imposing abstention until such time as the addict fully intends to quit.

Intention on the diet can be seen when you:

- *Take control of and be responsible for your actions*
- *Plan ahead to make the next day(s) special*
- *Act confidently to get 100% of what you want in everything.*

If you continue to experience willpower problems on the diet, go back and spend more time reviewing your motivation in Step 1 of the diet – and try getting a friend to help you.

What happens if you forget yourself and pig-out?

So often a momentary lapse in the face of temptation or a sudden craving leads to despair, and then on to complete abandonment of a rational eating programme. If you slip up, or even pig-out, forgive yourself and forget about it – but don't make a regular habit of it! One slip will not destroy your diet, it will just slow down your fat loss a little, so do not make this a reason or an excuse to give up. Do not wallow in self-disgust and do not punish yourself either. Learning to deal with failure and to grow personally out of failure in a positive way is one of the most important life-enhancing processes that you can master. *Use this experience positively and do not waste it.* If a lapse occurs without significant temptation or external pressure, make a note of your *Bodyclock* reading at the time and use this for reference.

Flatulence

Normal healthy individuals on a conventional Western diet can expect to produce a couple of litres of gas per day as a by-product of the digestive process. There is nothing unusual about this. A switch to healthier food can sometimes lead to an increase in the production of intestinal gases, but this will cease as your body becomes more accustomed to the new regime. Provided you chew your food thoroughly and stick to the diet combinations and quantities, you should not experience problems – in fact, you may experience far less wind. If you do suffer with persistent flatulence on the *Bodyclock* Diet, you are advised to consult a physician, as this is more likely to stem from an intestinal ailment than a reaction to natural food.

Bowel movements

It is not uncommon to meet sedentary people living on junk food, cigarettes and alcohol who go for days between bowel movements and who frequently experience the unpleasant effects of constipation. Depending on your previous eating habits, a switch to the *Bodyclock* Diet could produce a major change in the number of bowel movements. Far from being bad, this is entirely good, showing that your body's waste disposal system is at last working properly and eliminating harmful residue. Perhaps more disturbing are very loose motions which may afflict some people during the first few days, depending on their system. Once again this is not bad, but does show that the body is taking the opportunity to naturally expel toxic waste. If it continues after the first couple of days, you should consult a doctor for expert advice.

Eating out

When you are invited out for dinner, don't be a diet bore – this will only produce the kind of reaction that will undermine your diet – but do be honest with your hosts about what you are trying to achieve so that they can plan a menu to suit the weight-conscious and everyone else. The chances are that at least one other person present will be trying to lose weight as well.

If you eat in restaurants regularly, particularly on those dreaded business lunches, make a list of places which offer simple food such as steamed fish, grilled meat, mixed salads and jacket potatoes. Avoid restaurants that only serve pizzas, fast food and fried food. Be especially cautious about anything covered in sauces, since these invariably have cream, butter, cheese or other diet-busting ingredients.

For eating out, the following list gives a guide to relatively 'safe' choices. There are different ethnic dishes to choose for different types of restaurant. We suggest that you keep a copy of this list with you if eating out is a significant part of your lifestyle.

Pub or canteen:
Salad sandwich

Baked Potato and salad/vegetables
Grilled steak and salad/vegetables
Omelette (occasionally) and salad/vegetables
Ham salad

Avoid: Ploughman's, steak and kidney pie, sausages and mash, shepherd's pie and peas, salt-beef sandwich, mayonnaise, butter and cream

English/French:
Grapefruit, consommé, oysters, smoked salmon
Grilled fish or lobster with salad/vegetables
Grilled meats and salad/vegetables
Fresh fruit salad (no topping)

Avoid: cream soups, pâté, anything potted, avocados, rich sauces, pies, profiteroles and other creamy puddings, cheeses

Indian:
Tandoori chicken and salad
Plain vegetable curry
1 or 2 poppadoms

Avoid: mango chutney, curries with thick sauces e.g. kormas, masalas, naan etc.

Greek:
Greek salad
Dolmades
Grilled fish and salad/vegetables
Kleftico and salad
Meat and vegetable kebabs (souvlakia)

Avoid: taramasalata, doner kebabs, moussaka, baklava, halva

Chinese:
Pancake roll
Beansprouts and boiled rice
Prawn chop suey
Chow mein

Avoid: all Chinese food as a rule – the frying process leaves a very high fat content and monosodium glutomate is usually added.

Italian:
Minestrone soup
Plain pasta with basil sauce or Parmesan
Spaghetti Napoletana
Grilled meat/fish and salad
Cheeseless vegetarian pizza

Avoid: rich pastas, regular pizzas, zabaglione, cassata, cheeses, salami

Spanish/Mexican:
Tomato salad
Gazpacho
Grilled meat/fish with salad/vegetables

Avoid: paella, chilli con carne with rice, guacamole dip

American:
Chicken (remove skin) and salad
Plain grilled regular hamburger and salad

Avoid: big hamburgers with buns, cheeseburgers, fries, fried onions, milk shakes, cola drinks, apple pies, relishes

Appendix I – Menus and Recipes

	Breakfast	Cals	Fbr	Fat	Lunch	Cals	Fbr	Fat	Dinner	Cals	Fbr	Fat	Total Cals	Total Fbr	Total Fat
	Prune Fluff	125	7.6	1.3	Tomato and Onion Sandwich	163	9.8	2.5	Chicken and Vegetable Stir-fry	342	9.7	4.8	951	45.1	9.4
1	Orange Juice (5fl oz)	55	0.0	0.0											
					Banana	88	4.0	0.8	Blackberry Baked Apple	133	14.0	0.0			
	Stewed Apricots	102	13.9	0.0	Tzatsiki	69	0.3	2.0	Stuffed Aubergine	252	15.8	7.0	981	54.2	17.0
2	Natural Low-fat Yogurt (5 oz)	75	0.0	2.5	Crudités	63	4.5	0.3	Mixed Salad	76	5.3	0.3			
					1 slice Wholemeal Pitta Bread	142	4.7	0.7	Brussels Sprouts	28	4.8	0.0			
					Pear	40	2.5	0.0	Stuffed Oranges	89	2.4	4.2			
	Blackberry Yogurt	91	4.0	2.5	Potato and Courgette Salad	185	5.3	2.3	Tomato Baked Fish	160	1.6	3.5	1011	41.6	14.1
3									Green Salad	29	3.0	0.0			
					Banana	88	4.0	0.8	Peas, Sweetcorn	204	12.8	0.0			
					Green Grapes (5oz)	85	1.5	0.0	Raspberry Yogurt Snow	124	9.4	5.0			
	Apple Sauce	40	2.4	0.0	Sunshine Omelette	218	3.8	12.6	Vegetable Kebabs and Rice	341	13.2	1.7	988	33.2	15.9
4	Orange Juice (5fl oz)	55	0.0	0.0	Green Salad	29	3.0	0.0	Mixed Salad	76	5.3	0.3			
					Peach	35	1.5	0.0	Ginger Pear Mousse	149	4.0	1.3			
	Apricot Drink	28	2.0	0.0	Ratatouille	105	7.6	3.5	Minced Beef with Roast Parsnips	291	9.0	16.0	966	41.6	20.3
5	Apple	50	3.0	0.0	Jacket Potato (7oz)	168	4.9	0.0	Carrots	24	3.2	0.0			
					Green Grapes (5oz)	85	1.5	0.0	Green Beans	8	3.6	0.0			
					Banana	88	4.0	0.8	Green Ginger Salad	74	2.8	0.0			
	Fruit and Nut Yogurt	249	7.4	11.5	Banana Sandwich	238	10.0	3.3	Prawn and Pepper Salad	239	11.7	4.7	952	44.3	19.5
6															
					Pear	40	2.5	0.0	Apricot Baked Apple	141	12.7	0.0			
	Spiced Grapefruit	26	0.5	0.0	Savoury Mushrooms on Toast	177	9.5	2.5	Spinach Dolmades	203	6.7	7.1	997	32.4	14.0
7									Mixed Salad	76	5.3	0.3			
					Pear	40	2.5	0.0	Brown Rice (2oz)	200	2.4	1.2			
					Green Grapes (5oz)	85	1.5	0.0	Banana Fool	145	4.0	2.9			

Daily allowance of ¼ pint of skimmed milk

Vegetable serving 4oz unless otherwise specified

	Breakfast	Cals	Fbr	Fat	Lunch	Cals	Fbr	Fat	Dinner	Cals	Fbr	Fat	Total Cals	Total Fbr	Total Fat
8	Banana Date Breakfast	137	5.9	0.8	Carrot and Raisin Salad	67	6.2	0.1	Hot Chicken	239	4.8	2.9	989	37.5	7.5
					Jacket Potato (7oz)	168	4.9	0.0	Sweetcorn	84	6.4	1.2			
					Pear	40	2.5	0.0	Broccoli	24	4.0	0.0			
					Natural Low-fat Yogurt (5 oz)	75	0.0	2.5	Tropical Salad	110	2.8	0.0			
9	Blackberry Apple Breakfast	86	4.4	1.3	Red Pepper Soup	78	1.9	3.7	Vegetable Risotto	329	10.5	7.7	1005	35	18.9
	Orange Juice (5fl oz)	55	0.0	0.0	1 slice Wholemeal Toast	60	2.4	1.0	Green Salad	29	3.0	0.0			
					Mixed Salad	76	5.3	0.3	Ginger Bananas with	128	5.0	3.7			
					Pear	40	2.5		Yogurt Snow	79	0.0	1.2			
10	Apple and Orange Yogurt	79	2.4	1.3	Tomatoes on Toast	166	7.6	2.5	Haddock with Grapefruit & Mushrooms	123	1.5	1.5	960	45	6.1
									Peas, Sweetcorn	204	12.8	0.0			
					Banana	88	4.0	0.8	Broccoli	24	4.0	0.0			
					Dates (2oz)	138	4.8	0.0	Hot Fruit Soufflé	93	7.9	0.0			
11	Citrus Starter	91	2.3	4.5	Fruity Cheese Plate	227	5.8	2.0	Minestrone Casserole	347	18.6	2.0	995	35.4	14.8
									Wholemeal Bread (1 slice per person)	60	2.4	1.0			
					Green Grapes (3oz)	51	0.9	0.0	Hot Bananas	174	5.4	5.3			
12	Raspberry Yogurt	89	4.2	2.5	Stuffed Pitta Bread	186	7.6	0.9	Garlic Steak and Mushrooms	216	2.8	5.6	982	33.8	13.2
	Orange Juice (5fl oz)	55	0.0	0.0					2 Grilled Tomatoes, Sweetcorn	100	8.0	1.2			
					Dried Dates (2oz)	138	4.8	0.0	Green Salad	29	3.0	0.0			
					Pear	40	2.5	0.0	Strawberry Cheese	84	0.9	3.0			
13	Half Ogen Melon	30	1.3	0.0	Cashew Coleslaw	178	10.2	7.6	Prawn Provençal	168	6.7	3.9	963	43.7	15.3
					Jacket Potato (7oz)	168	4.9	0.0	Green Beans	8	3.6	0.0			
					Dates (2oz)	138	4.8	0.0	Swede	24	3.2	0.0			
					Natural Low-fat Yogurt (5 oz)	75	0.0	2.5	Blackberry and Apple Fool	129	9.0	1.3			
14	Raspberry Apple Drink	41	4.9	0.0	Aubergine Pâté	168	4.7	13.0	Savoury Dutch Cakes	296	12.6	3.5	951	48.2	17.1
	Orange	42	2.4	0.0	Crudités	63	4.5	0.3	Mixed Salad	76	5.3	0.3			
									Peas	60	8.8	0.0			
					Green Grapes (5oz)	85	1.5	0.0	Pear Compôte	75	3.5				

Daily allowance of ¼ pint of skimmed milk

Vegetable serving 4oz unless otherwise specified

	Breakfast	Cals	Fbr	Fat		Cals	Fbr	Fat	Dinner	Cals	Fbr	Fat	Total Cals	Total Fbr	Total Fat
	Apple Sauce	40	2.4	0.0	Sweetcorn Soup	190	4.0	4.1	Spicy Fish Casserole	122	4.2	1.2	968	48.1	6.3
15	Orange Juice (5fl oz)	55	0.0	0.0	1 slice Wholemeal Toast	60	2.4	1.0	Brussels Sprouts, Peas	88	13.6	0.0			
					Dried Figs (2oz)	120	10.5	0.0	Roast Parsnips (5oz pp)	70	5.5	0.0			
					Pear	40	2.5	0.0	Pineapple Sorbet	138	3.0				
	Banana and Walnut Yogurt	200	4.4	7.0	Herby Cheese Salad	160	4.6	2.0	Spaghetti Napoletana	370	13.5	2.3	989	34.8	11.6
16									Mixed Salad	76	5.3	0.3			
					Apple	50	3.0	0.0	Banana Ice	88	4.0				
	Strawberry Apples	54	3.6	0.0	Herby Mushroom Pâté	60	3.5	3.5	Tuna and Corn Salad	272	15.5	7.2	971	48.4	14.2
17	Orange Juice (5fl oz)	55	0.0	0.0	1 slice Wholemeal Bread	60	2.4	1.0							
					Dried Dates (1oz),Green Grapes (5oz	154	3.9	0.0							
					Natural Low-fat Yogurt (5 oz)	75	0.0	2.5	Spiced Fruit Salad	196	19.5				
	Banana Date Breakfast	137	5.9	0.8	Gazpacho	40	2.9	0.0	Citrus Chicken	194	4.9	2.5	1001	35	10.5
18	Unsweetened Grape Juice	100	0.0	0.0	1 slice Wholemeal Bread	60	2.4	1.0	Mixed Salad	76	5.3	0.3			
	(5fl oz)				Pear, Sultanas (1oz)	110	4.5	0.0	Courgettes	20	2.0	0.0			
					Natural Low-fat Yogurt (5 oz)	75	0.0	2.5	Baked Apple	144	7.1	3.4			
	Raspberry Yogurt	89	4.2	2.5	Chinese Salad	149	7.0	3.0	Vegetable Stuffed Jacket Potato	354	12.5	0.8	1004	34.3	9.2
19	Orange Juice (5fl oz)	55	0.0	0.0	Nectarine	70	3.5	0.0	Green Salad	29	3.0	0.0			
					Orange	42	2.4	0.0							
									Banana Fruit Yogurt	171	1.7	2.9			
	Prune Whip	76	7.6	0.0	Mushroom Pasta	291	7.7	7.0	Spanish Omelette	237	7.7	12.3	963	37	19.3
20	Orange Juice (5fl oz)	55	0.0	0.0					Green Salad	29	3.0	0.0			
					Dried Figs (1oz)	60	5.2	0.0							
					Green Grapes (5oz)	85	1.5	0.0	Fruit Salad	85	4.3				

Daily allowance of $\frac{1}{4}$ pint of skimmed milk

Vegetable serving 4oz unless otherwise specified

Bodyclock DIET MENUS

DIET B

	Breakfast	Cals	Fbr	Fat	Lunch	Cals	Fbr	Fat	Dinner	Cals	Fbr	Fat	Total		
													Cals	Fbr	Fat
	Prune Fluff	125	7.6	1.3	Tomato and Onion Sandwich	163	9.8	2.5	Chicken and Vegetable Stir-fry	342	9.7	4.8	1214	52.9	11.9
1	Orange Juice (5fl oz)	55	0.0	0.0	Natural Low-fat Yogurt (5 oz)	75	0.0	2.5							
	Apple	50	3.0	0.0	Banana	88	4.0	0.8							
					Dates (2oz)	138	4.8	0.0	Blackberry Baked Apple	133	14.0	0.0			
	Stewed Apricots	102	13.9	0.0	Tzatsiki	69	0.3	2.0	Stuffed Aubergine	252	15.8	7.0	1223	71	17.0
2	Natural Low-fat Yogurt (5 oz)	75	0.0	2.5	Crudités	63	4.5	0.3	Mixed Salad	76	5.3	0.3			
	Orange Juice (5fl oz)	55	0.0	0.0	1 slice Wholemeal Pitta Bread	142	4.7	0.7	Brussels Sprouts	35	6	0			
					Pear, Dried Figs (3oz)	220	18.1	0.0	Stuffed Oranges	89	2.4	4.2			
	Blackberry Yogurt	91	4.0	2.5	Potato and Courgette Salad	185	5.3	2.3	Tomato Baked Fish	160	1.6	3.5	1242	47.8	16.6
3	Orange Juice (5fl oz)	55	0.0	0.0	Natural Low-fat Yogurt (5 oz)	75	0.0	2.5	Green Salad	29	3.0	0.0			
	Apple	50	3.0	0.0	Banana	88	4.0	0.8	Peas, Sweetcorn	255	16	0			
					Green Grapes (5oz)	85	1.5	0.0	Raspberry Yogurt Snow	124	9.4	5.0			
	Apple Sauce	40	2.4	0.0	Sunshine Omelette	218	3.8	12.6	Vegetable Kebabs and Rice	341	13.2	1.7	1219	37.6	18.7
4	Orange Juice (5fl oz)	55	0.0	0.0	Mixed Salad	76	5.3	0.3	Mixed Salad	76	5.3	0.3			
	Natural Low-fat Yogurt (5 oz)	75	0.0	2.5	Mango	100	2.0	0.0							
					Cherries (4oz)	44	1.6	0.0	Ginger Pear Mousse	149	4.0	1.3			
	Apricot Drink	28	2.0	0.0	Ratatouille	105	7.6	3.5	Minced Beef with Roast Parsnips	291	9.0	16.0	1172	55.7	22.8
5	Apple	50	3.0	0.0	Jacket Potato (9oz)	216	6.3	0.0	Carrots, Peas	105	15	0			
	Natural Low-fat Yogurt (5 oz)	75	0.0	2.5	Green Grapes (5oz)	85	1.5	0.0	Green Beans	10	4.5	0			
					Banana	88	4.0	0.8	Green Ginger Salad	74	2.8	0.0			
	Fruit and Nut Yogurt	249	7.4	11.5	Banana Sandwich	238	10.0	3.3	Prawn and Pepper Salad	239	11.7	4.7	1220	53.1	19.5
6	Orange Juice (5fl oz)	55	0.0	0.0											
	Peach	35	1.5	0.0	Dates (2oz)	138	4.8	0.0							
					2 Pears	80	5.0	0.0	Apricot Baked Apple	141	12.7	0.0			
	Spiced Grapefruit	26	0.5	0.0	Savoury Mushrooms on Toast	177	9.5	2.5	Spinach Dolmades	203	6.7	7.1	1206	37.5	16.5
7	Natural Low-fat Yogurt (5 oz)	75	0.0	2.5					Mixed Salad, Leeks	121	9.8	0.3			
	Orange Juice (5fl oz)	55	0.0	0.0	Pear	40	2.5	0.0	Brown Rice (2oz)	200	2.4	1.2			
					Green Grapes (7oz)	119	2.1	0.0	Banana Fool	145	4.0	2.9			

Daily allowance of ½ pint of skimmed milk

Vegetable serving 5oz unless otherwise specified

	Breakfast	Cals	Fbr	Fat	Lunch	Cals	Fbr	Fat	Dinner	Cals	Fbr	Fat	Total Cals	Total Fbr	Total Fat
	Banana Date Breakfast	137	5.9	0.8	Carrot and Raisin Salad	67	6.2	0.1	Hot Chicken	239	4.8	2.9	1239	41.5	10.3
8	Natural Low-fat Yogurt (5 oz)	75	0.0	2.5	Jacket Potato (9oz)	216	6.3	0.0	Sweetcorn	105	8	1.5			
	Unsweetened Grape Juice	100	0.0	0.0	Pear	40	2.5	0.0	Broccoli	30	5	0			
	(5fl oz)				Natural Low-fat Yogurt (5 oz)	75	0.0	2.5	Tropical Salad	110	2.8	0.0			
	Blackberry Apple Breakfast	86	4.4	1.3	Red Pepper Soup	78	1.9	3.7	Vegetable Risotto	329	10.5	7.7	1268	38.5	21.4
9	Natural Low-fat Yogurt (5 oz)	75	0.0	2.5	1 slice Wholemeal Toast	60	2.4	1.0	Green Salad	29	3.0	0.0			
	Orange Juice (5fl oz)	55	0.0	0.0	Mixed Salad	76	5.3	0.3	Ginger Bananas with	128	5.0	3.7			
					Banana, Sultanas (2oz)	228	6.0	0.0	Yogurt Snow	79	0.0	1.2			
	Apple and Orange Yogurt	79	2.4	1.3	Tomatoes on Toast	166	7.6	2.5	Haddock with Grapefruit & Mushrooms	123	1.5	1.5	1211	53.6	6.1
10	Orange Juice (5fl oz)	55	0.0	0.0					Peas, Sweetcorn	255	16	0			
	Sultanas (1oz)	70	2.0	0.0	Banana	88	4.0	0.8	Broccoli	30	5	0			
					Dates (3oz)	207	7.2	0.0	Hot Fruit Soufflé	93	7.9	0.0			
	Citrus Starter	91	2.3	4.5	Fruity Cheese Plate	227	5.8	2.0	Minestrone Casserole	347	18.6	2.0	1238	36	18.5
11	Natural Low-fat Yogurt (5 oz)	75	0.0	2.5					Wholemeal Bread (1 slice per person)	60	2.4	1.0			
	Orange Juice (5fl oz)	55	0.0	0.0					Hot Bananas with	174	5.4	5.3			
					Green Grapes (5oz)	85	1.5	0.0	Yogurt Snow	79	0.0	1.2			
	Raspberry Yogurt	89	4.2	2.5	Stuffed Pitta Bread	186	7.6	0.9	Garlic Steak & Mushrooms	216	2.8	5.6	1203	46.4	12.0
12	Orange Juice (5fl oz)	55	0.0	0.0					2 Grilled Tomatoes, Green Salad	45	4.6	0			
	Apple	50	3.0	0.0	Dried Dates (2oz)	138	4.8	0.0	Peas, Sweetcorn	255	16	0			
					Pear	40	2.5	0.0	Strawberry Cheese	84	0.9	3.0			
	Prune Fluff	125	7.6	1.3	Cashew Coleslaw	178	10.2	7.6	Prawn Provençal	168	6.7	3.9	1219	56.1	16.6
13	Orange Juice (5fl oz)	55	0.0	0.0	Jacket Potato (9oz)	216	6.3	0.0	Green Beans	10	4.5	0			
	Apple	50	3.0	0.0	Dates (2oz)	138	4.8	0.0	Swede	30	4	0			
					Natural Low-fat Yogurt (5 oz)	75	0.0	2.5	Blackberry and Apple Fool	129	9.0	1.3			
	Raspberry Apple Drink	41	4.9	0.0	Aubergine Pâté	168	4.7	13.0	Savoury Dutch Cakes	296	12.6	3.5	1217	55.7	20.3
14	Orange	42	2.4	0.0	Crudités	63	4.5	0.3	Mixed Salad	76	5.3	0.3			
	Natural Low-fat Yogurt (5 oz)	75	0.0	2.5	1 piece Wholemeal Pitta Bread	142	4.7	0.7	Peas	75	11	0			
					Green Grapes (7oz)	119	2.1	0.0	Pear Compôte	75	3.5				

Daily allowance of ¼ pint of skimmed milk

Vegetable serving 5oz unless otherwise specified

	Breakfast	Cals	Fbr	Fat		Cals	Fbr	Fat	Dinner	Cals	Fbr	Fat	Total Cals	Total Fbr	Total Fat
15	Apple Sauce	40	2.4	0.0	Sweetcorn Soup	190	4.0	4.1	Spicy Fish Casserole	122	4.2	1.2	1253	58.1	16.1
	Orange Juice (5fl oz)	55	0.0	0.0	1 slice Wholemeal Toast	60	2.4	1.0	Brussels Sprouts, Peas	110	17	0			
	Natural Low-fat Yogurt (5 oz)	75	0.0	2.5	Banana, Dried Figs (3oz)	268	19.6	0.8	Roast Parsnips	70	5.5	0.0			
					Pumpkin Seeds (1tbsp)	80	0.0	6.5	Pineapple Sorbet	138	3.0				
16	Banana and Walnut Yogurt	200	4.4	7.0	Herby Cheese Salad	160	4.6	2.0	Spaghetti Napoletana	370	13.5	2.3	1229	37.8	14.1
	Unsweetened Grape Juice	100	0.0	0.0					Mixed Salad	76	5.3	0.3			
	(5fl oz)				Nectarine	65	3.0	0.0	Natural Low-fat Yogurt (5 oz)	75	0.0	2.5			
					Apple	50	3.0	0.0	Banana Ice	88	4.0				
17	Strawberry Apples	54	3.6	0.0	Herby Mushroom Pâté	60	3.5	3.5	Tuna and Corn Salad	272	15.5	7.2	1218	53.8	16.7
	Orange Juice (5fl oz)	55	0.0	0.0	1 slice Wholemeal Bread	60	2.4	1.0							
	Natural Low-fat Yogurt (5 oz)	75	0.0	2.5	Dried Dates (3oz),Green Grapes (7oz	326	9.3	0.0							
					Natural Low-fat Yogurt (5 oz)	75	0.0	2.5	Spiced Fruit Salad	196	19.5				
18	Banana Date Breakfast	137	5.9	0.8	Gazpacho	40	2.9	0.0	Citrus Chicken	194	4.9	2.5	1226	48.5	13.0
	Unsweetened Grape Juice	100	0.0	0.0	1 slice Wholemeal Bread	60	2.4	1.0	Mixed Salad	76	5.3	0.3			
	(5fl oz)				Pear, Sultanas (2oz)	180	6.5	0.0	Courgettes, Peas	100	13.5	0			
	Natural Low-fat Yogurt (5 oz)	75	0.0	2.5	Natural Low-fat Yogurt (5 oz)	75	0.0	2.5	Baked Apple	144	7.1	3.4			
19	Raspberry Yogurt	89	4.2	2.5	Chinese Salad	149	7.0	3.0	Vegetable Stuffed Jacket Potato	354	12.5	0.8	1199	51.8	9.2
	Orange Juice (5fl oz)	55	0.0	0.0	2 Nectarines	140	7.0	0.0	Green Salad	29	3.0	0.0			
	Apple	50	3.0	0.0	Orange	42	2.4	0.0	Peas	75	11.0	0.0			
									Banana Fruit Yogurt	171	1.7	2.9			
20	Prune Whip	76	7.6	0.0	Mushroom Pasta	291	7.7	7.0	Spanish Omelette	237	7.7	12.3	1229	48.1	22.1
	Orange Juice (5fl oz)	55	0.0	0.0					Mixed Salad	76	5.3	0.3			
	Apple	50	3.0	0.0	Dried Figs (2oz)	120	10.4	0.0	Natural Low-fat Yogurt (5 oz)	75	0.0	2.5			
					Green Grapes (7oz)	119	2.1	0.0	Fruit Salad	85	4.3				

Daily allowance of ¼ pint of skimmed milk

Vegetable serving 5oz unless otherwise specified

	Breakfast	Cals	Fbr	Fat	Lunch	Cals	Fbr	Fat	Dinner	Cals	Fbr	Fat	Total Cals	Total Fbr	Total Fat
	Prune Fluff	125	7.6	1.3	2 Tomato and Onion Sandwiches	326	19.6	5.0	Chicken and Vegetable Stir-fry	342	9.7	4.8	1468	65.1	14.4
1	Orange Juice (7fl oz)	77	0.0	0.0	Natural Low-fat Yogurt (5 oz)	75	0.0	2.5							
	Apple	50	3.0	0.0	Banana	88	4.0	0.8							
					Dried Dates (3oz)	207	7.2	0.0	Blackberry Baked Apple	133	14.0	0.0			
	Stewed Apricots	102	13.9	0.0	Tzatsiki	69	0.3	2.0	Stuffed Aubergine	252	15.8	7.0	1434	79.4	17.7
2	Natural Low-fat Yogurt (5 oz)	75	0.0	2.5	Crudités	63	4.5	0.3	Mixed Salad	76	5.3	0.3			
	Orange Juice (7fl oz)	77	0.0	0.0	2 pieces Wholemeal Pitta Bread	284	9.4	1.4	Brussels Sprouts	42	7	0			
					2 Pears, Dried Figs (3oz)	260	20.6	0.0	Stuffed Oranges	89	2.4	4.2			
	Blackberry Yogurt	91	4.0	2.5	Potato and Courgette Salad	185	5.3	2.3	Tomato Baked Fish	160	1.6	3.5	1437	55.6	17.4
3	Orange Juice (7fl oz)	77	0.0	0.0	Natural Low-fat Yogurt (5 oz)	75	0.0	2.5	Green Salad	29	3.0	0.0			
	Apple	50	3.0	0.0	2 Bananas	176	8.0	1.6	Peas, Sweetcorn	306	19	0			
					Green Grapes (7oz)	119	2.1	0.0	Raspberry Yogurt Snow	124	9.4	5.0			
	Apple Sauce	40	2.4	0.0	Sunshine Omelette	218	3.8	12.6	Vegetable Kebabs and Rice	341	13.2	1.7	1463	40.8	19.9
4	Orange Juice (7fl oz)	77	0.0	0.0	Mixed Salad	76	5.3	0.3	Brown Rice (2oz additional to recipe)	200	2.4	1.2			
	Natural Low-fat Yogurt (5 oz)	75	0.0	2.5	Mango	100	2.0	0.0	Mixed Salad	76	5.3	0.3			
					Cherries (6oz)	66	2.4	0.0	Ginger Pear Mousse	149	4.0	1.3			
	Apricot Drink	28	2.0	0.0	Ratatouille	105	7.6	3.5	Minced Beef with Roast Parsnips	291	9.0	16.0	1439	69.3	23.6
5	2 Apples	100	6.0	0.0	Jacket Potato (12oz)	288	8.4	0.0	Carrots, Peas	126	18	0			
	Natural Low-fat Yogurt (5 oz)	75	0.0	2.5	Green Grapes (7oz)	119	2.1	0.0	Green Beans	12	5	0			
					2 Bananas	176	8.0	1.6	Green Ginger Salad	74	2.8	0.0			
	Fruit and Nut Yogurt	249	7.4	11.5	2 Banana Sandwiches	476	20.0	6.6	Prawn and Pepper Salad	239	11.7	4.7	1480	63.1	22.8
6	Orange Juice (7fl oz)	77	0.0	0.0											
	Peach	35	1.5	0.0	Dried Dates (2oz)	138	4.8	0.0							
					2 Pears	80	5.0	0.0	Apricot Baked Apple	141	12.7	0.0			
	Spiced Grapefruit	26	0.5	0.0	Savoury Mushrooms on Toast	177	9.5	2.5	Spinach Dolmades	203	6.7	7.1	1437	40.8	17.7
7	Natural Low-fat Yogurt (5 oz)	75	0.0	2.5					Mixed Salad, Leeks	130	10.7	0.3			
	Orange Juice (7fl oz)	77	0.0	0.0	Pear	40	2.5	0.0	Brown Rice (4oz)	400	4.8	2.4			
					Green Grapes (7oz)	119	2.1	0.0	Banana Fool	145	4.0	2.9			

Daily allowance of ½ pint of skimmed milk

Vegetable serving 6oz unless otherwise specified

Day	Breakfast	Cals	Fbr	Fat	Lunch	Cals	Fbr	Fat	Dinner	Cals	Fbr	Fat	Total Cals	Total Fbr	Total Fat
	Banana Date Breakfast	137	5.9	0.8	Carrot and Raisin Salad	67	6.2	0.1	Hot Chicken	239	4.8	2.9	1463	47.7	10.6
8	Natural Low-fat Yogurt (5 oz)	75	0.0	2.5	Jacket Potato (12oz)	288	8.4	0.0	Sweetcorn	126	10	2			
	Unsweetened Grape Juice	140	0.0	0.0	Green Grapes (7oz), Pear	125	4.0	0.0	Broccoli	36	6	0			
	(7fl oz)				Natural Low-fat Yogurt (5 oz)	75	0.0	2.5	Tropical Salad	110	2.8	0.0			
	Blackberry Apple Breakfast	86	4.4	1.3	Red Pepper Soup	78	1.9	3.7	Vegetable Risotto	329	10.5	7.7	1498	47.3	23.4
9	Natural Low-Fat Yogurt (5 oz)	75	0.0	2.5	3 slices Wholemeal Toast	180	7.2	3.0	Green Salad	29	3.0	0.0			
	Orange Juice (7fl oz)	77	0.0	0.0	Mixed Salad	76	5.3	0.3	Ginger Bananas with	128	5.0	3.7			
					2 Bananas, Sultanas (2oz)	316	10.0	0.0	Yogurt Snow	79	0.0	1.2			
	Apple and Orange Yogurt	79	2.4	1.3	Tomatoes on Toast	166	7.6	2.5	Haddock with Grapefruit & Mushrooms	123	1.5	1.5	1435	59.8	8.6
10	Orange Juice (7fl oz)	77	0.0	0.0	Natural Low-fat Yogurt (5 oz)	75	0.0	2.5	Peas, Sweetcorn	306	19	0			
	Sultanas (2oz)	140	4.0	0.0	Banana	88	4.0	0.8	Broccoli	36	6	0			
					Dried Dates (3oz)	207	7.2	0.0	Hot Fruit Soufflé	93	7.9	0.0			
	Citrus Starter	91	2.3	4.5	Fruity Cheese Plate	227	5.8	2.0	Minestrone Casserole	347	18.6	2.0	1474	43.8	21.5
11	Natural Low-fat Yogurt (5 oz)	75	0.0	2.5					⅓ Wholemeal French Stick (4 oz)	240	9.6	4.0			
	Orange Juice (7fl oz)	77	0.0	0.0					Hot Bananas with	174	5.4	5.3			
					Green Grapes (7oz)	119	2.1	0.0	Yogurt Snow	79	0.0	1.2			
	Raspberry Yogurt	89	4.2	2.5	2 Stuffed Pitta Breads	372	15.2	1.8	Garlic Steak and Mushrooms	216	2.8	5.6	1462	57.2	12.9
12	Orange Juice (7fl oz)	77	0.0	0.0					2 Grilled Tomatoes, Green Salad	45	4.6	0			
	Apple	50	3.0	0.0	Dried Dates (2oz)	138	4.8	0.0	Peas, Sweetcorn	306	19.2	0			
					Pear	40	2.5	0.0	Strawberry Cheese	84	0.9	3.0			
	Prune Fluff	125	7.6	1.3	Cashew Coleslaw	178	10.2	7.6	Prawn Provençal	168	6.7	3.9	1459	66.9	17.4
13	Orange Juice (7fl oz)	77	0.0	0.0	Jacket Potato (12oz)	288	8.4	0.0	Green Beans	12	5	0			
	2 Apples	100	6.0	0.0	Banana, Dates (2oz)	226	8.8	0.8	Swede	36	5	0			
					Natural Low-fat Yogurt (5 oz)	75	0.0	2.5	Blackberry and Apple Fool	129	9.0	1.3			
	Raspberry Apple Drink	41	4.9	0.0	Aubergine Pâté	168	4.7	13.0	Savoury Dutch Cakes	296	12.6	3.5	1462	66.6	21.8
14	Orange	42	2.4	0.0	Crudités	63	4.5	0.3	Mixed Salad	76	5.3	0.3			
	Natural Low-fat Yogurt (5 oz)	75	0.0	2.5	2 pieces Wholemeal Pitta Bread	284	9.4	1.4	Peas	90	13	0			
					Banana, Green Grapes (7oz)	207	6.1	0.8	Pear Compôte	75	3.5				

Daily allowance of ¼ pint of skimmed milk

Vegetable serving 6oz unless otherwise specified

	Breakfast	Cals	Fbr	Fat	Lunch	Cals	Fbr	Fat	Dinner	Cals	Fbr	Fat	Total		
													Cals	Fbr	Fat
	Apple Sauce	40	2.4	0.0	Sweetcorn Soup	190	4.0	4.1	Spicy Fish Casserole	122	4.2	1.2	1436	68	17.1
15	Orange Juice (7fl oz)	77	0.0	0.0	2 slices Wholemeal Toast	120	4.8	2.0	Brussels Sprouts, Peas	132	20	0			
	Natural Low-fat Yogurt (5 oz)	75	0.0	2.5	Banana, Dried Figs (3oz)	268	19.6	0.8	Roast Parsnips	84	7	0			
	Nectarine	65	3.0	0.0	Pumpkin Seeds (1tbsp)	80	0.0	6.5	Pineapple Sorbet	138	3.0				
	Banana and Walnut Yogurt	200	4.4	7.0	Herby Cheese Salad	160	4.6	2.0	Spaghetti Napoletana	370	13.5	2.3	1492	46.8	15.7
16	Unsweetened Grape Juice	140	0.0	0.0					Mixed Salad	76	5.3	0.3			
	(7fl oz)				2 Nectarines	130	6.0	0.0	Natural Low-fat Yogurt (5 oz)	75	0.0	2.5			
	Sultanas (1oz)	70	2.0	0.0	Apple	50	3.0	0.0	2 Banana Ices	176	8.0	1.6			
	Strawberry Apples	54	3.6	0.0	Herby Mushroom Pâté	60	3.5	3.5	Tuna and Corn Salad	272	15.5	7.2	1477	61	21.2
17	Orange Juice (7fl oz)	77	0.0	0.0	3 slices Wholemeal Toast	180	7.2	3.0							
	Natural Low-fat Yogurt (5 oz)	75	0.0	2.5	Dried Dates (3oz),Green Grapes (7oz	326	9.3	0.0	Spiced Fruit Salad	196	19.5	0.0			
	Orange	42	2.4	0.0	Natural Low-fat Yogurt (5 oz)	75	0.0	2.5	Natural Low-fat Yogurt (5 oz)	75	0.0	2.5			
	Banana Date Breakfast	137	5.9	0.8	Gazpacho	40	2.9	0.0	Citrus Chicken	194	4.9	2.5	1446	58.5	15.0
18	Unsweetened Grape Juice	140	0.0	0.0	3 slices Wholemeal Toast	180	7.2	3.0	Mixed Salad	76	5.3	0.3			
	(7fl oz)				2 Pears, Sultanas (2oz)	220	9.0	0.0	Courgettes, Peas	120	16	0			
	Natural Low-fat Yogurt (5 oz)	75	0.0	2.5	Natural Low-fat Yogurt (5 oz)	75	0.0	2.5	Baked Apple	144	7.1	3.4			
	Raspberry Yogurt	89	4.2	2.5	Chinese Salad	149	7.0	3.0	Vegetable Stuffed Jacket Potato	354	12.5	0.8	1441	57	18.2
19	Orange Juice (7fl oz)	77	0.0	0.0	2 Nectarines, Orange	182	9.4	0.0	Green Salad	29	3.0	0.0			
	2 Apples	100	6.0	0.0	Pumpkin Seeds (1 tbsp)	80	0.0	6.5	Peas	90	13	0			
					Natural Low-fat Yogurt (5 oz)	75	0.0	2.5	Banana Fruit Yogurt	171	1.7	2.9			
	Prune Whip	76	7.6	0.0	Mushroom Pasta made with	291	7.7	7.0	Spanish Omelette	237	7.7	12.3	1495	56.7	22.1
20	Orange Juice (7fl oz)	77	0.0	0.0	extra wholemeal pasta (2oz)	194	5.6	0.0	Mixed Salad	76	5.3	0.3			
	2 Apples	100	6.0	0.0	Dried Figs (2oz)	120	10.4	0.0	Natural Low-fat Yogurt (5 oz)	75	0.0	2.5			
					Green Grapes (7oz)	119	2.1	0.0	Fruit Salad	85	4.3	0.0			

Daily allowance of ¼ pint of skimmed milk

Vegetable serving 6oz unless otherwise specified

	Breakfast	Cals	Fbr	Fat	Lunch	Cals	Fbr	Fat	Dinner	Cals	Fbr	Fat	Total		
													Cals	Fbr	Fat
									Avocado Dip and Crudités	171	6.5	8.1			
	Porridge	226	4.0	4.0	Cheese and Cucumber Sandwich	177	6.1	2.8	Ginger Beef	361	5.8	15.6	1250	35.7	32.9
1									Green Beans	8	3.6	0.0			
									Cauliflower	16	2.4	0.0			
	Pear	40	2.5	0.0	Banana	88	4.0	0.8	Kiwi Lemon Cheese	118	0.8	1.6			
									Horseradish Tomatoes	36	1.2	1			
	Honey on Toast	299	6.0	14.0	Greek Salad	153	7.0	13.0	Coronation Chicken	299	10.8	7.2	1236	54.3	37.2
2									Mangetouts, Sweetcorn	144	15.2	1.2			
					Apple	50	3.0	0.0	Courgettes	20	2.0	0.0			
	Banana	88	4.0	0.8	Orange	42	2.4	0.0	Red Fruit Salad	60	2.7				
									Spinach Cheese Pâté with Crudités	115	6.3	0.9			
	Tomato Beans on Toast	226	19.8	2.1	Avocado Salad	122	3.5	7.8	Salmon with Watercress Sauce	329	0.9	11.4	1250	53.6	26.9
3					Jacket Potato (7oz)	168	4.9	0.0	Broccoli	24	4.0	0.0			
									Mixed Salad	76	5.3	0.3			
					Pear	40	2.5	0.0	Hot Berry Pudding	105	6.4	4.4			
									Curry Dip and Crudités	80	4.5	0.9			
	Tomato Scrambled Eggs	138	0.9	9.0	Leek and Potato Soup	236	10.3	0.0	Beefburgers with Tomato Sauce	262	3.7	19.5	1239	42.5	38.4
4					1 slice Wholemeal Toast	60	2.4	1.0	Sweetcorn	84	6.4	1.2			
									Critical Salad	117	6.8	0.3			
	Apple	50	3.0	0.0	Pear	40	2.5	0.0	Peach Freeze	127	2.0	6.5			

Daily allowance of ¼ pint of skimmed milk

Vegetable serving 4oz unless otherwise specified

	Breakfast	Cals	Fbr	Fat	Lunch	Cals	Fbr	Fat	Dinner	Cals	Fbr	Fat	Total Cals	Total Fbr	Total Fat
									Avocado and Grapefruit Cocktail	123	1.5	7.8			
	Banana Muesli and Yogurt	243	10.6	5.7	Lemon Spaghetti	246	5.8	2.2	Celebration Salad	352	13.2	18.5	1259	50	35.2
5					Green Salad	29	3.0	0.0							
					Pear	40	2.5	0.0	Apricot Ice Cream	181	13.4	1.0			
	Breakfast Compôte	154	11.8	1.4	Hot Herb Loaf	394	7.2	26.0	Vegetable Curry and Rice	375	10.3	4.7	1224	34.6	34.7
6									Cucumber and Tomato Raita	33	1.0	0.6			
									Onion Relish	42	2.8	0.0			
					Green Grapes (5oz)	85	1.5	0.0	1 Poppadom, 1 tbsp Mango Chutney	96		2.0			
									Stuffed Pears	66	2.4	2.8			
	Honey Raisin Crêpes	242	4.6	1.5	Mackerel Pâté	170	0.0	10.8	Beef Stroganoff	271	4.5	7.4	1274	38.5	31.4
7					Crudités	63	4.5	0.3	Critical Salad	117	6.8	0.3			
									Brussels Sprouts	28	4.8	0.0			
	Banana	88	4.0	0.8	Apple	50	3.0	0.0	Spicy Peaches	134	3.9	7.5			
									Tomato and Orange Soup	76	4.3	1.0			
	Sweetcorn Fritters	98	4.0	2.0	Brown Rice Salad	452	15.7	14.3	4oz Honey Roast Chicken (without skin)	195	0.0	9.5	1233	48.4	34.2
8									Parsnips, Peas	116	13.2	0.0			
									Brussels Sprouts	28	4.8	0.0			
	Green Grapes (5oz)	85	1.5	0.0					Apple Crumble	138	4.9	7.4			

Daily allowance of ½ pint of skimmed milk

Vegetable serving 4oz unless otherwise specified

	Breakfast	Cals	Fbr	Fat	Lunch	Cals	Fbr	Fat	Dinner	Cals	Fbr	Fat	Total		
													Cals	Fbr	Fat
									Avocado Dip and Crudités	171	6.5	8.1			
	Porridge	226	4.0	4.0	Cheese and Cucumber Sandwich	177	6.1	2.8	Ginger Beef	361	5.8	15.6	1494	42	32.9
1	Unsweetened Grape Juice	100	0.0	0.0					Green Beans	10	4.5	0.0			
	(5fl oz)				Dates (2oz)	138	4.8	0.0	Cauliflower	20	3.0	0.0			
	Pear	40	2.5	0.0	Banana	88	4.0	0.8	Kiwi Lemon Cheese	118	0.8	1.6			
									Horseradish Tomatoes	36	1.2	1.0			
	Honey on Toast	299	6.0	14.0	Greek Salad	153	7.0	13.0	Coronation Chicken	299	10.8	7.2	1490	63.4	40
2					Natural Low-fat Yogurt (5 oz)	75	0.0	2.5	Mangetouts, Sweetcorn	180	19.0	1.5			
	Dates (2oz)	138	4.8	0.0	Apple	50	3.0	0.0	Courgettes	25	2.5	0.0			
	Banana	88	4.0	0.8	Orange	42	2.4	0.0	Red Fruit Salad	60	2.7				
									Spinach Cheese Pâté with Crudités	115	6.3	0.9			
	Tomato Beans on Toast	226	19.8	2.1	Avocado Salad	122	3.5	7.8	Salmon with Watercress Sauce	329	0.9	11.4	1467	60	30.2
3					Jacket Potato (9oz)	216	6.3	0	Broccoli	30	5.0	0.0			
					Natural Low-fat Yogurt (5 oz)	75	0.0	2.5	Mixed Salad	76	5.3	0.3			
	Banana	88	4.0	0.8	Pear	40	2.5	0.0	Hot Berry Pudding	105	6.4	4.4			
									Curry Dip and Crudités	80	4.5	0.9			
	Tomato Scrambled Eggs	138	0.9	9.0	Leek and Potato Soup	236	10.3	0.0	Beefburgers with Tomato Sauce	262	3.7	19.5	1495	51.3	38.7
4	Orange Juice (5fl oz)	55	0.0	0.0	1 slice Wholemeal Toast	60	2.4	1.0	Sweetcorn	105	8.0	1.5			
	Orange	42	2.4	0.0	Dates (2oz)	138	4.8	0.0	Critical Salad	117	6.8	0.3			
	Apple	50	3.0	0.0	Pear	40	2.5	0.0	Peach Freeze	127	2.0	6.5			

Daily allowance of ¼ pint of skimmed milk

Vegetable serving 5oz unless otherwise specified

	Breakfast	Cals	Fbr	Fat	Lunch	Cals	Fbr	Fat	Dinner	Cals	Fbr	Fat	Total Cals	Total Fbr	Total Fat
									Avocado and Grapefruit Cocktail	123	1.5	7.8			
	Banana Muesli and Yogurt	243	10.6	5.7	Lemon Spaghetti	246	5.8	2.2	Celebration Salad	352	13.2	18.5	1497	54.8	35.2
5	Unsweetened Grape Juice	100	0.0	0.0	Green Salad	29	3.0	0.0							
	(5fl oz)				Dates (2oz)	138	4.8	0.0							
					Pear	40	2.5	0.0	Apricot Ice Cream	181	13.4	1.0			
	Breakfast Compôte	154	11.8	1.4	Hot Herb Loaf	394	7.2	26.0	Vegetable Curry and Rice	375	10.3	4.7	1484	45.4	35.8
6	Orange Juice (5fl oz)	55	0.0	0.0	Critical Salad	117	6.8	0.3	Cucumber and Tomato Raita	33	1.0	0.6			
					Banana	88	4.0	0.8	Onion Relish	42	2.8	0.0			
					Green Grapes (5oz)	85	1.5	0.0	1 Poppadom, 1tbsp Mango Chutney	96		2.0			
	Honey Raisin Crêpes	242	4.6	1.5					Stuffed Pears	66	2.4	2.8			
	Unsweetened Grape Juice	100	0.0	0.0	Mackerel Pâté	170	0.0	10.8	Beef Stroganoff	271	4.5	7.4	1521	42.7	33.9
7	(5fl oz)				Crudités	63	4.5	0.3	Critical Salad	117	6.8	0.3			
	Natural Low-fat Yogurt (5 oz)	75	0.0	2.5	Nectarine	65	3.0	0.0	Brussels Sprouts	35	6.0	0.0			
	Banana	88	4.0	0.8	Apple	50	3.0	0.0	Spicy Peaches	134	3.9	7.5			
									Tomato and Orange Soup	76	4.3	1.0			
	Sweetcorn Fritters	98	4.0	2.0	Brown Rice Salad	452	15.7	14.3	4oz Honey Roast Chicken (without skin)	195	0.0	9.5	1495	61.7	35
8									Parsnips, Peas	145	16.5	0.0			
	Banana	88	4.0	0.8					Brussels Sprouts	35	6.0	0.0			
	Dates (2oz)	138	4.8	0.0	Green Grapes (5oz)	85	1.5	0.0	Apple Crumble	138	4.9	7.4			

Daily allowance of ½ pint of skimmed milk

Vegetable serving 5oz unless otherwise specified

	Breakfast	Cals	Fbr	Fat	Lunch	Cals	Fbr	Fat	Dinner	Cals	Fbr	Fat	Total Cals	Total Fbr	Total Fat
					2 Cheese and				Avocado Dip and Crudités	171	6.5	8.1			
	Porridge	226	4.0	4.0	Cucumber Sandwiches	354	12.2	5.6	Ginger Beef	361	5.8	15.6	1754	50.0	38.2
1	Unsweetened Grape Juice	100	0.0	0.0	Natural Low-fat Yogurt (5 oz)	75	0.0	2.5	Green Beans	13	5.6	0.0			
	(5fl oz)				Dates (2oz)	138	4.8	0.0	Cauliflower	25	3.8	0.0			
	Pear	40	2.5	0.0	Banana	88	4.0	0.8	Kiwi Lemon Cheese	118	0.8	1.6			
	Honey on Toast	299	6.0	14.0					Horseradish Tomatoes	36	1.2	1			
	Unsweetened Grape Juice	100	0.0	0.0	Greek Salad	153	7.0	13.0	Coronation Chicken	299	10.8	7.2	1768	70.8	40.4
2	(5fl oz)				Natural Low-fat Yogurt (5 oz)	75	0.0	2.5	Mangetouts, Sweetcorn	225	23.8	1.9			
	Dates (3oz)	207	7.2	0.0	Apple	50	3.0	0.0	Courgettes	31	3.1	0.0			
	Banana	88	4.0	0.8	Mango	100	2.0	0.0	Red Fruit Salad	60	2.7				
									Spinach Cheese Pâte with Crudités	115	6.3	0.9			
	Tomato Beans on Toast	226	19.8	2.1	Avocado Salad	122	3.5	7.8	Salmon with Watercress Sauce	329	0.9	11.4	1785	68.2	30.2
3	Unsweetened Grape Juice	100	0.0	0.0	Jacket Potato (12oz)	288	8.4	0.0	Broccoli	38	6.3	0.0			
	(5fl oz)				Natural Low-fat Yogurt (5 oz)	75	0.0	2.5	Mixed Salad	76	5.3	0.3			
	Banana	88	4.0	0.8	Pear, Dates (2oz)	178	7.3	0.0	Hot Berry Pudding	105	6.4	4.4			
									Curry Dip and Crudités	80	4.5	0.9			
	Tomato Scrambled Eggs	138	0.9	9.0	Leek and Potato Soup	236	10.3	0.0	Beefburgers with Tomato Sauce	262	3.7	19.5	1730	57.7	40.1
4	Orange Juice (7fl oz)	77	0.0	0.0	2 slices Wholemeal Toast	120	4.8	2.0	Sweetcorn	131	10.0	1.9			
	Mango	100	2.0	0.0	Dried Dates (3oz)	207	7.2	0.0	Critical Salad	117	6.8	0.3			
	Apple	50	3.0	0.0	Pear	40	2.5	0.0	Peach Freeze	127	2.0	6.5			

Daily allowance of ¼ pint of skimmed milk

Vegetable serving 6oz unless otherwise specified

	Breakfast	Cals	Fbr	Fat	Lunch	Cals	Fbr	Fat	Dinner	Cals	Fbr	Fat	Total Cals	Total Fbr	Total Fat
					Lemon Spaghetti	246	5.8	2.2	Avocado and Grapefruit Cocktail	123	1.5	7.8			
	Banana Muesli and Yogurt	243	10.6	5.7	Wholemeal Spaghetti (1 oz additional to recipe)	97	2.8	2.2	Celebration Salad	352	13.2	18.5	1722	63.9	37.7
5	Unsweetened Grape Juice	100	0.0	0.0	Critical Salad	117	6.8	0.3							
	(5fl oz)				Dates (2oz)	138	4.8	0.0							
					2 Pears	80	5.0	0.0	Apricot Ice Cream	181	13.4	1.0			
	Breakfast Compôte	154	11.8	1.4	Hot Herb Loaf	394	7.2	26.0	Vegetable Curry and Rice	375	10.3	4.7	1738	53.0	37.8
6	Orange Juice (7fl oz)	77	0.0	0.0	Critical Salad	117	6.8	0.3	Cucumber and Tomato Raita	33	1.0	0.6			
					2 Bananas	176	8.0	0.8	Onion Relish	42	2.8	0.0			
	Apple	50	3.0	0.0	Green Grapes (7oz)	119	2.1	0.0	2 Poppadoms, 1 tbsp Mango Chutney	156		4.0			
	Honey Raisin Crêpes	242	4.6	1.5					Stuffed Pears	66	2.4	2.8			
	Unsweetened Grape Juice	140	0.0	0.0	Mackerel Pâté	170	0.0	10.8	Beef Stroganoff	271	4.5	7.4	1762	46.3	34.7
7	(7fl oz)				Crudités	63	4.5	0.3	Critical Salad	117	6.8	0.3			
	Natural Low-fat Yogurt (5 oz)	75	0.0	2.5	Green Grapes (7oz)	119	2.1	0.0	Brussels Sprouts	44	7.5	0.0			
	2 Bananas	176	8.0	1.6	Mango	100	2.0	0.0	Spicy Peaches	134	3.9	7.5			
	Sweetcorn Fritters	98	4.0	2.0					Tomato and Orange Soup	76	4.3	1.0			
	Unsweetened Grape Juice	140	0.0	0.0	Brown Rice Salad	452	15.7	14.3	4oz Honey Roast Chicken (without skin)	195	0.0	9.5	1755	67.3	37.5
8	(7fl oz)								Parsnips, Peas	181	20.6	0.0			
	Banana	88	4.0	0.8	Natural Low-fat Yogurt (5 oz)	75	0.0	2.5	Brussels Sprouts	44	7.5	0.0			
	Dates (2oz)	138	4.8	0.0	Green Grapes (5oz)	85	1.5	0.0	Apple Crumble	138	4.9	7.4			

Daily allowance of ¼ pint of skimmed milk

Vegetable serving 6oz unless otherwise specified

Bodyclock Diet recipes

BREAKFAST – PROTEIN

Apple and Orange Yogurt

Metric/Imperial	*American*
2 oranges, peeled and segmented	2 oranges, peeled and segmented
2 dessert apples, sliced	2 dessert apples, sliced
375g/10oz natural low-fat yogurt	1⅓ cups unflavoured low-fat yogurt

1. Stir the orange segments and apple slices into the yogurt.
2. Divide between individual serving dishes.
3. Serve chilled.

Apple Sauce

Metric/Imperial	*American*
4 red dessert apples, chopped	4 red dessert apples, chopped
150ml/5fl oz apple juice	⅔ cup apple juice
½ tsp ground cinnamon	½ tsp ground cinnamon

1. Purée the apples and juice until smooth.
2. Pour into individual dishes and sprinkle with cinnamon.
3. Serve immediately.

Apricot Drink

Metric/Imperial	*American*
450g/1lb fresh apricots, stoned	3 cups fresh apricots, pitted
260ml/8fl oz orange juice	1 cup orange juice
pinch of coriander	pinch of coriander

1. Liquidize ingredients.
2. Pour into glasses and serve.

Blackberry Apple Breakfast

Metric/Imperial	*American*
4 dessert apples, chopped	4 dessert apples, chopped
275g/10oz natural low-fat yogurt	$1\frac{1}{3}$ cups unflavoured low-fat yogurt
100g/4oz blackberries	$\frac{3}{4}$ cup blackberries

1. Mix the apples and yogurt and divide between individual serving dishes.
2. Purée the blackberries and spoon over the top of the apple mixture.
3. Serve chilled.

Blackberry Yogurt

Metric/Imperial	*American*
225g/8oz blackberries	1½ cups blackberries
4 tbsp water	5 tbsp water
575g/20oz natural low-fat yogurt	2⅔ cups unflavoured low-fat yogurt

1. Stew the blackberries in the water for a few minutes until just tender.
2. Leave to cool, then stir into the yogurt.
3. Serve chilled.

Citrus Starter

Metric/Imperial	*American*
2 oranges	2 oranges
1 grapefruit	1 grapefruit
25g/1oz seedless raisins	3 tbsp seedless raisins
25g/1oz chopped walnuts	3 tbsp chopped walnuts
1 tbsp clear honey	1 tbsp clear honey

This is best made the night before.

1. Peel the oranges and grapefruit, remove the pith and divide into segments in a bowl.
2. Add the raisins, walnuts and honey and mix well.
3. Cover with clingfilm and refrigerate overnight.
4. Serve the next morning in individual bowls.

Fruit and Nut Yogurt

Metric/Imperial	*American*
4 dessert apples, chopped	4 dessert apples, chopped
50g/2oz dried apricots	⅓ cup dried apricots
50g/2oz raisins	⅓ cup raisins
50g/2oz nuts, chopped	½ cup nuts, chopped
575g/20oz natural low-fat yogurt	2⅔ cups unflavoured low-fat yogurt

1. Mix together all the ingredients.
2. Serve chilled.

Prune Fluff

Metric/Imperial	*American*
225g/8oz dried prunes	1½ cups dried prunes
200ml/7fl oz water	1 cup water
juice of half an orange	juice of half an orange
1 tbsp clear honey	1 tbsp clear honey
275g/10oz natural low-fat yogurt	1¼ cups unflavoured low-fat yogurt

This must be made the night before.

1. Soak the prunes in the water overnight.
2. By the next morning, the prunes should have absorbed the water. Remove the stones.
3. Liquidize the prune flesh, orange juice, honey and yogurt until well mixed.
4. Serve chilled in individual bowls.

Prune Whip

Metric/Imperial	*American*
225g/8oz dried prunes	1½ cups dried prunes
200ml/7fl oz apple juice	1 cup apple juice
½ tsp ground cinnamon	½ tsp ground cinnamon

This must be made the night before.

1. Soak the prunes in the apple juice overnight.
2. By the next morning, the prunes should have absorbed the water. Remove the stones.
3. Purée the prunes and soaking liquid with the cinnamon until smooth.
4. Serve chilled in individual bowls.

Raspberry Apple Drink

Metric/Imperial	*American*
3 dessert apples, chopped	3 dessert apples, chopped
175g/6oz raspberries	1 cup raspberries
150ml/5fl oz water	⅔ cup water
1 tsp finely chopped mint	1 tsp finely chopped mint

1. Liquidize ingredients.
2. Pour into glasses and serve.

Raspberry Yogurt

Metric/Imperial	*American*
225g/8oz raspberries	1½ cups raspberries
575g/20oz natural low-fat yogurt	2⅔ cups unflavoured low-fat yogurt

1. Stir the raspberries into the yogurt.
2. Serve chilled.

Spiced Grapefruit

Metric/Imperial	*American*
2 grapefruit	2 grapefruit
1 tbsp clear honey	1 tbsp clear honey
½ tsp ground ginger	½ tsp ground ginger
½ tsp ground cinnamon	½ tsp ground cinnamon

This is best made the night before.

1. Cut the grapefruit in half and remove the segments, discarding any pith and skin.
2. Mix the segments in a bowl with the honey and spices.
3. Pile the mixture back into the grapefruit shells and chill overnight before serving.

Stewed Apricots

Metric/Imperial	*American*
225g/8oz dried apricots	1½ cups dried apricots
300ml/10fl oz unsweetened orange juice	1⅓ cups unsweetened orange juice
300ml/10fl oz water	1⅓ cups water

This must be made the night before.

1. Soak the apricots overnight in the orange juice and water.
2. Stew the apricots in the soaking liquid in a covered saucepan until just tender.
3. Serve hot or cold.

Strawberry Apples

Metric/Imperial	*American*
225g/8oz strawberries	1½ cups strawberries
4 dessert apples, sliced	4 dessert apples, sliced

1. Purée the strawberries.
2. Divide the apples between individual serving dishes.
3. Pour the strawberry purée over the top and serve.

BREAKFASTS – STARCH

Banana and Walnut Yogurt

Metric/Imperial	American
4 bananas, sliced	4 bananas, sliced
25g/1oz walnuts, chopped	¼ cup walnuts, chopped
575g/20oz natural low-fat yogurt	2⅔ cups unflavoured low-fat yogurt

1. Mix together all the ingredients.
2. Serve chilled.

Banana Date Breakfast

Metric/Imperial	American
4 bananas	4 bananas
75g/3oz dried dates, chopped	¾ cup dried dates, chopped
150ml/5fl oz grape juice	⅔ cup grape juice

1. Purée the bananas, dates and raisin juice until smooth.
2. Pour into individual serving dishes and serve.

LUNCHES SNACKS – PROTEIN

Chinese Salad

Metric/Imperial	*American*
1 head Chinese leaves, shredded	1 head Chinese leaves, shredded
100g/4oz lean boiled ham	½ cup lean boiled ham
3 red dessert apples, chopped	3 red dessert apples, chopped
3 tbsp lemon juice	3 tbsp lemon juice
100g/4oz green grapes, halved	⅔ cup green grapes
4 sticks celery, chopped	4 sticks celery, chopped
4 spring onions, chopped	4 salad onions, chopped
freshly ground black pepper	freshly ground black pepper
dressing	dressing

1. Put the Chinese leaves into a shallow salad bowl.
2. Remove any fat and chop the ham.
3. Toss the apples in the lemon juice.
4. Mix together the ham, apples, grapes, celery, onions and pepper to taste with the dressing.
5. Pile onto the Chinese leaves in the salad bowl.

Fruity Cheese Plate

Metric/Imperial	***American***
2 oranges, peeled and segmented	2 oranges, peeled and segmented
2 dessert apples, quartered	2 dessert apples, quartered
2 peaches, sliced	2 peaches, sliced
2 kiwi fruit, sliced	2 kiwi fruit, sliced
225g/8oz strawberries	2 cups strawberries
1 small pineapple, sliced	1 small pineapple, sliced
450g/1lb low-fat cottage cheese	2 cups low-fat cottage cheese

Adapt the combination of fruits to taste, using any fresh fruit except bananas and melon, which do not combine well.

1. Pile the cottage cheese in the middle of individual serving plates.
2. Arrange the fruit round the sides of the plates.

Herby Cheese Salad

Metric/Imperial	*American*
1 iceberg lettuce	1 iceberg lettuce
1 cucumber, diced	1 cucumber, diced
1 green pepper, diced	1 green pepper, diced
4 spring onions, sliced	4 salad onions, sliced
1 tbsp chopped chives	1 tbsp chopped chives
1 tbsp chopped dill	1 tbsp chopped dill
1 tbsp chopped tarragon	1 tbsp chopped tarragon
450g/1lb low-fat cottage cheese	2 cups low-fat cottage cheese

1. Arrange the lettuce leaves in a shallow salad bowl.
2. Mix together the cucumber, green pepper, spring onions, chives, herbs and cottage cheese.
3. Pile into the centre of the salad bowl and serve.

Sunshine Omelette

Metric/Imperial	*American*
225g/8oz beansprouts	4 cups beansprouts
1 tbsp soy sauce	1 tbsp soy sauce
8 free-range eggs	8 free-range eggs
150ml/5fl oz water	⅔ cup water
freshly ground black pepper	freshly ground black pepper
225g/8oz sweetcorn	1½ cups kernel corn

1. Mix together the beansprouts and soy sauce.
2. Beat together the eggs, water and black pepper to taste.
3. Mix in the sweetcorn.
4. Heat a non-stick omelette pan and pour in a quarter of the egg mixture.
5. As the bottom begins to set, pull in from the edges of the pan with a spatula and tip the pan so that the uncooked egg runs into the space made.
6. When the surface is almost set, remove from the heat and slide the omelette onto a serving plate.
7. Pile a quarter of the beansprout mixture on to half of the omelette, and fold over to serve.
8. Repeat steps 4 to 7 for the remaining three omelettes.

LUNCHES SNACKS – STARCH

Aubergine Pâté and Crudités*

Metric/Imperial	*American*
2 large aubergines	2 large aubergines
3 garlic cloves, crushed	3 garlic cloves, crushed
1 small onion, finely chopped	1 small onion, finely chopped
4 tbsp tahini (sesame seed paste)	4 tbsp tahini (sesame seed paste)
3 tbsp chopped parsley	3 tbsp chopped parsley
½ tsp ground cumin	½ tsp ground cumin
freshly ground black pepper	freshly ground black pepper

1. Prick the aubergines all over with a fork and cut in half.
2. Place on a grill-pan rack, cut side down, and grill under low heat until the skins start to blister and the flesh feels soft.
3. Squeeze out as much of the bitter juice as possible, then peel and chop.
4. Add the garlic, onion, tahini, parsley, cumin and black pepper to taste.
5. Liquidize until smooth
6. Serve chilled.

**See p. 190.*

Banana Sandwich

Metric/Imperial	*American*
8 slices wholemeal bread	8 slices wholewheat bread
4 bananas, sliced	4 bananas, sliced
2 tbsp lemon juice (optional)	2 tbsp lemon juice (optional)

1. Mash the bananas in a bowl.
2. If not eating immediately, add lemon juice and mix well to prevent browning.
3. Cover four of the slices of bread with the banana mixture.
4. Top with the remaining four slices of bread.
5. Cut each sandwich diagonally in half.

Carrot and Raisin Salad

Metric/Imperial	*American*
1 iceberg lettuce	1 iceberg lettuce
225g/8oz carrots, grated	1½ cups carrots, grated
50g/2oz raisins	⅓ cup seedless raisins
1 tsp soy sauce	1 tsp soy sauce
1 tbsp natural low-fat yogurt	1 tbsp unflavoured low-fat yogurt
chopped parsley to garnish	chopped parsley to garnish

1. Tear the lettuce leaves into a salad bowl
2. Mix the carrots and raisins and pile on the lettuce.

3. Mix the yogurt and soy sauce and pour over the grated carrot.
4. Garnish with chopped parsley.

Cashew Coleslaw

Metric/Imperial	*American*
225g/8oz firm white cabbage, shredded	3 cups firm white cabbage, shredded
100g/4oz green cabbage, shredded	1½ cups green cabbage, shredded
6 carrots, grated	6 carrots, grated
4 green dessert apples, thinly sliced	4 green dessert apples, thinly sliced
2 onions, thinly sliced	2 onions, thinly sliced
50g/2oz cashew nuts, toasted	½ cup cashew nuts, toasted
2 tbsp parsley	2 tbsp parsley
dressing	dressing

1. Place all the ingredients in a large salad bowl.
2. Toss well and serve.

Gazpacho

Metric/Imperial	*American*
6 tomatoes, chopped	6 tomatoes, chopped
3 garlic cloves, crushed	3 garlic cloves, crushed
1 hot pepper	1 hot pepper
juice of 1 lemon	juice of 1 lemon
1 cucumber, chopped	1 cucumber, chopped

1 onion, chopped	1 onion, chopped
1 green pepper, chopped	1 green pepper, chopped
1 red pepper, chopped	1 red pepper, chopped
3 tbsp parsley, finely chopped	3 tbsp parsley, finely chopped
freshly ground black pepper	freshly ground black pepper

1. Liquidize the tomatoes, garlic, hot pepper and lemon juice with half the cucumber, onion and red and green peppers.
2. Add the remaining cucumber, onion, green and red peppers.
3. Add the parsley and freshly ground black pepper to taste and mix well.
4. Serve chilled.

Herby Mushroom Pâté

Metric/Imperial	*American*
1 tbsp cold pressed olive oil	1 tbsp cold pressed olive oil
1 onion, finely chopped	1 onion, finely chopped
450g/1lb mushrooms, roughly chopped	4 cups mushrooms, roughly chopped
3 garlic cloves, crushed	3 garlic cloves, crushed
1 tbsp tomato purée	1 tbsp tomato purée
2 tbsp chopped parsley	2 tbsp chopped parsley
1 tsp chopped thyme	1 tsp chopped thyme
freshly ground black pepper	freshly ground black pepper

1. Heat the oil in a pan.
2. Fry the onion until softened.
3. Stir in the mushrooms, garlic and tomato purée.
4. Cover and cook for 10 minutes.
5. Liquidize until smooth with the parsley, thyme and black pepper to taste.
6. Serve chilled in individual dishes.

Mushroom Pasta

Metric/Imperial	*American*
225g/8oz wholemeal pasta	½lb wholewheat pasta
3 garlic cloves, crushed	3 garlic cloves, crushed
350g/12oz mushrooms, roughly chopped	3 cups mushrooms, roughly chopped
1 tbsp cold pressed olive oil	1 tbsp cold pressed olive oil
75g/3oz low-fat fromage frais	⅓ cup low-fat fromage frais
2 tbsp chopped parsley	3 tbsp chopped parsley
freshly ground black pepper	freshly ground black pepper
25g/1oz grated Parmesan cheese	¼ cup grated Parmesan cheese

1. Cook the pasta as directed on the packet.
2. Meanwhile, fry the garlic and mushrooms in the olive oil until very soft.
3. Stir in the cooked pasta, fromage frais, parsley and pepper to taste.
4. Serve sprinkled with the Parmesan cheese.

Potato and Courgette Salad

Metric/Imperial	*American*
675g/1½lb scrubbed small new potatoes	1½lb scrubbed small new potatoes
350g/12oz courgettes, sliced	2¼ cups zucchini, sliced
finely grated rind and juice of 1 orange	finely grated rind and juice of 1 orange
2 tsp olive oil	2 tsp olive oil
1 tbsp cider vinegar	1 tbsp cider vinegar
1 tbsp chopped parsley	1 tbsp chopped parsley
2 spring onions, finely chopped	2 salad onions, finely chopped
freshly ground black pepper	freshly ground black pepper
chopped parsley to garnish	chopped parsley to garnish
snipped chives to garnish	snipped chives to garnish

1. Steam the potatoes or cook them in boiling water until just tender.
2. Remove from the water and drain.
3. Steam the courgettes for 5 minutes or add them to the boiling water and simmer for 3 minutes until just tender.
4. Drain the courgettes and put them in a salad bowl with the potatoes.
5. Mix the orange rind and juice, olive oil, vinegar, parsley and onions in a bowl and season to taste with black pepper.
6. Pour on to the potatoes and courgettes whilst they are still warm. Toss gently to mix.

7. Just before serving, toss again and sprinkle on the parsley and chives.
8. Serve cold.

Ratatouille

Metric/Imperial	*American*
1 tbsp olive oil	1 tbsp olive oil
2 medium onions, roughly chopped	2 medium onions, roughly chopped
4 garlic cloves, crushed	4 garlic cloves, crushed
350g/12oz courgettes, sliced	2¼ cups courgettes, sliced
2 green peppers, roughly chopped	2 green peppers, roughly chopped
2 aubergines, in 2½cm/1in pieces	2 eggplants, in 1in pieces
450g/1lb tomatoes, roughly chopped	2 cups tomatoes, roughly chopped
1 tbsp chopped basil	1 tbsp chopped basil
freshly ground black pepper	freshly ground black pepper
1 tbsp chopped parsley to garnish	1 tbsp chopped parsley to garnish

1. Heat the oil in a large saucepan.
2. Fry the onions and garlic for 5 minutes.
3. Add the courgettes, peppers and aubergines and fry for a further 5 minutes, stirring.
4. Add the tomatoes, basil and freshly ground black pepper to taste.
5. Cover and simmer for 25 minutes.
6. Sprinkle with the parsley and serve hot or cold.

Red Pepper Soup

Metric/Imperial	*American*
4 red peppers	4 red peppers
1 onion, chopped	1 onion, chopped
2 garlic cloves, crushed	2 garlic cloves, crushed
1 tbsp cold pressed olive oil	1 tbsp cold pressed olive oil
600ml/1 pint water or vegetable stock	2⅔ cups water or vegetable stock
450ml/¾ pint tomato juice	2 cups tomato juice
2 tbsp natural low-fat yogurt	2 tbsp unflavoured low-fat yogurt
freshly ground black pepper	freshly ground black pepper

1. Bring a large pan of water to the boil and leave the peppers in it for 5 minutes.
2. Fry the onions and garlic in the oil until softened.
3. Chop the peppers roughly.
4. Liquidize the peppers, onion, garlic, water or stock, tomato juice and add freshly ground black pepper to taste.
5. Chill, then pour into individual bowls.
6. Swirl a little yogurt into each bowl.
7. If serving hot, reheat gently, then allow to cool slightly before adding yogurt.

Savoury Mushrooms on Toast

Metric/Imperial
1 onion, chopped
2 garlic cloves, crushed
450g/1lb mushrooms, chopped
1 tbsp soy sauce
8 slices wholemeal bread

American
1 onion, chopped
2 garlic cloves, crushed
4 cups mushrooms, chopped
1 tbsp soy sauce
8 slices wholewheat bread

1. Fry the onion and garlic without fat in a heavy-based non-stick saucepan for 5 minutes. Stir frequently to prevent sticking.
2. Add the mushrooms and cook gently until just softened.
3. Toast the bread while the mushrooms are cooking.
4. Stir the soy sauce into the mushrooms.
5. Serve the mushroom mixture on the hot toast.

Stuffed Pitta Bread

Metric/Imperial
4 wholemeal pitta breads
1 radicchio
225g/8oz mixed sprouts
2 carrots, grated
1 yellow pepper, sliced
4 spring onions, sliced

American
4 wholewheat pitta breads
1 radicchio
4 cups mixed sprouts
2 carrots, grated
1 yellow pepper, sliced
4 salad onions, sliced

½ cucumber, sliced	½ cucumber, sliced
2 tbsp natural low-fat yogurt	2 tbsp unflavoured low-fat yogurt
1 tsp chilli powder	1 tsp chilli powder

1. Slit each pitta bread along one side.
2. Tear the radicchio leaves into a bowl.
3. Mix with the remaining ingredients.
4. Fill the pitta breads with the mixture.

Sweetcorn Soup

Metric/Imperial	*American*
350g/12oz sweetcorn	2⅔ cups kernel corn
1.2 litres/2 pints water or vegetable stock	5 cups water or vegetable stock
450ml/¾ pint skimmed milk	2 cups skimmed milk
1 onion, finely chopped	1 onion, finely chopped
1 tsp mustard powder	1 tsp mustard powder
4 drops Tabasco sauce	4 drops Tabasco sauce
1 tbsp tahini (optional)	1 tbsp tahini (optional)
½ green pepper, finely chopped	½ green pepper, finely chopped
freshly ground black pepper	freshly ground black pepper

1. Mix together the sweetcorn, water or stock, milk, onion, mustard powder, Tabasco sauce and tahini.
2. Bring to the boil in a saucepan and simmer for 5 minutes.

3. Liquidize until smooth.
4. Serve hot or chilled, garnished with chopped green pepper and freshly ground black pepper.

Tomato and Onion Sandwich

Metric/Imperial	*American*
8 slices wholemeal bread	8 slices wholewheat bread
4 medium tomatoes, sliced	4 medium tomatoes, sliced
4 spring onions, finely chopped	4 salad onions, finely chopped

1. Cover four of the slices of bread with the tomatoes.
2. Sprinkle with the chopped onions.
3. Top with the remaining four slices of bread.
4. Cut each sandwich diagonally in half.
5. Cover with clingfilm and leave for 1 hour before serving.

Tomatoes on Toast

Metric/Imperial	*American*
450g/1lb tomatoes, chopped	2 cups tomatoes, chopped
8 slices wholemeal bread	8 slices wholewheat bread

1. Cook the tomatoes slowly in a saucepan until softened.
2. Toast the bread.
3. Divide the tomatoes between the slices of toast and serve.

Tzatsiki

Metric/Imperial	*American*
450g/1lb natural low-fat yogurt	2 cups unflavoured low-fat yogurt
1 cucumber, peeled and grated	1 cucumber, peeled and grated
3 garlic cloves, crushed	3 garlic cloves, crushed
freshly ground black pepper	freshly ground black pepper
1 tbsp chopped mint	1 tbsp chopped mint

1. Drain any liquid from the cucumber.
2. Mix together the cucumber, yogurt, garlic and pepper to taste.
3. Chill well, then sprinkle on the mint before serving.

DINNERS/MAIN MEALS – PROTEIN

Chicken and Vegetable Stir-fry

Metric/Imperial	*American*
4 boneless chicken breasts, skinned	4 boneless chicken breasts, skinned
1 tbsp soy sauce	1 tbsp soy sauce
1 tsp root ginger, finely chopped	1 tsp root ginger, finely chopped
4 tbsp water or vegetable stock	4 tbsp water or vegetable stock
2 tsp cold pressed olive oil	2 tsp cold pressed olive oil
2 medium onions, chopped	2 medium onions, chopped
1 green pepper, thinly sliced	1 green pepper, thinly sliced
3 carrots, cut into matchsticks	3 carrots, cut into matchsticks
225g/8oz mushrooms, sliced	2 cups mushrooms, sliced
225g/8oz baby corn cobs	1½ cups baby corn cobs
175g/6oz green beans, sliced	¾ cup green beans, sliced
175g/6oz mangetout	1 cup mangetout
225g/8oz beansprouts	4 cups beansprouts

1. Cube the chicken and mix with the soy sauce, ginger and water or stock.
2. Leave to stand for 30 minutes.
3. Heat the oil in a wok or large frying pan and stir-

fry the chicken mixture and onions for 3 minutes over high heat.

4. Add the pepper, carrots, mushrooms, baby corn, green beans, mangetout and beansprouts and stir-fry for a further 3 minutes.
5. Serve immediately.

Citrus Chicken

Metric/Imperial	*American*
4 boneless chicken breasts, skinned	4 boneless chicken breasts, skinned
freshly ground black pepper	freshly ground black pepper
½ tsp ground cinnamon	½ tsp ground cinnamon
2 large lemons	2 large lemons
2 large oranges	2 large oranges
parsley to garnish	parsley to garnish

1. Rub the chicken breasts with the pepper and ground cinnamon and put in an ovenproof casserole dish.
2. Squeeze the juice from one of the lemons and pour over the chicken.
3. Grate the rind from the other lemon and one of the oranges.
4. Peel the lemon and both of the oranges and chop the flesh roughly.
5. Mix the chopped flesh with the grated rind and pour over the chicken.
6. Cover and cook in a preheated moderately hot oven (200°C/400°F, Gas Mark 6) for 1 hour, or until tender.

Garlic Steak and Mushrooms

Metric/Imperial	*American*
4 × 100g/4oz lean rump or sirloin steaks	4 × ¼lb lean rump or sirloin steaks
1 tsp oregano	1 tsp oregano
1 tsp basil	1 tsp basil
1 tsp thyme	1 tsp thyme
1 tsp majoram	1 tsp marjoram
freshly ground black pepper	freshly ground black pepper
4 garlic cloves, crushed	4 garlic cloves, crushed
150ml/¼ pint water or vegetable stock	⅔ cup water or vegetable stock
450g/1lb mushrooms, sliced	4 cups mushrooms, sliced.

1. Cut off any fat from the steak.
2. Sprinkle the herbs, black pepper to taste and half the garlic on to both sides of the steaks and press in well – with a meat hammer if you have one.
3. Leave as long as possible for the flavours to penetrate the meat.
4. Simmer the mushrooms, water and remaining garlic for 10 minutes.
5. Meanwhile, heat the grill on high for 5 minutes and grill the steak for 1 minute.
6. Turn the steak over the grill on medium heat until cooked to taste.
7. Serve the steak with the mushrooms and their juice poured over.

Haddock with Grapefruit and Mushrooms

Metric/Imperial	*American*
4 haddock fillets, boned and skinned	4 haddock fillets, boned and skinned
3 spring onions, finely chopped	3 salad onions, finely chopped
2 grapefruit	2 grapefruit
100g/4oz mushrooms, sliced	1 cup mushrooms, sliced

1. Arrange the fish fillets in the bottom of an oven-proof dish.
2. Sprinkle the spring onions over the fish.
3. Grate the rind from the grapefruit and sprinkle this on top.
4. Cover with the mushrooms.
5. Squeeze the juice from one grapefruit and pour over the mushrooms.
6. Peel and segment the other grapefruit and arrange the segments on the top of the mushrooms.
7. Cover and bake in a preheated moderate oven (180°C/350°F, Gas Mark 4) for 30 minutes.
8. Serve hot.

Hot Chicken

Metric/Imperial

4 boneless chicken breasts, skinned
2 onions, chopped
1 cooking apple, chopped
2 garlic cloves, crushed
100g/4oz peas
2 tbsp curry powder
1 tsp ground cinnamon
1 tsp ground ginger
300ml/½ pint skimmed milk

American

4 boneless chicken breasts, skinned
2 onions, chopped
1 cooking apple, chopped
2 garlic cloves, crushed
¾ cup peas
2 tbsp curry powder
1 tsp ground cinnamon
1 tsp ground ginger
1⅓ cup skimmed milk

1. Cook the chicken gently in a heavy-based non-stick pan until browned.
2. Remove from the pan and add the onions, apple and garlic and cook for a further 3 minutes, stirring to prevent sticking.
3. Stir in the peas, curry powder, cinnamon, ginger and milk.
4. Bring to the boil and return the chicken to the pan.
5. Simmer, covered, for 45 minutes or until the chicken is tender.
6. Serve hot.

Minced Beef with Roast Parsnips

Metric/Imperial	*American*
675g/1½lb parsnips, scrubbed	1½lb parsnips, scrubbed
450g/1lb very lean minced beef	1lb very lean minced beef
1 large onion, finely chopped	1 large onion, finely chopped
1 stick celery, finely chopped	1 stick celery, finely chopped
2 carrots, finely chopped	2 carrots, finely chopped
1 garlic clove, crushed	1 garlic clove, crushed
2 tbsp tomato purée	2 tbsp tomato purée
freshly ground black pepper	freshly ground black pepper
100g/4oz mushrooms, sliced	1 cup mushrooms, sliced
300ml/½ pint water	1⅓ cups water

1. Cut the parsnips into large chunks.
2. Place in a pan of cold water and bring to the boil.
3. Drain well and place on a non-stick baking tray in a preheated moderately hot oven (200°C/400°F, Gas Mark 6) for 30 minutes, or until soft.
4. Meanwhile, heat a large non-stick frying pan and cook the beef until browned, stirring regularly.
5. Drain off any fat which has come from the meat.
6. Add the onion, celery, carrots, garlic, purée, mushrooms, water and black pepper to taste.
7. Stir well and simmer for 20 minutes.
8. Serve hot with the parsnips.

Prawn and Pepper Salad

Metric/Imperial	*American*
1 curly endive	1 curly endive
1 radicchio	1 radicchio
1 cucumber, chopped	1 cucumber, chopped
2 green peppers, chopped	2 green peppers, chopped
4 tomatoes, quartered then halved	4 tomatoes, quartered then halved
450g/1lb cooked prawns	1lb cooked shrimps
175g/6oz cooked peas	1 cup cooked peas
175g/6oz small cauliflower florets	1½ cups small cauliflower florets
175g/6oz button mushrooms	1½ cups button mushrooms
225g/8oz mixed sprouts	4 cups mixed sprouts
1 tbsp sesame seeds, toasted	1 tbsp sesame seeds, toasted
dressing	dressing

1. Tear the endive and radicchio leaves into a shallow salad bowl.
2. Mix together the cucumber, peppers, tomatoes, prawns, peas, cauliflower, mushrooms, mixed sprouts and dressing.
3. Pile into the salad bowl, sprinkle with the sesame seeds and serve.

Prawn Provençal

Metric/Imperial	*American*
½ tbsp cold pressed olive oil	½ tbsp cold pressed olive oil
2 medium onions, sliced	2 medium onions, sliced
2 garlic cloves, crushed	2 garlic cloves, crushed
2 sticks celery, sliced	2 sticks celery, sliced
1 green pepper, sliced	1 green pepper, sliced
175g/6oz mushrooms, sliced	1½ cups mushrooms, sliced
100g/4oz peas	¾ cup peas
350g/12oz tomatoes, roughly chopped	1½ cups tomatoes, roughly chopped
1 tbsp tomato purée	1 tbsp tomato purée
300ml/½ pint vegetable stock or water	1⅓ cups vegetable stock or water
2 tbsp chopped parsley	2 tbsp chopped parsley
freshly ground black pepper	freshly ground black pepper
350g/12oz cooked prawns	1½ cups cooked shrimp

1. Heat the oil in a large frying pan and fry the onions for 5 minutes until soft.
2. Add the garlic, celery, green pepper and mushrooms and fry for a further 5 minutes.
3. Stir in the peas, tomatoes, tomato purée, vegetable stock or water, parsley and black pepper to taste.
4. Simmer over a medium heat until the sauce thickens.
5. Add the prawns and simmer gently for a further 5 minutes.
6. Serve hot.

Spanish Omelette

Metric/Imperial	*American*
2 onions, chopped	2 onions, chopped
1 garlic clove, crushed	1 garlic clove, crushed
½ green pepper, chopped	½ green pepper, chopped
½ red pepper, chopped	½ red pepper, chopped
225g/8oz mushrooms, sliced	2 cups mushrooms, sliced
225g/8oz tomatoes, chopped	1 cup tomatoes, chopped
100g/4oz peas	¾ cup peas
100g/4oz sweetcorn	¾ cup kernel corn
8 free-range eggs	8 free-range eggs
150ml/5fl oz water	⅔ cup water
1 tbsp parsley, chopped	1 tbsp parsley, chopped
freshly ground black pepper	freshly ground black pepper

1. Fry the onions, garlic and peppers without oil in a large heavy-based non-stick frying pan until soft. Stir to prevent sticking.
2. Add mushrooms, tomatoes, peas and sweetcorn. Stir well and cook for 2 minutes.
3. Beat together the eggs, water, parsley and black pepper to taste.
4. Add to the mixture in the frying pan, stir round and cook over medium heat, shaking the pan to prevent sticking.
5. When the bottom is just cooked, put the pan under a preheated moderate grill for a few minutes to cook the top.
6. Cut into wedges to serve.

Spicy Fish Casserole

Metric/Imperial	*American*
3 large tomatoes, sliced	3 large tomatoes, sliced
2 celery sticks, finely chopped	2 celery sticks, finely chopped
50g/2oz mushrooms, sliced	½ cup mushrooms, sliced
1 large onion, sliced	1 large onion, sliced
2 carrots, sliced	2 carrots, sliced
freshly ground black pepper	freshly ground black pepper
1 garlic clove, crushed	1 garlic clove, crushed
pinch of grated nutmeg	pinch of grated nutmeg
1 tsp chopped parsley	1 tsp chopped parsley
1 tsp chopped basil	1 tsp chopped basil
1 bay leaf	1 bay leaf
450g/1lb cod fillets	1lb cod fillets
3 tbsp cider vinegar	3 tbsp cider vinegar
150ml/¼ pint water	⅔ cup water

1. Arrange half the tomato slices in the bottom of an ovenproof dish.
2. Cover with the celery, mushrooms, onion and carrot
3. Season with the black pepper, garlic, nutmeg, parsley, basil and bay leaf.
4. Cut the fish into bite-sized pieces and add them to the dish.
5. Cover with the remaining tomato slices.
6. Pour on the vinegar and water.
7. Cover and bake in a preheated moderate oven (180°C/350°F, Gas Mark 4) for 40 minutes.
8. Serve hot.

Stuffed Aubergine

Metric/Imperial	*American*
4 large aubergines	4 large eggplants
2 large onions, chopped	2 large onions, chopped
1 tbsp cold pressed olive oil	1 tbsp cold pressed olive oil
4 garlic cloves, crushed	4 garlic cloves, crushed
450g/1lb mushrooms, sliced	4 cups mushrooms, sliced
450g/1lb tomatoes, roughly chopped	2 cups tomatoes, roughly chopped
2 tbsp tomato purée	2 tbsp tomato purée
225g/8oz low-fat cottage cheese	1 cup low-fat cottage cheese
2 tsp chopped thyme	2 tsp chopped thyme
2 tsp chopped parsley	2 tsp chopped parsley
freshly ground black pepper	freshly ground black pepper
25g/1oz grated Parmesan cheese	¼ cup grated Parmesan cheese

1. Prick the aubergines all over with a fork and cut in half.
2. Place cut side down on a non-stick baking sheet and bake in a preheated moderately hot oven (200°C/400°F, Gas Mark 6) for 30 minutes.
3. Meanwhile, fry the onions in the oil until softened.
4. Stir in the garlic, mushrooms, tomatoes and tomato purée and cook for a further 5 minutes.
5. Add the cottage cheese, thyme, parsley and black pepper to taste. Mix well and remove from the heat.

6. Scoop the flesh from the aubergines, being careful not to break the skins, and mash roughly.
7. Add to the mixture in the frying pan and mix well.
8. Pile into the aubergine skins and sprinkle the Parmesan cheese on top.
9. Heat through under a preheated hot grill and serve immediately.

Tomato Baked Fish

Metric/Imperial	*American*
4 halibut fillets, boned and skinned	4 halibut fillets, boned and skinned
1 medium onion, thinly sliced	1 medium onion, thinly sliced
1 green pepper, thinly sliced	1 green pepper, thinly sliced
2 large tomatoes, chopped	2 large tomatoes, chopped
2 tsp chopped fresh oregano	2 tsp chopped fresh oregano
300ml/½ pint tomato juice	1⅓ cup tomato juice
freshly ground black pepper	freshly ground black pepper

1. Arrange the fish fillets in the bottom of an ovenproof dish.
2. Cover with the onion, green pepper and tomatoes.
3. Mix the oregano with the tomato juice and pour over the top of the mixture.

4. Season with the black pepper.
5. Cover and bake in a preheated moderately hot oven (200°C/400°F, Gas Mark 6) for 30 minutes.
6. Serve hot.

Tuna and Corn Salad

Metric/Imperial	*American*
1 iceberg lettuce	1 iceberg lettuce
1 cucumber, sliced	1 cucumber, sliced
2 carrots, sliced	2 carrots, sliced
1 red pepper, sliced	1 red pepper, sliced
4 tomatoes, quartered	4 tomatoes, quartered
400g/14oz can tuna in brine, well drained	14oz can tuna in brine, well drained
350g/12oz sweetcorn	2¼ cups kernel corn
225g/8oz button mushrooms, halved	2 cups button mushrooms, halved
350g/12oz green beans, cooked	1½ cups green beans, cooked
4 spring onions, sliced	4 salad onions, sliced
1 tbsp pumpkin seeds	1 tbsp pumpkin seeds
dressing	dressing
8 black olives	8 black olives

1. Tear the lettuce leaves into a shallow salad bowl.
2. Mix together the cucumber, carrots, pepper, tomatoes, tuna, sweetcorn, mushrooms, green beans, spring onions and pumpkin seeds.
3. Pile into the salad bowl.
4. Pour the dressing over the salad, garnish with the olives and serve.

DINNERS/MAIN MEALS – STARCH

Minestrone Casserole

Metric/Imperial	*American*
2 onions, sliced	2 onions, sliced
3 carrots, sliced	3 carrots, sliced
2 leeks, sliced	2 leeks, sliced
2 celery sticks, sliced	2 celery sticks, sliced
225g/8oz parsnips, diced	1⅓ cups parsnips, diced
1 turnip, diced	1 turnip, diced
2 garlic cloves, crushed	2 garlic cloves, crushed
225g/8oz wholemeal pasta	2 cups wholewheat pasta
1.2 litres/2 pints water or vegetable stock	5 cups water or vegetable stock
freshly ground black pepper	freshly ground black pepper
350g/12oz tomatoes, roughly chopped	1½ cups tomatoes, roughly chopped
½ small cabbage, shredded	½ small cabbage, shredded
225g/8oz green beans, sliced	1 cup green beans, sliced
25g/1oz grated Parmesan cheese	¼ cup grated Parmesan cheese
parsley to garnish	parsley to garnish

1. Put the onions, carrots, leeks, celery, parsnips, turnip, garlic, pasta and water or stock in a large pan.

2. Add pepper to taste, stir well and bring to the boil.
3. Cover and simmer for 30 minutes.
4. Add the tomatoes, cabbage and beans and simmer for a further 5 minutes.
5. Serve hot in individual bowls, garnished with Parmesan and parsley.

Savoury Dutch Cakes

Metric/Imperial	*American*
1kg/2lb unpeeled potatoes	2lb unpeeled potatoes
225g/8oz broccoli or brussels sprouts, chopped	3 cups broccoli or brussels sprouts, chopped
225g/8oz cabbage, chopped	3 cups cabbage, chopped
1 tbsp olive oil	1 tbsp olive oil
4 onions, finely chopped	4 onions, finely chopped
½ tsp nutmeg	½ tsp nutmeg
freshly ground black pepper	freshly ground black pepper
50ml/2fl oz skimmed milk	¼ cup skimmed milk

The broccoli, sprouts and cabbage can be replaced with any leftover cooked green vegetables.

1. Bake, boil or steam the potatoes in their skins.
2. Steam the broccoli or sprouts and cabbage until just tender.
3. Heat the oil in a frying pan and fry the onion for 5 minutes.

4. Mash the potatoes with the nutmeg, black pepper and skimmed milk.
5. Mix together the potatoes, broccoli or sprouts, cabbage and onions.
6. Form into twelve round cakes.
7. Grill under a moderate heat for 15 minutes.

Spaghetti Napoletana

Metric/Imperial	*American*
350g/12oz wholemeal spaghetti	¾lb wholewheat spaghetti
2 tsp cold pressed olive oil	2 tsp cold pressed olive oil
175g/6oz mushrooms, sliced	1½ cups mushrooms, sliced
1 green pepper, chopped	1 green pepper, chopped
2 carrots, chopped	2 carrots, chopped
2 onions, chopped	2 onions, chopped
3 garlic cloves, crushed	3 garlic cloves, crushed
450g/1lb tomatoes, chopped	2 cups tomatoes, chopped
2 tbsp tomato purée	2 tbsp tomato purée
1 tbsp oregano	1 tbsp oregano
freshly ground black pepper	freshly ground black pepper

1. Cook the spaghetti without salt in boiling water according to the packet instructions.
2. Fry the mushrooms, pepper, carrots, onions and garlic in the oil for 5 minutes.

3. Add the tomatoes, purée, oregano and pepper to taste.
4. Cook for a further 5 minutes until the sauce has thickened.
5. Drain the cooked spaghetti and pour the sauce over.
6. Serve hot.

Spinach Dolmades

Metric/Imperial	*American*
12 large spinach leaves, stalks removed	12 large spinach leaves, stalks removed
1 onion, chopped	1 onion, chopped
2 garlic cloves, crushed	2 garlic cloves, crushed
175g/6oz mushrooms, chopped	1½ cups mushrooms, chopped
100g/4oz brown rice, cooked	½ cup brown rice, cooked
50g/2oz cashew nuts, nuts, chopped	½ cup cashew nuts, chopped
1 tbsp chopped mint	1 tbsp chopped mint
1 tbsp chopped coriander	1 tbsp chopped coriander
freshly ground black pepper	freshly ground black pepper
2 tbsp water or vegetable stock	2 tbsp water or vegetable stock

1. Bring a large pan of water to the boil and plunge the spinach leaves into the water.
2. Leave for 3 minutes, then drain and leave to cool on a board.

3. Fry the onion without fat in a heavy-based non-stick pan until softened. Stir regularly to prevent sticking.
4. Add the garlic and mushrooms and cook, stirring, for a further 2 minutes.
5. Remove from the heat and stir in the rice, nuts, herbs and black pepper to taste.
6. Add enough water to moisten, then divide the mixture between the spinach leaves.
7. Fold over both sides of the leaves, then roll up to form parcels.
8. Lay the spinach parcels in a shallow non-stick ovenproof dish, cover and bake in a preheated moderately hot oven (200°C/400°F, Gas Mark 6) for 45 minutes.
9. Serve hot or cold.

Vegetable Kebabs with Rice

Metric/Imperial	*American*
2 green peppers, cut in 2½cm/1in pieces	2 green peppers, cut in 1in pieces
2 red peppers, cut in 2½cm/1in pieces	2 red peppers, cut in 1in pieces
2 medium onions, cut in 2½cm/1in pieces	2 medium onions, cut in 1in pieces
1 aubergine, cut in 2½cm/1in pieces	1 eggplant, cut in 1in pieces
350g/12oz courgettes, thickly sliced	2¼ cups courgettes, thickly sliced
475g/1lb tomatoes, quartered	1lb tomatoes, quartered

350g/12oz cauliflower florets	3 cups cauliflower florets
350g/12oz button mushrooms	3 cups button mushrooms
1 tsp chopped thyme	1 tsp chopped thyme
1 tsp chopped oregano	1 tsp chopped oregano
1 tsp chopped marjoram	1 tsp chopped marjoram
1 tsp chopped parsley	1 tsp chopped parsley
freshly ground black pepper	freshly ground black pepper
225g/8oz brown rice	1 cup brown rice
225g/8oz sweetcorn	2 cups kernel corn

1. Thread the vegetable pieces on to eight skewers.
2. Put the kebabs on a non-stick baking sheet and sprinkle with the herbs and pepper.
3. Cover with foil and bake in a preheated moderate oven (180°C/350°F, Gas Mark 4) for 35 minutes.
4. Meanwhile, cook the rice according to the packet instructions.
5. Cook the sweetcorn and mix with the cooked rice.
6. Serve the kebabs on a bed of the rice sweetcorn.

Vegetable Risotto

Metric/Imperial	*American*
2 onions, sliced	2 onions, sliced
2 garlic cloves, crushed	2 garlic cloves, crushed
225g/8oz brown rice	1 cup brown rice
900ml/1½ pints water or vegetable stock	4 cups water or vegetable stock
1 red pepper, chopped	1 red pepper, chopped
225g/8oz courgettes, sliced	1½ cups courgettes, sliced
225g/8oz green beans	1 cup green beans
225g/8oz carrots, sliced	1½ cups carrots, sliced
50g/2oz cashew nuts	½ cup cashew nuts
1 tbsp chopped parsley	1 tbsp chopped parsley
1 tbsp soy sauce	1 tbsp soy sauce
freshly ground black pepper	freshly ground black pepper

1. Fry the onions and garlic without fat in a heavy-based non-stick pan for 5 minutes or until softened. Stir frequently to prevent sticking.
2. Add the rice and water or vegetable stock and bring to the boil.
3. Cover and simmer for 20 minutes.
4. Add the red pepper, courgettes, green beans, carrots, chopped parsley, soy sauce, and freshly ground black pepper to taste.
5. Cover then simmer for a further 10 minutes, adding more water if necessary.
6. Add the cashew nuts, stir well and cook over low heat for a further 5 minutes.
7. Serve hot.

Vegetable Stuffed Jacket Potato

Metric/Imperial	*American*
4 × 350g/12oz baking potatoes	4 × ¾lb baking potatoes
1 green pepper, chopped	1 green pepper, chopped
1 red pepper, chopped	1 red pepper, chopped
100g/4oz mushrooms, sliced	1 cup mushrooms, sliced
100g/4oz sweetcorn	¾ cup kernel corn
8 spring onions, chopped	8 salad onions, chopped
100g/4oz mixed sprouts	2 cups mixed sprouts
100g/4oz natural low-fat yogurt	½ cup unflavoured low-fat yogurt
1 tbsp chopped parsley	1 tbsp chopped parsley
freshly ground black pepper	freshly ground black pepper

1. Scrub the potatoes, prick the skins and bake in a hot oven (220°C/425°F, Gas Mark 7) for 1½ hours or until soft.
2. Mix the remaining ingredients together in a bowl.
3. Cut the potatoes in two and pile the mixture on each half.
4. Serve hot.

SIDE SALADS AND DRESSING

Basic Vinaigrette Dressing

Metric/Imperial	*American*
50ml/2fl oz cider vinegar	¼ cup cider vinegar
1 tbsp lemon juice	1 tbsp lemon juice
½ tsp basil	½ tsp basil
½ tsp French mustard	½ tsp French mustard

1. Put all the ingredients into a screw-topped jar and shake well.
2. Pour over the salad just before serving.

Garden Salad Dressing

Metric/Imperial	*American*
3g/½ tsp green pepper, minced	1½ tsp green pepper, minced
3g/½ tsp onion, minced	1½ tsp onion, minced
25g/1oz carrot, minced	1½ tbsp carrot, minced
60ml/2fl oz cider vinegar	¼ cup cider vinegar
100ml/3fl oz tomato juice	⅓ cups tomato juice

1. Put all the ingredients into a screw-topped jar and shake well.
2. Pour over the salad just before serving.

Green Salad

Metric/Imperial	*American*
½ iceberg lettuce	½ iceberg lettuce
½ cucumber, chopped	½ cucumber, chopped
2 spring onions, sliced	2 salad onions, sliced
1 green pepper, sliced	1 green pepper, sliced
100g/4oz beansprouts	2 cups beansprouts
1 stick celery, sliced	1 stick celery, sliced
dressing	dressing

1. Tear the lettuce leaves into a salad bowl.
2. Add the other ingredients and toss.

Herb and Garlic Dressing

Metric/Imperial	*American*
120ml/4 fl oz cider vinegar	½ cup cider vinegar
60ml/2fl oz water	¼ cup water
1 garlic clove, crushed	1 garlic clove, crushed
2 tsp chopped parsley	2 tsp chopped parsley
1 tsp basil	1 tsp basil
½ tsp dill	½ tsp dillweed
½ tsp thyme	½ tsp thyme
¼ tsp celery seed	¼ tsp celery seed
½ tsp parsley	½ tsp parsley

1. Pull all the ingredients into a screw-topped jar and shake well.
2. Pour over the salad just before serving.

Huguenot Dressing

Metric/Imperial	*American*
100g/3½oz natural low-fat yogurt	½ cup unflavoured low-fat yogurt
2 tbsp tomato purée	2 tbsp tomato purée
½ tsp Meaux mustard	½ tsp Meaux mustard
½ garlic clove, crushed	½ garlic clove, crushed
½ tbsp shallots, finely chopped	½ tbsp scallions, finely chopped

1. Put all the ingredients into a bowl and mix well.
2. Pour over the salad just before serving.

Minty Fruit Juice Dressing

Metric/Imperial	*American*
150ml/¼ pint fresh orange or grapefruit juice	⅔ cup fresh orange or grapefruit juice
2 tsp chopped mint	2 tsp chopped mint
freshly ground black pepper	freshly ground black pepper

1. Put all the ingredients into a bowl and mix well.
2. Pour over the salad just before serving.

Mixed Salad

Metric/Imperial	*American*
½ iceberg lettuce	½ iceberg lettuce
½ cucumber, chopped	½ cucumber, chopped
2 spring onions, sliced	2 salad onions, sliced
1 green pepper, sliced	1 green pepper, sliced
100g/4oz beansprouts	2 cups beansprouts
1 stick celery, sliced	1 stick celery, sliced
2 carrots, grated	2 carrots, grated
2 tomatoes, quartered	2 tomatoes, quartered
4 radishes, sliced	4 radishes, sliced
100g/4oz baby corn cobs, sliced	¾ cup baby corn cobs, sliced
dressing	dressing

1. Tear the lettuce leaves into a salad bowl.
2. Add the other ingredients and toss.

St Clements Vinaigrette

Metric/Imperial	*American*
120ml/4fl oz cider vinegar	½ cup cider vinegar
4 tbsp lemon juice	4 tbsp lemon juice
4 tbsp orange juice	4 tbsp orange juice
grated rind of 1 lemon	grated rind of 1 lemon
½ tsp French mustard	½ tsp French mustard
freshly ground black pepper	freshly ground black pepper

1. Put all the ingredients into a screw-topped jar and shake well.
2. Pour over the salad just before serving.

Spicy Tomato Dressing

Metric/Imperial	*American*
100ml/3fl oz tomato juice	⅓ cup tomato juice
2 tbsp lemon juice	2 tbsp lemon juice
2 tsp Worcestershire sauce	2 tsp Worcestershire sauce
1 tbsp snipped chives	1 tbsp snipped chives
freshly ground black pepper	freshly ground black pepper

1. Put all the ingredients into a bowl and mix well.
2. Pour over the salad just before serving.

PUDDINGS – PROTEIN

Apricot Baked Apples

Metric/Imperial	*American*
4 large cooking apples	4 large cooking apples
100g/4oz dried apricots, chopped	$\frac{3}{4}$ cup dried apricots, chopped
150ml/5fl oz unsweetened orange juice	$\frac{2}{3}$ cup unsweetened orange juice
1 tsp cinnamon	1 tsp cinnamon
200ml/7fl oz water	1 cup water

1. Soak the apricots in the orange juice with the cinnamon overnight.
2. Core the apples, leaving 0.5cm/$\frac{1}{4}$ inch at the bottom to hold the filling.
3. Cut through the skin round the centre of each apple to prevent them bursting when cooked.
4. Fill the apple centres with the apricot mixture.
5. Put the apples in a shallow baking dish and add the water.
6. Cover with a lid or foil and bake in a preheated moderately hot oven (200°C/400°F, Gas Mark 6) for about 30 minutes or until cooked.
7. Serve hot or cold.

Baked Apples

Metric/Imperial	*American*
4 large cooking apples	4 large cooking apples
1½ tbsp raisins	1½ tbsp raisins
1½ tbsp dried dates, chopped	1½ tbsp dried dates, chopped
1½ tbsp nuts, chopped	1½ tbsp nuts, chopped
1 tsp cinnamon	1 tsp cinnamon
200ml/7fl oz water	1 cup water

1. Core the apples, leaving 0.5cm/¼ inch at the bottom to hold the filling.
2. Cut through the skin round the centre of each apple to prevent them bursting when cooking.
3. Mix together the raisins, dates, nuts and cinnamon and fill the apple centres with the mixture.
4. Put the apples in a shallow baking dish and add the water.
5. Cover with a lid or foil and bake in a preheated moderately hot oven (200°C/400°F, Gas Mark 6) for about 30 minutes or until cooked.
6. Serve hot or cold.

Blackberry and Apple Fool

Metric/Imperial	*American*
225g/8oz blackberries	1½ cups blackberries
2 cooking apples, sliced	2 cooking apples, sliced
Finely grated rind and juice of 1 lemon	Finely grated rind and juice of 1 lemon

2 tbsp honey	2 tbsp honey
275g/10oz natural low-fat yogurt	1⅓ cups unflavoured low-fat yogurt

1. Reserve 4 blackberries for decoration. Stew the blackberries, apples, lemon rind and juice and honey in a covered saucepan for 15 minutes or until the apples are just tender.
2. Stir in the honey and yoghurt and purée.
3. Pour into individual glass dishes and decorate with the reserved blackberries.
4. Serve hot or cold.

Blackberry Baked Apples

Metric/Imperial	*American*
4 large cooking apples	4 large cooking apples
450g/1lb blackberries	3 cups blackberries
200ml/7fl oz water	1 cup water
1 tbsp honey	1 tbsp honey
finely grated rind and juice of 1 large orange	finely grated rind and juice of 1 large orange

1. Core the apples, leaving 0.5cm/¼ inch at the bottom to hold the filling.
2. Cut through the skin round the centre of each apple to prevent them bursting when cooked.
3. Fill the apple centres with a quarter of the blackberries.
4. Put the apples in a shallow baking dish and add the water.

5. Cover with a lid or foil and bake in a preheated moderately hot oven (200°C/400°F, Gas Mark 6) for about 30 minutes or until cooked.
6. Meanwhile, stew the remaining blackberries for a few minutes with the honey and the orange rind and juice.
7. Mash or liquidize the blackberries to a sauce and serve over the baked apples.

Fruit Salad

Metric/Imperial	*American*
1 green dessert apple, sliced	1 green dessert apple, sliced
1 orange, peeled and segmented	1 orange, peeled and segmented
1 peach, sliced	1 peach, sliced
1 pear, sliced	1 pear, sliced
225g/8oz strawberries, halved	1½ cups strawberries, halved
100g/4oz green grapes, halved	⅔ cup green grapes, halved
100g/4oz cherries, stoned	1 cup cherries, pitted
2 tbsp lemon juice	2 tbsp lemon juice
2 tbsp orange juice	2 tbsp orange juice

1. Mix together the fruit and lemon juice.
2. Cover and chill before serving.

Green Ginger Salad

Metric/Imperial	*American*
2 green dessert apples, sliced	2 green dessert apples, sliced
1 tbsp lemon juice	1 tbsp lemon juice
2 kiwi fruit, thinly sliced	2 kiwi fruit, thinly sliced
225g/8oz green grapes, halved	1⅓ cups green grapes, halved
1 piece stem ginger, sliced	1 piece stem ginger, sliced
4 tbsp apple juice	4 tbsp apple juice

1. Mix the apple slices and lemon juice together.
2. Add the kiwi fruit, grapes, ginger and apple juice.
3. Mix and serve in individual dishes.

Hot Fruit Soufflé

Metric/Imperial	*American*
175g/6oz mixed dried fruit	1 cup mixed dried fruit
450ml/15fl oz water	2 cups water
finely grated rind and juice of 1 lemon	finely grated rind and juice of 1 lemon
1 tbsp honey	1 tbsp honey
4 egg whites	4 egg whites

1. Soak the fruit overnight in the water, lemon rind and juice and honey.
2. Put the fruit in a pan and simmer for 30 minutes.
3. Make up the liquid to 150ml/5fl oz/⅔ cup with water.

4. Purée the fruit and liquid until smooth in an electric blender, then leave to cool.
5. Beat the egg whites until stiff, then fold into the purée.
6. Pour into a 1¾ litre/2½ pint/7 cup soufflé dish and bake in a preheated moderately hot oven (200°C/400°F, Gas Mark 6) for 20 minutes.
5. Serve immediately.

Pineapple Sorbet

Metric/Imperial	*American*
1 × 1.5kg/3lb pineapple	1 × 3lb pineapple
finely grated rind and juice of 1 large orange	finely grated rind and juice of 1 large orange
2 egg whites	2 egg whites

1. Cut the pineapple in half lengthwise and scoop out the pineapple flesh, discarding the central core.
2. Liquidize the pineapple flesh to a purée with the orange rind and juice.
3. Pour the purée into a bowl and freeze until half frozen.
4. Beat well to break down the ice crystals.
5. Beat the egg whites until stiff, then fold into the pineapple mixture.
6. Pile the mixture into the pineapple shells and freeze.
7. Allow to soften for 10 minutes at room temperature before serving.

Raspberry Yogurt Snow

Metric/Imperial	*American*
450g/1lb raspberries	3 cups raspberries
2 egg whites	2 egg whites
1 tbsp clear honey	1 tbsp clear honey
275g/10oz natural low-fat yogurt	1⅓ cups unflavoured low-fat yogurt
grated rind of ½ lemon	grated rind of ½ lemon
25g/1oz flaked almonds, toasted	¼ cup flakes almonds, toasted

1. Divide the raspberries between four glass dishes.
2. Whisk the egg whites until stiff.
3. Whisk in the honey until very thick.
4. Fold in the yogurt and lemon rind gently.
5. Spoon over the raspberries and sprinkle with the almonds.
6. Serve immediately.

Spiced Fruit Salad

Metric/Imperial	*American*
100g/4oz dried prunes	¾ cup dried prunes
100g/4oz dried pears	¾ cup dried pears
100g/4oz dried peaches	¾ cup dried peaches
100g/4oz dried apricots	¾ cup dried apricots
1 cinnamon stick	1 cinnamon stick
2 cloves	2 cloves

300ml/10fl oz unsweetened orange juice	1⅓ cups unsweetened orange juice
300ml/10fl oz water	1⅓ cups water

1. Soak the fruit and spices overnight in the orange juice and water.
2. Stew the fruit in the soaking liquid in a covered saucepan until just tender.
3. Serve hot or cold.

Strawberry Cheese

Metric/Imperial	*American*
2 tbsp clear honey	2 tbsp clear honey
175g/6oz strawberries	1 cup strawberries
175g/6oz low-fat curd cheese	¾ cup low-fat curd cheese

1. Liquidize the honey and half the strawberries to a purée
2. Beat the cheese until smooth, then fold in the strawberry mixture.
3. Slice the remaining strawberries, and put in the bottom of individual serving dishes, reserving four slices for decoration.
4. Spoon the strawberry mixture into the serving dishes and decorate with the reserved strawberry slices.
5. Serve chilled.

Stuffed Oranges

Metric/Imperial

2 large oranges, halved
1 dessert apple, peeled and chopped
1 tbsp raisins
1 tbsp hazelnuts, toasted and chopped
100g/4oz low-fat fromage frais
4 slices of orange

American

2 large oranges, halved
1 dessert apple, peeled and chopped
1 tbsp raisins
1 tbsp hazelnuts, toasted and chopped
½ cup low-fat fromage frais
4 slices of orange

1. Scoop out the orange flesh, keeping the shells intact.
2. Chop the orange flesh, discarding any pith, and put in a bowl.
3. Add the apple, raisins and hazlenuts and mix well.
4. Pile mixture into the orange halves.
5. Stir the fromage frais well, then put a tablespoon on top of each orange.
6. Cut each orange slice to the centre and turn out to form twists.
7. Top each orange with a twist and chill before serving.

Tropical Salad

Metric/Imperial	*American*
1 small pineapple, sliced	1 small pineapple, sliced
1 kiwi fruit, sliced	1 kiwi fruit, sliced
1 mango, sliced	1 mango, sliced
1 papaya, sliced	1 papaya, sliced
1 lime, cut into wedges	1 lime, cut into wedges

1. Arrange the fruit slices on serving plates.
2. Cover and chill.
3. Serve with lime wedges.

PUDDINGS – STARCH

Banana Fool

Metric/Imperial	*American*
4 ripe bananas, sliced	4 ripe bananas, sliced
150g/5oz natural low-fat yogurt	⅔ cup unflavoured low-fat yogurt
150g/5oz low-fat fromage frais	⅔ cup low-fat fromage frais
4 green grapes	4 green grapes

1. Purée the bananas in a liquidizer.
2. Stir in the yogurt and fromage frais and mix well.
3. Pour into individual serving dishes and chill.
4. Decorate with the grapes and serve.

Banana Fruit Yogurt

Metric/Imperial	*American*
575g/20oz natural low-fat yogurt	2⅔ cups unflavoured low-fat yogurt
2 ripe bananas, sliced	2 ripe bananas, sliced
100g/4oz green grapes, halved	⅔ cup green grapes, halved
50g/2oz dates, chopped	⅓ cup dates, chopped

1. Mix all the ingredients together in a large bowl.
2. Serve chilled.

Banana Ice

Metric/Imperial	*American*
4 ripe bananas, peeled	4 ripe bananas, peeled
1 tsp grated nutmeg	1 tsp grated nutmeg

1. Put the bananas on a plastic tray and freeze until solid.
2. Remove half an hour before serving, allow to soften slightly in the refrigerator.
3. Sprinkle with nutmeg and serve.

Ginger Bananas

Metric/Imperial	*American*
4 ripe bananas, sliced	4 ripe bananas, sliced
1 piece preserved ginger, finely chopped	1 piece preserved ginger, finely chopped
25g/1oz flaked almonds, toasted	¼ cup flaked almonds, toasted

1. Divide the bananas between individual dishes.
2. Sprinkle the ginger and almonds over the top.
3. Serve with Yogurt Snow (see p. 160).

Ginger Pear Mousse

Metric/Imperial	*American*
1kg/2lbs pears, chopped	2lbs pears, chopped
finely grated rind and juice of 1 lemon	finely grated rind and juice of 1 lemon
¼ tsp ground ginger	¼ tsp ground ginger
4 pieces preserved ginger	4 pieces preserved ginger
2 tbsp syrup from preserved ginger	2 tbsp syrup from preserved ginger
2 egg whites	2 egg whites
275g/10oz natural low-fat yogurt	1⅓ cups unflavoured low-fat yogurt
15g/½oz gelatine	2 envelopes gelatine
2 tbsp water	2 tbsp water

1. Cook the pears gently in a pan for 10 minutes with the lemon rind and juice, ground and preserved ginger and syrup.
2. Remove the preserved ginger and set aside, then liquidize the pear mixture, egg yolks and yogurt to a smooth purée.
3. Chop two of the pieces of ginger and slice the other two.
4. Sprinkle the gelatine over the water in a small cup and stand the cup in a pan of hot water, stirring until the gelatine has dissolved.
5. Stir the gelatine and chopped ginger into the purée and leave in a cool place until setting.
6. Beat the egg whites until stiff, then fold into the mixture.

7. Spoon into individual glass dishes or a serving bowl and chill.
8. Decorate with the slices of preserved ginger, and serve.

Hot Bananas

Metric/Imperial	*American*
100ml/3fl oz grape juice	⅓ cup grape juice
1 tbsp honey	1 tbsp honey
½ tsp ground cinnamon	½ tsp ground cinnamon
4 bananas, halved	4 bananas, halved
50g/2oz raisins	⅓ cup raisins
25g/1oz walnuts, chopped	¼ cup walnuts, chopped

1. Heat the grape juice, honey and cinnamon in a pan.
2. Add the bananas and raisins, bring to the boil, then simmer for a few minutes until the bananas are tender.
3. Put the bananas on a serving dish, pour over the liquid and sprinkle with the chopped nuts.
4. Serve hot.

Pear Compôte

Metric/Imperial	*American*
4 ripe pears, peeled	4 ripe pears, peeled
150ml/5fl oz unsweetened grape juice	$\frac{2}{3}$ cup unsweetened grape juice
2 tsp ground cinnamon	2 tsp ground cinnamon
50g/2oz raisins	$\frac{1}{3}$ cup raisins

1. Stand the pears in a deep saucepan, just wide enough to hold them upright.
2. Add the grape juice, cinnamon and raisins.
3. Cover the pan and simmer for 30 minutes or until the pears are just tender.
4. Serve hot or cold.

Yogurt Snow

Metric/Imperial	*American*
2 egg whites	2 egg whites
3 tbsp clear honey	3 tbsp clear honey
275g/10oz natural low-fat yogurt	$1\frac{1}{4}$ cups unflavoured low-fat yogurt

1. Whisk the egg whites until stiff.
2. Whisk in the honey until very thick.
3. Fold in the yogurt gently.
4. Serve immediately as a substitute for cream.

Bodyclock CRITICAL RECIPES

BREAKFAST – PROTEIN

Breakfast Compôte

Metric/Imperial	*American*
100g/4oz dried prunes	¾ cup dried prunes
100g/4oz dried apricots	¾ cup dried apricot
450ml/¾ pint water	2 cups water
2 oranges	2 oranges
150g/5oz natural low-fat yogurt	⅔ cup unflavoured low-fat yogurt
25g/1oz wheatgerm	¼ cup wheatgerm

1. Simmer the prunes and apricots in the water for 15 minutes, then leave to cool.
2. Peel the oranges, remove the pith and divide into segments.
3. Mix the oranges with the dried fruit and liquid and divide between individual serving dishes.
4. Spoon the yogurt over the fruit and sprinkle the wheatgerm on top.

Tomato Scrambled Eggs

Metric/Imperial
6 free-range eggs
4 tbsp skimmed milk
freshly ground black pepper
1 small onion, finely chopped
2 tomatoes, chopped

American
6 free-range eggs
4 tbsp skimmed milk
freshly ground black pepper
1 small onion, finely chopped
2 tomatoes, chopped

1. Beat the eggs with the milk and black pepper to taste.
2. Fry the onion without fat in a non-stick pan until softened, stirring to prevent sticking.
3. Pour in the eggs and stir over a low heat until beginning to set.
4. Stir in the tomatoes and remove from the heat.
5. Serve immediately.

BREAKFASTS – STARCH

Banana Muesli

Metric/Imperial	*American*
50g/2oz rolled oats	½ cup rolled oats
25g/1oz wheatgerm	¼ cup wheatgerm
50g/2oz bran	½ cup bran
1 tbsp chopped mixed nuts	1 tbsp chopped mixed nuts
25g/1oz raisins	¼ cup raisins
25g/1oz dried dates, chopped	¼ cup dried dates, chopped
300ml/½ pint skimmed milk	1⅓ cups skimmed milk
2 bananas, sliced	2 bananas, sliced
150g/5oz natural low-fat yogurt	⅔ cups unflavoured low-fat yogurt

1. Mix together all ingredients except the bananas and yogurt.
2. Divide between individual bowls.
3. Top with the bananas and yogurt and serve.

Honey Raisin Crêpes

Metric/Imperial	*American*
100g/4oz wholemeal self-raising flour	1 cup wholewheat self-rising flour
1 free-range egg yolk, beaten	1 free-range egg yolk, beaten

300ml/½ pint skimmed milk	1⅓ cup skimmed milk
4 tbsp honey	4 tbsp honey
100g/4oz raisins	1 cup raisins
¼ tsp nutmeg	¼ tsp nutmeg

1. Put the flour in a bowl and make a well in the centre.
2. Pour in the egg yolk and milk and beat well until smooth.
3. Mix together the honey, raisins and nutmeg.
4. Heat a 20cm/8in non-stick heavy-based frying pan and pour in enough batter to thinly coat the bottom of the pan.
5. Tilt the pan to spread the batter evenly and cook until the top of the batter is set and the underside golden brown. Turn and cook the other side.
6. Slide on to a warm plate, cover and stand over a pan of hot water to keep warm.
7. Make a further seven crêpes.
8. Spread each crêpe with a spoonful of the honey mixture and serve.

Honey on Toast

Metric/Imperial	*American*
8 slices wholemeal bread	8 slices wholewheat bread
50g/2oz unsalted butter	¼ cup unsalted butter
4 tbsp honey	4 tbsp honey

Porridge

Metric/Imperial	*American*
1.2 litres/2 pints water	5 cups water
225g/8oz medium-cut oatmeal	2 cups medium-cut oatmeal
300ml/½ pint skimmed milk	1⅓ cups skimmed milk

1. Bring the water to the boil in a heavy-based saucepan.
2. Stir in the oatmeal and cook gently for 3 minutes, until starting to thicken.
3. Pour into individual bowls and serve with the milk.

Sweetcorn Fritters

Metric/Imperial	*American*
2 tbsp wholemeal flour	2 tbsp wholewheat flour
1 large free-range egg yolk, beaten	1 large free-range egg yolk, beaten
5 tbsp skimmed milk	5 tbsp skimmed milk
200g/7oz sweetcorn kernels	1⅓ cups kernel corn
2 spring onions, sliced	2 salad onions, sliced
freshly ground black pepper to taste	freshly ground black pepper to taste

1. Liquidize the ingredients to a batter, with small chunks of sweetcorn remaining.
2. Heat a non-stick heavy-based frying pan and

add 2 tablespoons of the batter at a time, cooking for 2 minutes on each side.
3. Serve immediately.

Tomato Beans on Toast

Metric/Imperial	*American*
4 slices wholemeal bread	4 slices wholewheat bread
2 × 440g/15oz cans baked beans	2 × 15oz cans baked beans
4 tomatoes, chopped	4 tomatoes, chopped

Use reduced sugar and salt baked beans.

Mix the tomatoes with the beans before heating and serving on the toast.

LUNCHES/SNACKS – PROTEIN

Greek Salad

Metric/Imperial	*American*
1 iceberg lettuce	1 iceberg lettuce
4 large tomatoes, quartered	4 large tomatoes, quartered
1 cucumber, cubed	1 cucumber, cubed
1 large onion, sliced	1 large onion, sliced
1 green pepper, sliced	1 green pepper, sliced
175g/6oz feta cheese, cubed	1½ cups feta cheese, cubed
12 black olives	12 black olives
dressing	dressing

1. Tear the lettuce leaves into a large salad bowl.
2. Halve the tomato quarters and add to the bowl.
3. Add the cucumber, onion, pepper, cheese, olives and dressing.
4. Toss well and serve.

Mackerel Pâté and Crudités*

Metric/Imperial	*American*
225g/8oz smoked mackerel, skinned	½lb smoked mackerel, skinned
100g/4oz low-fat curd cheese or fromage frais	½ cup low-fat curd cheese or fromage frais

**See p. 190.*

1 tbsp creamed horseradish
juice of 1 lemon
1 tbsp chopped parsley
½ tsp paprika
freshly ground black pepper
lemon twists and parsley sprigs to garnish

1 tbsp creamed horseradish
juice of 1 lemon
1 tbsp chopped parsley
½ tsp paprika
freshly ground black pepper
lemon twists and parsley springs to garnish

1. Flake the mackerel in a bowl.
2. Add the curd cheese or fromage frais, horseradish, lemon juice, parsley, paprika and black pepper to taste.
3. Mix well and pile into a small serving dish or individual ramekins.
4. Garnish with the lemon twists and parsley and serve chilled.

LUNCHES/SNACKS – STARCH:

Avocado Salad

Metric/Imperial

1 frisee or curly endive
1 bunch watercress, separated into sprigs
1 avocado, peeled and sliced
½ cucumber
dressing
1 tbsp sesame seeds, toasted

American

1 frisee or curly endive
1 bunch watercress, separated into sprigs
1 avacado, peeled and sliced
½ cucumber
dressing
1 tbsp sesame seeds, toasted

1. Tear the frisee leaves into a large salad bowl.
2. Add the watercress sprigs and sliced avocado.
3. Halve the cucumber lengthwise, slice thinly and add to the salad.
4. Add the dressing and sesame seeds, toss well and serve.

Brown Rice Salad

Metric/Imperial

100g/4oz brown rice
100g/4oz frozen peas
100g/4oz sweetcorn
150ml/¼ pint piquant tomato dressing
1 red pepper, finely chopped

American

½ cup brown rice
¾ cup frozen peas
¾ cup kernel corn
⅔ cup piquant tomato dressing
1 red pepper, finely chopped

50g/2oz cashew nuts	½ cup cashew nuts
1 small onion, finely chopped	1 small onion, finely chopped
freshly ground black pepper	freshly ground black pepper

1. Cook the rice in boiling water for 30 minutes or as instructed.
2. Add the peas and sweetcorn and simmer for 3 minutes.
3. Drain thoroughly and put in a serving dish.
4. Add the dressing whilst the vegetables are still warm and toss well.
5. When the salad mixture has cooled, add the red pepper, nuts, onion and pepper to taste.
6. Mix well and serve cold.

Curd Cheese and Cucumber Sandwich

Metric/Imperial	*American*
8 slices wholemeal bread	8 slices wholewheat bread
100g/4oz low-fat curd cheese	½ cup low-fat curd cheese
½ cucumber, thinly sliced	½ cucumber, thinly sliced

1. Spread four of the slices of bread with the curd cheese.
2. Cover with the cucumber slices.
3. Top with the remaining four slices of bread.
4. Cut each sandwich diagonally in half and serve.

Hot Herb Loaf

Metric/Imperial	*American*
1 wholemeal French stick	1 wholemeal French stick
100g/4oz unsalted butter	½ cup unsalted butter
4 garlic cloves, crushed	4 garlic cloves, crushed
1 tsp chopped parsley	1 tsp chopped parsley
1 tsp chopped oregano	1 tsp chopped oregano
1 tsp chopped marjoram	1 tsp chopped marjoram
1 tsp chopped thyme	1 tsp chopped thyme
freshly ground black pepper	freshly ground black pepper

1. Cut slits in the French stick to within ½cm/¼in of the bottom.
2. Beat together the butter, garlic, herbs and pepper.
3. Spread each side of the slits generously with the butter mixture.
4. Cover the bread with foil.
5. Bake for 10 minutes in a hot oven (220°C/425°F, Gas Mark 7).
6. Serve hot.

Leek and Potato Soup

Metric/Imperial	*American*
450ml/¾ pint water or vegetable stock	2 cups water or vegetable stock
1 large onion, sliced	1 large onion, sliced
3 leeks, cleaned and sliced	3 leeks, cleaned and sliced
3 large potatoes, scrubbed and sliced	3 large potatoes, scrubbed and sliced
freshly ground black pepper	freshly ground black pepper
chopped parsley to garnish	chopped parsley to garnish

1. Bring the water or vegetable stock to the boil in a large pan.
2. Add the onion, leeks, potatoes and black pepper to taste and bring back to the boil.
3. Simmer for 30 minutes.
4. Liquidize until smooth and pour into individual soup bowls.
5. Garnish with chopped parsley and serve.

Lemon Spaghetti

Metric/Imperial	*American*
225g/8oz wholemeal spaghetti	½lb wholewheat spaghetti
grated rind and juice of 2 lemons	grated rind and juice of 2 lemons
4 garlic cloves, crushed	4 garlic cloves, crushed

2 spring onions, finely chopped	2 salad onions, finely chopped
175g/6oz low-fat fromage frais	¾ cup fromage frais
25g/1oz grated Parmesan cheese	¼ cup grated Parmesan cheese
freshly ground black pepper	freshly ground black pepper
1 tbsp chopped parsley	1 tbsp chopped parsley

1. Cook the spaghetti as directed on the packet.
2. Meanwhile, mix together the lemon rind and juice, garlic, onions and fromage frais in a saucepan.
3. Heat gently until hot, but *do not boil.*
4. Drain the pasta well and mix with the lemon sauce.
5. Serve sprinkled with the cheese and black pepper to taste, and garnish with the parsley.

STARTERS – PROTEIN

Avocado and Grapefruit Cocktail

Metric/Imperial	*American*
8 lettuce leaves	8 lettuce leaves
1 avocado pear	1 avocado pear
juice of 1 lemon	juice of 1 lemon
2 grapefruit	2 grapefruit
1 tbsp chopped mint	1 tbsp chopped mint
1 tbsp sesame seeds, toasted	1 tbsp sesame seeds, toasted
mint sprigs to garnish	mint sprigs to garnish

1. Shred the lettuce and divide equally between four serving dishes.
2. Peel the avocado lengthwise, remove stones and slice into a bowl.
3. Add the lemon juice and mix gently.
4. Halve the grapefruit and divide into segments in the bowl.
5. Add the mint and stir the mixture gently.
6. Divide the avocado and grapefruit mixture equally between the dishes and sprinkle with the sesame seeds.
7. Garnish with the mint sprigs and serve immediately.

Avocado Dip

Metric/Imperial

1 avocado, stoned and peeled
juice of 1 lemon
juice of ½ orange
1 garlic clove, crushed
1 small onion, finely chopped
1 tbsp chopped parsley
1 tbsp chopped basil
1 tbsp chopped mint
freshly ground black pepper

American

1 avocado, pitted and peeled
juice of .1 lemon
juice of ½ orange
1 garlic clove, crushed
1 small onion, finely chopped
1 tbsp chopped parsley
1 tbsp chopped basil
1 tbsp chopped mint
freshly ground black pepper

1. Liquidize all the ingredients.
2. Serve with crudités (*see p. 190*).

Curry Dip

Metric/Imperial

150g/5oz natural low-fat yogurt
½ tsp curry powder
¼ tsp ground cumin
¼ tsp lemon juice
freshly ground black pepper

American

⅔ cup unflavoured low-fat yogurt
½ tsp curry powder
¼ tsp ground cumin
¼ tsp lemon juice
freshly ground black pepper

1. Mix together all the ingredients.
2. Serve chilled.

Horseradish Tomatoes

Metric/Imperial	*American*
4 large tomatoes, sliced	4 large tomatoes, sliced
3 tbsp natural low-fat yogurt	3 tbsp unflavoured low-fat yogurt
1 tbsp creamed horseradish	1 tbsp creamed horseradish
chopped parsley to garnish	chopped parsley to garnish

1. Arrange the tomatoes in individual serving dishes.
2. Mix the yogurt and horseradish.
3. Spoon over the tomatoes and sprinkle with the parsley.

Spinach Cheese Pâté

Metric/Imperial	*American*
225g/8 oz low-fat curd cheese	1 cup low-fat curd cheese
100g/4oz spinach, cooked	1½ cups spinach, cooked
3 drops Tabasco sauce	3 drops Tabasco sauce
juice of ½ lemon	juice of ½ lemon
½ tsp nutmeg	½ tsp nutmeg
freshly ground black pepper	freshly ground black pepper
lemon twists to garnish	lemon twists to garnish

1. Beat the curd cheese until smooth.

2. Chop the spinach and beat into the curd cheese.
3. Add the Tabasco, lemon juice, nutmeg and pepper to taste and mix thoroughly.
4. Chill, and garnish with lemon twists to serve.

Stuffed Pears

Metric/Imperial	*American*
2 pears, halved and cored	2 pears, halved and cored
2 tbsp lemon juice	2 tbsp lemon juice
100g/4oz low-fat cottage cheese	½ cup low-fat cottage cheese
1 tbsp walnuts, chopped	1 tbsp walnuts, chopped
freshly ground black pepper	freshly ground black pepper
1 celery stick, chopped	1 celery stick, chopped
1 carrot, grated	1 carrot, grated
½ bunch watercress leaves, chopped	½ bunch watercress leaves, chopped

1. Brush the pears with the lemon juice.
2. Mix together the cottage cheese, walnuts and freshly ground black pepper to taste.
3. Pile the mixture on to the pear halves.
4. Mix together the celery, carrot and watercress and arrange on serving plates.
5. Put the pear halves on top and serve.

Tomato and Orange Soup

Metric/Imperial	*American*
1kg/2lb tomatoes, chopped	4 cups tomatoes, chopped
1 onion, chopped	1 onion, chopped
1 carrot, grated	1 carrot, grated
2 tbsp chopped basil	2 tbsp chopped basil
2 tbsp grated orange rind	2 tbsp grated orange rind
4 tbsp orange juice	4 tbsp orange juice
900ml/1½ pints vegetable stock or water	4 cups vegetable stock or water
225g/8oz natural low-fat yogurt	1 cup unflavoured low-fat yogurt
¼ tsp grated nutmeg	¼ tsp grated nutmeg
freshly ground black pepper to taste	freshly ground black pepper to taste
1 tbsp snipped chives to garnish	1 tbsp snipped chives to garnish

1. Simmer the tomatoes, onion, carrot, basil, orange rind and vegetable stock or water for 15 minutes.
2. Liquidize, then sieve back into the pan.
3. Stir in the yogurt, nutmeg and black pepper to taste and heat gently – *do not boil.*
4. Serve hot or cold, garnished with the chives.

DINNERS/MAIN MEALS – PROTEIN

Beefburger with Tomato Sauce

Metric/Imperial	*American*
1 tsp cold pressed olive oil	1 tsp cold pressed olive oil
3 onions, finely chopped	3 onions, finely chopped
3 garlic cloves, crushed	3 garlic cloves, crushed
1 green pepper, finely chopped	1 green pepper, finely chopped
350g/12oz tomatoes, chopped	1½ cups tomatoes, chopped
1 tbsp tomato purée	1 tbsp tomato purée
1 tbsp chopped basil	1 tbsp chopped basil
freshly ground black pepper	freshly ground black pepper
450g/1lb extra lean minced beef	1lb extra lean minced beef

1. Heat the oil in a frying pan and fry half the onions and garlic with the green pepper for 5 minutes.
2. Stir in the tomatoes, purée, basil and black pepper to taste.
3. Bring to the boil, then cover and simmer for 20 minutes.
4. Meanwhile, mix well together the beef and the remaining onions and garlic, with freshly ground black pepper to taste.
5. Divide the mixture into eight, form into balls, then flatten each ball into a burger shape.

Alternatively, use a burger maker, if you have one.

6. Cook to taste under a hot grill, turning half-way through the cooking time.
7. Liquidize the tomato sauce, if desired.
8. Serve the burger with the sauce poured over.

Beef Stroganoff

Metric/Imperial	*American*
450g/1lb fillet or rump steak	1lb fillet or rump steak
150g/5oz low-fat fromage frais	⅔ cup low-fat fromage frais
150ml/¼ pint water or vegetable stock	⅔ cup water or vegetable stock
2 tbsp soy sauce	2 tbsp soy sauce
2 tbsp chopped parsley	2 tbsp chopped parsley
freshly ground black pepper	freshly ground black pepper
½ tbsp cold pressed olive oil	½ tbsp cold pressed olive oil
2 onions, sliced	2 onions, sliced
1 crushed garlic clove	1 crushed garlic clove
1 stick celery, finelysliced	1 stick celery, finely sliced
450g/1lb mushrooms, sliced	1lb mushrooms, sliced

1. Remove any fat from the steak and cut into stripes across the grain about 5cm/2in long.
2. Mix together the fromage frais, stock, soy sauce, parsley and black pepper in a jug.

3. Heat the oil in a large frying pan or wok and stir-fry the onions for 3 minutes.
4. Add the beef and stir-fry a further 5 minutes until browned.
5. Add the garlic, celery and mushrooms and stir-fry for a further 5 minutes.
6. Remove from the heat and allow to cool slightly.
7. Stir in the yogurt mixture.
8. Return to the heat and warm gently but *do not boil.*
9. Serve immediately.

Celebration Salad

Metric/Imperial	*American*
175g/6oz red cabbage, shredded	2¼ cups red cabbage, shredded
2 celery sticks, chopped	2 celery sticks, chopped
2 large carrots, grated	2 large carrots, grated
2 green dessert apples, chopped	2 green dessert apples, chopped
100g/4oz dried apricots, chopped	½ cup dried apricots, chopped
2 satsumas, peeled and segmented	2 satsumas, peeled and segmented
50g/2oz raisins	⅓ cup raisins
50g/2oz walnuts, roughly chopped	½ cup walnuts, roughly chopped
100g/4oz Stilton cheese, cubed	1 cup Stilton cheese, cubed
150ml/¼ pint fresh orange juice	⅔ cup fresh orange juice

1 tbsp cider vinegar	1 tbsp cider vinegar
1 tbsp chopped parsley	1 tbsp chopped parsley
freshly ground black pepper	freshly ground black pepper

This can be stored for several days if refrigerated in an airtight container.

1. Mix all the ingredients well in a salad bowl.
2. Serve cold.

Coronation Chicken

Metric/Imperial	***American***
½ iceberg lettuce	½ iceberg lettuce
1 frisee or curly endive	1 frisee or curly endive
175g/6oz beansprouts	3 cups beansprouts
½ cucumber, thinly sliced	½ cucumber, thinly sliced
4 spring onions, sliced	4 salad onions, sliced
2 tbsp lemon juice	2 tbsp lemon juice
1 tbsp curry powder	1 tbsp curry powder
1 small onion, finely chopped	1 small onion, finely chopped
2 green dessert apples, sliced	2 green dessert apples, sliced
75g/3oz dried apricots, chopped	½ cup dried apricots, chopped
150g/5oz natural low-fat yogurt	⅔ cup unflavoured low-fat yogurt
4 tbsp low-fat fromage frais	4 tbsp low-fat fromage frais
450g/1lb cooked chicken meat, cubed	1lb cooked chicken meat, cubed

1. Tear the iceberg and endive leaves into a large salad bowl.
2. Add the beansprouts, cucumber and spring onions.
3. Mix together in a bowl the lemon juice, curry powder, chopped onion, apple, apricots, yogurt and fromage frais.
4. Stir in the chicken cubes and mix well.
5. Pile into the salad bowl and serve.

Ginger Beef

Metric/Imperial	*American*
450g/1lb fillet or rump steak	1lb fillet or rump steak
2 tbsp soy sauce	2 tbsp soy sauce
2½cm/1in root ginger, grated	1in root ginger, grated
grated rind and juice of 1 orange	grated rind and juice of 1 orange
1 tbsp cold pressed olive oil	1 tbsp cold pressed olive oil
1 onion, sliced into rings	1 onion, sliced into rings
1 stick celery, finely sliced	1 stick celery, finely sliced
2 carrots, finely sliced	2 carrots, finely sliced
1 green pepper, finely sliced	1 green pepper finely sliced
100g/4oz mangetout	¾ cup mangetout
50g/2oz cashew nuts	½ cup cashew nuts
100g/4oz beansprouts	2 cups beansprouts

1. Remove any fat from the steak and cut into strips across the grain about 5cm/2in long.
2. Put the soy sauce, ginger and orange rind and juice into a bowl and stir in the beef strips.
3. Leave to marinate for at least 15 minutes.
4. Heat the oil in a large frying pan or wok and stir-fry the onions for 3 minutes.
5. Add the beef and stir-fry a further 5 minutes until browned.
6. Add the marinade, celery, carrots, pepper, mangetout, nuts and beansprouts and stir-fry for a further 5 minutes.
7. Serve immediately.

Honey Roast Chicken

Metric/Imperial	*American*
1 tbsp honey	1 tbsp honey
4 spring onions, chopped	4 salad onions, chopped
1 tsp finely chopped stem ginger	1 tsp finely chopped stem ginger
1 tbsp soy sauce	1 tbsp soy sauce
150ml/¼ pint sherry or vegetable stock	⅔ cup sherry or vegetable stock
1 × 1½kg/3lb chicken	1 × 1½kg chicken
1 tsp potato flour	1 tsp potato flour
300ml/½ pint water or vegetable stock	1⅓ cups water or vegetable stock

1. Mix together the honey, onions, ginger, soy sauce and sherry or stock.

2. Clean the chicken and brush with the honey mixture.
3. Put in a roasting tin and cover with foil.
4. Roast in a preheated moderate oven (180°C/350°F, Gas Mark 4) for 1½ hours or until the chicken is cooked through, basting regularly with the honey sauce. Remove the foil for the last 15 minutes of cooking time.
5. Remove the chicken from the tin and keep warm. Pour away all but 1 tablespoon of the fat and juices in the roasting tin.
6. Mix the potato flour with a little of the water or stock and stir into the remaining chicken juices.
7. Make up any remaining honey basting mixture to 300ml/½ pint/1⅓ cups with the water or vegetable stock and gradually blend into the potato flour mixture in the roasting tin.
8. Cook gently for 3 minutes, being careful not to overheat as the gravy will go thin again.
9. Carve the chicken and serve with the gravy.

Salmon with Watercress Sauce

Metric/Imperial	*American*
675g/1½lb salmon steaks	1½lb salmon steaks
600ml/1 pint vegetable stock or water	2⅔ cups vegetable stock or water
1 onion, thinly sliced	1 onion, thinly sliced
1 carrot, thinly sliced	1 carrot, thinly sliced
1 lemon, thinly sliced	1 lemon, thinly sliced
1 tbsp chopped parsley	1 tbsp chopped parsley

1 bay leaf	1 bay leaf
1 tsp basil	1 tsp basil
1 tsp thyme	1 tsp thyme
freshly ground black pepper	freshly ground black pepper
1 bunch watercress	1 bunch watercress
2 sprigs mint	2 sprigs mint
150g/5oz natural low-fat yogurt	⅔ cup unflavoured low-fat yogurt
1 garlic clove, crushed	1 garlic clove, crushed
1 tsp lemon juice	1 tsp lemon juice

1. Arrange the fish steaks in a single layer in a large pan or fish kettle.
2. Pour in the water or vegetable stock.
3. Cover the fish with the onion, carrot, lemon slices and bay leaf and sprinkle with the basil, thyme and black pepper.
4. Bring to the boil, simmer gently for 1 minute, then remove from the heat.
5. Leave for 10 minutes to finish cooking.
6. Meanwhile, blanch the watercress and mint in boiling water for 2 minutes.
7. Drain well, then liquidize with the yogurt, garlic, lemon juice and black pepper until smooth.
8. Heat through gently, but *do not boil*.
9. Serve over the warm fish steaks.

DINNERS/MAIN MEALS – STARCH

Cucumber and Tomato Raita

Metric/Imperial
1 small cucumber
4 tomatoes
275g/10oz natural low-fat yogurt
2 tbsp chopped mint
freshly ground black pepper

American
1 small cucumber
4 tomatoes
1¼ cups unflavoured low-fat yogurt
2 tbsp chopped mint
freshly ground black pepper

1. Slice the cucumber and tomatoes thinly and arrange in a serving dish.
2. Mix the yogurt, mint and pepper to taste.
3. Pour over the salad and serve chilled.

Onion Relish

Metric/Imperial
225g/8oz Spanish onion, thinly sliced
2 tbsp lemon juice
½ tsp paprika
¼ tsp cayenne pepper
paprika to garnish

American
½lb Spanish onion, thinly sliced
2 tbsp lemon juice
½ tsp paprika
¼ tsp cayenne pepper
paprika to garnish

1. Mix the ingredients together well.
2. Leave to stand for an hour.
3. Sprinkle with paprika and serve.

Vegetable Curry and Rice

Metric/Imperial	*American*
225g/8oz brown rice	1 cup brown rice
1 tbsp cold pressed olive oil	1 tbsp cold pressed olive oil
1 large onion, sliced	1 large onion, sliced
2 garlic cloves, crushed	2 garlic cloves, crushed
1 tbsp finely chopped root ginger	1 tbsp finely chopped root ginger
2 tbsp curry powder	2 tbsp curry powder
450ml/¾ pint water or vegetable stock	1 cups water or vegetable stock
freshly ground black pepper	freshly ground black pepper
2 medium potatoes, diced	2 medium potatoes, diced
3 carrots, sliced	3 carrots, sliced
225g/8oz cauliflower florets	2 cups cauliflower florets
225g/8oz green beans, sliced	1 cup green beans, sliced

This recipe may be adapted for whichever vegetables you have on hand.

1. Cook the brown rice according to packet instructions.
2. Meanwhile, heat the oil in a large pan.
3. Fry the onion for 5 minutes until softened.
4. Add the garlic, ginger and curry powder and fry for a further 1 minute, stirring to prevent sticking.

5. Add the stock, potatoes, and carrots and bring to the boil.
6. Cover and simmer gently for 15 minutes.
7. Add the beans and simmer for a further 10 minutes.
8. Serve hot on a bed of the drained brown rice.

SIDE SALADS AND DRESSINGS

Critical Salad

Metric/Imperial	*American*
½ iceberg lettuce	½ iceberg lettuce
½ cucumber, chopped	½ cucumber, chopped
2 spring onions, sliced	2 salad onions, sliced
1 green pepper, sliced	1 green pepper, sliced
100g/4oz beansprouts	2 cups beansprouts
1 stick celery, sliced	1 stick celery, sliced
2 carrots, grated	2 carrots, grated
2 tomatoes, quartered	2 tomatoes, quartered
4 radishes, sliced	4 radishes, sliced
100g/4oz baby corn cobs, sliced	¾ cup baby corn cobs, sliced
100g/4oz mushrooms, sliced	1 cup mushrooms, sliced
1 dessert apple, chopped	1 dessert apple, chopped
50g/2oz raisins	⅓ cup raisins
dressing	dressing

1. Tear the lettuce leaves into a salad bowl.
2. Add the other ingredients and toss.

Crudités

Metric/Imperial	*American*
¼ cucumber, cut into sticks	¼ cucumber, cut into sticks
1 red pepper, cut into strips lengthwise	1 red pepper, cut into strips lengthwise
3 carrots, cut into sticks	3 carrots, cut into sticks
100g/4oz baby corn cobs	¾ cup baby corn cobs
100g/4oz button mushrooms	1 cup button mushrooms
175g/6oz cauliflower florets	1½ cups cauliflower florets

1. Arrange the vegetables on a serving plate or in individual glasses.
2. Serve with a dip.

East West Dressing

Metric/Imperial	*American*
2 pieces stem ginger	2 pieces preserved ginger
150g/5oz natural low-fat yogurt	⅔ cup unflavoured low-fat yogurt
¼ tsp ground ginger	¼ tsp ground ginger

1. Rinse the stem ginger and chop finely.
2. Put into a bowl with the yogurt and ground ginger and mix well.
3. Pour over the salad just before serving.
4. Serve with a cucumber or citrus fruit salad.

Lemon Dream Dressing

Metric/Imperial	*American*
150g/5oz natural low-fat yogurt	⅔ cup unflavoured low-fat yogurt
finely grated rind and juice of ½ lemon	finely grated rind and juice of ½ lemon
1 small onion, finely chopped	1 small onion, finely chopped
1 tbsp chopped parsley	1 tbsp chopped parsley
1 tbsp snipped chives	1 tbsp snipped chives
1 tbsp chopped mint	1 tbsp chopped mint
freshly ground black pepper	freshly ground black pepper

1. Put all the ingredients into a bowl and mix well.
2. Pour over the salad just before serving.

Thousand and One Island Dressing

Metric/Imperial	*American*
100ml/3fl oz tomato juice	1⅓ cups tomato juice
1 tbsp low-fat cottage cheese, sieved	1 tbsp low-fat cottage cheese, sieved
⅔ tbsp dill pickles, chopped	⅔ tbsp dill pickles, chopped
⅔ tbsp green pepper, chopped	⅔ tbsp green pepper, chopped
½ tsp dry mustard	½ tsp dry mustard
1 tsp chopped onion	1 tsp chopped onion

1. Liquidize the ingredients until smooth.
2. Chill before serving.

PUDDINGS – PROTEIN

Apple Crumble

Metric/Imperial	*American*
6 green dessert apples, sliced	6 green dessert apples, sliced
2 tsp lemon juice	2 tsp lemon juice
½ tsp ground cinnamon	½ tsp ground cinnamon
50ml/2fl oz water	¼ cup water
1 tbsp unsalted butter	1 tbsp unsalted butter
40g/1½oz oat bran	⅓ cup oat bran
2 tbsp chopped walnuts	2 tbsp chopped walnuts

1. Mix the apples, lemon juice, cinnamon and water and put in the bottom of an ovenproof dish.
2. Melt the butter and stir in the oat bran and walnuts.
3. Sprinkle over the apples and bake in a preheated moderately hot oven (200°C/400°F, Gas Mark 6) for about 30 minutes.
4. Serve warm or cold.

Apricot Ice Cream

Metric/Imperial	*American*
225g/8oz dried apricots	1½ cups dried apricots
350ml/12fl oz apple juice	1⅔ cups apple juice
2 egg whites	2 egg whites
1 tbsp honey	1 tbsp honey

225g/8oz natural low-fat yogurt	1 cup unflavoured low-fat yogurt

1. Soak the apricots in water for 2 hours.
2. Discard the water and simmer the apricots and apple juice for 20 minutes in a covered pan.
3. Liquidize, then leave until cold.
4. Add the yogurt and mix well.
5. Whisk the egg whites until stiff, then gradually whisk in the honey.
6. Fold into the apricot purée.
7. Pour into a freezer container and freeze until solid.
8. Leave to soften in the refrigerator for 30 minutes before serving.

Hot Berry Pudding

Metric/Imperial	*American*
225g/8oz strawberries	1½ cups strawberries
225g/8oz raspberries	1½ cups raspberries
1 tbsp honey	1 tbsp honey
150g/5oz natural low-fat yogurt	⅔ cup unflavoured low-fat yogurt
25g/1oz ground almonds	¼ cup ground almonds
2 egg whites	2 egg whites

1. Put the fruit in a baking dish and spoon over the honey.
2. Beat together the yogurt and ground almonds.
3. Beat the egg whites until stiff, then fold into the yogurt mixture.

4. Spoon over the fruit, then bake in preheated moderately hot oven (200°/400°F, Gas Mark 6) for 20 minutes.
5. Serve immediately.

Kiwi Lemon Cheese

Metric/Imperial	*American*
225g/8oz low-fat cottage cheese, sieved	1 cup low-fat cottage cheese, sieved
150g/5oz natural low-fat yogurt	⅔ cup unflavoured low-fat yogurt
2 tbsp honey	2 tbsp honey
rind and juice of 1 lemon	rind and juice of 1 lemon
1 tbsp powdered gelatine	1 tbsp powdered gelatine
4 tbsp water	4 tbsp water
2 egg whites	2 egg whites
2 kiwi fruit, peeled and sliced	2 kiwi fruit, peeled and sliced

1. Beat together well the cottage cheese, yogurt, honey, lemon rind and juice.
2. Dissolve the gelatine in the water in a heatproof bowl over hot water.
3. Stir the gelatine into the cheese mixture.
4. Whisk the egg whites until they form soft peaks, then fold into the cheese mixture.
5. Pour into individual glass dishes or a flan dish and leave in a cool place to set.
6. Decorate with the kiwi slices and serve.

Peach Freeze

Metric/Imperial	*American*
450g/16oz natural low-fat yogurt	2¼ cups unflavoured low-fat yogurt
1 tsp powdered ginger	1 tsp powdered ginger
2 tbsp lemon juice	2 tbsp lemon juice
4 peaches, stoned and diced	4 peaches, stoned and diced
25g/1oz chopped nuts	¼ cup chopped nuts

1. Mix together the yogurt, ginger and lemon juice.
2. Stir in the peaches and nuts.
3. Pour into a mould or plastic bowl and freeze for 3 hours or until firm.
4. Dip the mould or bowl almost to the top in a bowl of hot water for 10 seconds.
5. Put a plate upside-down on the top of the mould or bowl, then turn them over so that the pudding comes out on to the plate.
6. Leave for 5 minutes, then serve.

Red Fruit Salad

Metric/Imperial	*American*
50g/2oz raspberries	½ cup raspberries
2 tbsp Cointreau	2 tbsp Cointreau
2 peaches, sliced	2 peaches, sliced
175g/6oz strawberries, sliced	1 cup strawberries

1. Sieve the raspberries into a bowl and stir in the Cointreau.

2. Add the peaches and strawberries and mix gently to cover with the raspberry sauce.
3. Serve chilled.

Spicy Peaches

Metric/Imperial	***American***
4 large peaches, halved and stoned	4 large peaches, halved and stoned
juice of 2 oranges	juice of 2 oranges
2 tbsp strawberry fruit purée	2 tbsp strawberry fruit purée
1 cinnamon stick	1 cinnamon stick
2 cloves	2 cloves
½ tsp allspice	½ tsp allspice
50g/2oz ground almonds	½ cup ground almonds
1 tbsp finely chopped preserved ginger	1 tbsp finely chopped preserved ginger
1 tbsp honey	1 tbsp honey

1. Scoop out a tablespoon of flesh from the middle of each peach half and chop.
2. Mix with the almonds, ginger and honey and spoon into the hollows in the peach halves.
3. Put the peach halves in a baking dish.
4. Heat the orange juice, strawberry purée and spices gently in a small pan for a few minutes, then bring to the boil.
5. Pour over the peaches, then bake in a preheated moderate oven (180°C/350°F, Gas Mark 4) for 20 minutes or until the peaches are tender. Serve hot or cold.

Appendix II – All About Food

All About Food

Technology has revolutionized the food that most people eat today compared with what was consumed only a hundred years ago. Yet it would take our bodies thousands of years to evolve to the stage where they could run properly on fuel so different from what they were designed to use – and we must remember that the basic reason for eating is to provide our bodies with the fuel they need. For the average person, most of the calories required are just for maintaining the basic body functions such as digestion, breathing etc. Since the typical modern diet is mismatched to the human body in evolutionary terms, we need to rematch this evolutionary balance in order to attain successful and permanent weight loss – as well as good health.

The *Bodyclock* diet strategy is to provide your body with the food it is designed to consume. So what foods *are* our bodies designed to eat?

Anthropologists have discovered from studies of fossilized teeth and intestines that our early ancestors lived mainly on fruit, and our current digestive system is very similar to that of our fruit-eating cousins, the apes. However, we are not suggesting that the only way to slimness, health and happiness is to live on bananas and grape-fruits! Just remember that fresh fruit is a very important part of a healthy diet and the nutrients it provides give us a good indication of what our bodies need.

Many people feel that they already know what is good for them – or, at least, they know what they like! – and in the wake of pronouncements by experts about what we should or should not be eating, the issue has almost become one of human rights for some junk-food addicts! Yet although we may think that our eyes, noses and mouths tell us what is good, our senses sometimes deceive us. These reactions are left over from prehistory when initially mother's milk, and then the ripe fruits which formed the basic diet of our ancestors, would be sweet and – in the case of the fruits – shiny and highly coloured. Our senses are now being tricked, so that our primeval reactions to sweet, shiny, brightly-coloured (but healthy) foods are being abused by a food industry dedicated to make its sweet, shiny, highly-coloured – and processed – produce attractive and profitable, regardless of the cost to our health.

Their success in deceiving our senses is illustrated by the fact that some people are now being diagnosed as suffering from 'marginal malnutrition' as a result of living on junk food and in children this has been linked with learning difficulties. Scientific research is currently investigating the effect of diet on behaviour: how mineral deficiency and additives associated with poor diet can seemingly lead to violent and erratic behaviour, for example.

Apart from issues of general health and well-being, good eating habits are essential to reduce excess body fat. So what food should we be eating and how do we avoid 'junk'?

Not all food is the same

Food is the fuel on which our bodies run, and they work better when running on high-quality fuel. The quality of food is determined by the extent of which it provides the nutrients essential for creating and maintaining life, for providing energy and growth and repairs. These nutrients are: *vitamins, minerals, aminio acids (from protein), glucose (from carbohydrates), lipids (from fats) and water.*

We also need fibre, to help food and waste products pass smoothly through our digestive system.

However, different foods provide varying amounts of these nutrients and also different amounts of calories (the units used to measure the amount of energy in food). If we eat too many calories, the surplus is stored as fat. Furthermore, we don't need the same amount of each type of nutrient.

Let's look at an example. Can you guess what the following have in common?:

8oz bar of milk chocolate
Big Mac, french fries and milk shake
8oz peanuts
8 baked potatoes
65 figs
250 sticks of celery

The answer is that they all have roughly the same

energy content – that is, the same number of calories. In fact, they have about as many calories as the daily allowance in most standard diets. You could choose any one of them for your daily diet and probably lose weight, but there are two major problems. Firstly, they contain entirely different quantities, quality and nutrients. A comparison between the chocolate and the celery clearly highlights a difference:

	Fat	*Fibre*	*Vitamin C*	*Sugar*	*Calories*
8oz chocolate	56g	–	–	100g	1300
250 sticks celery	–	190g	750mg	–	1300

To our bodies, either of these presents something of an overdose, but they react quite differently to overdosing on the Vitamin C and fibre (which can be expelled quite easily and healthily) as compared with the fat and sugar (which just serve to make us fat and unhealthy). When you see a chocolate bar advertised as a 'high energy' snack, this really means a 'high fat and sugar' snack.

Secondly, the list demonstrates one other important quality that some foods are easier to eat than others. For instance, the burger, french fries and milk-shake can be devoured in as little as two to three minutes by voracious youngsters outside fast-food outlets – just as a snack. And for those of us with a sweet tooth – how long would the chocolate last? Nor would it stop us feeling hungry for the rest of the day. In fact, as we see later when considering the effects of sugar, it would make us hungrier!

But how long would it take to eat 8 baked potatoes, or 65 figs, or, worse still, 250 celery sticks? For many of us it would be physically impossible to consume most of these within the course of a day, because we have natural control mechanisms which restrict our appetites for natural foods and tell us that we are full. One of our biggest allies in this is fibre, which would be present in large quantities in these amounts, but hardly (or not at all) in the processed snack or chocolate.

Incidentally, we can see here the origin of certain 'miracle food' diets, based on eating unlimited quantities of one particular food. It is practically impossible to overeat one type of food – as long as it is natural and unprocessed – but this is unlikely to provide all the nutrients needed by the body and so will not be healthy. Our bodies retain effective control mechanisms that operate on evolutionary balanced food, but sadly these do not work so well on 'revolutionary' food.

The food we need and the food we eat

We have already established that the nutrients we need are vitamins, minerals, amino acids (from protein) glucose (from carbohydrates), lipids (from fats) and water, plus fibre. A hundred years ago, eating a reasonable quantity of a variety of the foods available would probably have given us sufficient amounts of all the nutrients needed, without making us fat. However, the changes in the average diet since then have sent these nutritional requirements out of balance.

Let us consider each in turn:

Vitamins and minerals

These are only required in small doses and are supplied by a balanced diet of different foods. Severe cases of vitamin deficiency are rare in Western countries, but there is always a problem where diets have too little food, or too few variations of nutritious food. Although many dieters fall victim to vitamin and mineral deficiencies because their diets concentrate on one particular type of food, the *Bodyclock* Diet is well balanced and in combination with the exercise programme will ensure that you become slim as well as properly nourished!

Amino acids

These are needed to build muscles, blood, skin, hair, nails, and the internal organs, and are essential in our diet. They are made from proteins, and it is highly unlikely that anyone in a Western country would eat insufficient protein. If anything, we eat far more than we need, which gives rise to a number of problems. Firstly, protein is normally found only in foods which are quite high in fat, such as cheese (33% fat) and roast lamb (26%), so that by eating more protein that we need, we also consume far more fat than we need. However, we can keep excess fat to a minimum by eating lean meat, chicken, white fish and low-fat cheese rather than fatty meat, oily fish and high-fat cheeses.

Secondly, the Western diet tends to be high in animal rather than vegetable protein, therefore high in animal rather than vegetable fat – remember that, as discussed earlier, man did not evolve as a meat eater. Thirdly, proteins are difficult to digest, dairy products in particular. Finally, proteins contain little water, yet a lot of water is needed to digest them. The body must take water from anywhere it can in order to digest the protein and this can lead to dehydration and difficulties in eliminating wastes – one of the vital functions of water.

The now-discredited high protein diets appeared to be successful in the short term because the body had to use all the water it could find to digest the protein – therefore the weight loss was almost entirely water. As soon as more water was taken in – whether from other food or from drinks – the body would replenish its stores of water and the weight would be regained.

The *Bodyclock* Diet includes carefully controlled quantities of lower-fat protein foods, so that the body receives just as much as it needs for good health.

Glucose

Glucose provides our basic supply of energy and is produced from the digestion of carbohydrates. The Western diet does tend to be high in carbohydrates – but unfortunately of the wrong kind. This has led to much confusion for dieters, who associate all carbohydrates with fattening foods Our diet should be high in complex, or unrefined, carbohydrates such as fruit, vegetables and wholegrain cereals and cereal products such as wholemeal bread. One reason for this is that it ensures we eat plenty of fibre, since fibre is in fact the part of complex carbohydrates which the body does not digest – of which more later. Fruit and vegetables are also the kind of foods we have evolved to eat. However, the average diet tends to be high in simple, or refined, carbohydrates – the renowned pure, white and deadly refined sugar being by far the worst offender!

The *Bodyclock* Diet includes plenty of unrefined carbohydrates for maximum health and energy.

Lipids

Lipids are the most concentrated source of energy in the body, acting as an energy store and carrier for certain essential vitamins, as well as protecting the organs and insulating the body. They are supplied to the body from the fats that we eat, therefore some fat in the diet is essential. The problem is that we all tend to eat far too much fat – often without realizing it; in fact, on average, 40 per cent of our calories come from fat! Fat contains twice as many calories as protein or carbohydrate, weight for weight, and it tends to come in very concentrated forms: 1 ounce of butter contains over 200 calories, about the same as 3 slices of bread or 40 celery sticks. Animal fat increases cholesterol levels in the blood, which are linked with an increased risk of heart disease and other serious health problems. Many processed and convenience foods are high in fat – it makes foods taste palatable and it's cheap. Whatever else can be said about it, fat is without doubt the number one enemy of the dieter: eating fat *makes* you fat!

The *Bodyclock* Diet is low in fat, providing just the minimum needed for health and energy.

Water

Pure water is the liquid fuel upon which your body depends. It is vital for the correct operation of the liver and kidneys, which flush away toxins, as well as for a whole host of other important biological functions. In the Western diet water tends to come from polluted sources such as tea, coffee and alcohol, which are loaded with toxins. Alcohol is by far the worst problem in that it is high in calories, stimulates the appetite and dehydrates the body. Our bodies need water in as pure a state as possible – remember that some fat is caused by toxins which the body cannot eliminate, and the best way to ensure that the liver and kidneys are operating at maximum efficiency to clear toxins is to drink as much pure water as you can.

To reiterate the advice in Chapter 4, tap water is no longer as pure as it should be, and is best filtered before drinking. Some of the most expensive spring waters – including those in fancy packages – can give you a most unwelcome dose of sodium and nitrates amongst other things, especially if you drink several litres. So choose carefully and ensure that you buy the brands with the lowest sodium and nitrate content. Water is also present in many foods; fruit and vegetables are particularly high in water, so should form an important part of the diet.

The *Bodyclock* Diet includes drinking as much pure water as possible and eating plenty of fresh fruit and vegetables. Tea and coffee should be replaced by herbal and decaffeinated filter varieties, while alcohol should be excluded altogether.

Fibre

Fibre is the indigestible part of carbohydrate, and although it cannot make you lose weight by itself, it plays a very important role in a healthy diet. Many diseases prevalent in the West – including heart disease, constipation, diabetes and bowel cancer – are extremely rare when the staple diet is high in fibre. Fibre increases the rate at which waste products pass through the digestive system and helps to reduce the level of cholesterol in the blood.

As far as losing weight is concerned, fibre-rich food helps in a number of ways. It needs more chewing, so that we can't just swallow it without realizing how much we are eating, and it absorbs water and swells in the stomach so that we feel full sooner. The fibre in naturally sweet foods, such as dried fruit, also prevents the rebound hunger effect of refined sugar discussed in the next section.

The *Bodyclock* Diet is high in fibre.

Sugar

Refined sugar is probably the worst food of the lot. It is high in calories, has certain bad effects on our bodies, is put in most manufactured foods and yet has no nutritional value whatsoever. It is certainly not a food we have evolved to eat – refined sugar didn't exist 200 years ago – yet the average Westerner consumes about 500 calories' worth a day, which is between half and one-third of a day's calorie allowance on most diets! This is a perfect example of our senses being tricked. Our ancestors would include certain sweet foods, but these were fruit, where the sugar is natural and bound up with plenty of fibre, and therefore impossible to overeat.

We are deceived by the sweet taste of refined sugar into thinking that we are eating the same healthy, natural sweet food as our forebears. Refined sugar (which includes all processed sugar, brown or white, molasses, treacle, syrup or whatever) is concentrated so that it is very easy to eat large quantities of it without feeling full – therefore very easy to eat lots of excess calories without realizing it.

This is particularly the case with convenience foods, where the sugar is hidden effectively. Always check labels, remembering that even soups and vegetables are packed with sugar! Ignore the sugar industry's stories about high energy food – all this means is high calories, and as long as we eat a balanced diet, our bodies get all the energy they need.

Apart from the obvious calorie problem posed for the dieter by sugar, it also plays another devious trick: it is converted almost instantly to glucose, but not a form which is usable for energy. It is absorbed by the bloodstream through the roof of the mouth and so provides an instant 'hit'. Reacting to this overdose by releasing insulin to quickly lower the blood sugar level, the body craves more sugar – and feels hunger, even though there is no need for food.

Not surprisingly, sugar forms no part of the *Bodyclock* Diet! A little honey is occasionally used, but this is processed naturally by bees!

Salt

The typical Western diet contains very high quantities of salt although, as with sugar, much of this comes from processed foods where it is used as a preservative, leavening agent and flavour enhancer. Salt is particularly associated with water retention and high blood pressure: it forces water out of the body's cells into the surrounding tissue, so that the cells have to replace the lost water from the food we eat and the liquids we drink. The body therefore becomes bloated with the excess water, which causes a gain in weight. It also makes elimination of waste more difficult because the water needed for elimination has been diverted to replace that lost from the cells.

Although salt is not banned entirely on the *Bodyclock* Diet, it should not be used in cooking and should never be added to food without tasting it first – and then only sea salt, and very sparingly.

Additives

Under this heading come all types of artificial food additives, preservatives, flavourings, colourings etc. A few of these are beneficial, but many are known to be actually dangerous and no one seems sure about the remainder. A number of additives used in some countries are banned in others because of their associated risks, some are thought to be carcinogenic, others are linked with allergy reactions, liver problems and arthritis, amongst other things.

Most people would prefer to avoid the risk of eating them, but this is not as easy as it seems; the food industry uses more all the time as it attempts to extend the shelf-life of products and increase profits. The average person eats 11 lbs of additives per year! Of course, added to the basic health risk is the fact that the body cannot always eliminate all the toxins and so it deposits them as fat.

The *Bodyclock* Diet is based on fresh, unprocessed food so as to minimize the risks of unwanted additives.

Food basis of the Bodyclock Diet

In summary, the food basis of the *Bodyclock* Diet is food which is:

- *Naturally evolved*
- *Balanced in vitamins, minerals and other nutrients*
- *Low in fat*
- *High in water*
- *High in fibre*
- *Low in sugar*
- *Low in salt*
- *Low in chemicals and processed foods*

We will now consider in more detail how these principles are used in two steps:

- *Choosing food*
- *Eating and digestion*

Choosing Food

Food Types

Using the food basis described, food can be divided into the three groups below:

	Naturally Evolved	*Fat*	*Fibre*	*Sugar*	*Chemicals/ Salt*	*Calories*
1. *Safe foods:* Fruits, vegetables, salads	high	low	high	nil	nil	low
2. *Concentrated foods:* Proteins, starches, sweets, oils	vary	vary	vary	nil	nil	vary
3. *Danger foods:* Processed, fatty, or salty preserved foods, food with additives and sugars	low	high	low	high	high	high

Our bodies have evolved to be healthiest and slimmest on an evolutionary 'balanced' diet – this is a balance between safe and concentrated foods. The danger foods are a risk to health if consumed in quantity and to the exclusion of the other types of food, but more important to us is that they leave their mark as permanent fat.

Let us consider the foods in each of these groups:

1. *Safe foods:*

The fresh foods listed below are 'safe' and allowed in generous quantities throughout the *Bodyclock* Diet programme:

Fruits:
Apples, Apricots, Blackberries, Cherries, Grapefruit, Grapes, Lemons, Loganberries, Mangoes, Oranges, Peaches, Pears, Pineapple, Raspberries, Rhubarb, Strawberries, Tangerines.

Salads:
Beansprouts, Beetroot, Carrots, Celery, Cucumber, Endive, Mushrooms, Mustard and Cress, Onions, Radishes, Red Cabbage, Sea Kale, Tomatoes, Watercress.

Vegetables:
Asparagus, Aubergines, Broccoli, Brussels Sprouts, Cabbage, Cauliflower, Courgettes, French Beans, Leeks, Marrow, Onions, Parsnips, Peas, Runner Beans, Spinach, Swedes, Sweet Corn, Turnips.

Drinks:
Filtered water, herbal tea, mineral water.

2. *Concentrated foods:*

The food groups listed below are 'concentrated' and allowed in controlled amounts during the *Bodyclock* Diet. These foods have beneficial qualities but higher calorie and fat content than the safe foods, as well as varying amounts of dietary fibre.

Animal and vegetable proteins:
Butter, Cheeses, Eggs, Nuts,

Lean Meats – Beef, Chicken, Game, Lamb, Pork, Turkey.

Starches:
Brown Rice, Oats, Potatoes, Wholewheat breads & flour, Wholewheat pastas.

Vegetable fats and oils:
Avocado Pears, Vegetable Oils, Olives.

Sweets:
Bananas, Currants, Dates, Figs, Honey, Prunes, Raisins, Sultanas.

Drinks:
Fruit juice, filter coffee, skimmed milk, tea.

It is recommended that you minimize your intake of saturated animal fats, which create cholesterol in the blood. Use cold pressed olive oil or safflower oil, which is high in linoleic acid, rather than butter – and then only in small quantities. Both of these oils are beneficial in the transportation of fat soluble vitamins and fatty acids. Margarines should be avoided because they are highly processed and high in chemicals – this of course includes the low-fat spreads so beloved of the dieter. If you must have fat, use them very sparingly, but try to do without.

Danger foods:
The foods listed below are to be considered 'dangerous' and do not form any part of the *Bodyclock* Diet programme. These foods are generally low in dietary fibre and high in fat, salt, sugar, chemicals

and calories. They have little or no nutritional value – so why eat them?

All fast foods, take-aways e.g. Hamburgers, fries etc.
Canned meats, and most canned foods in general
Crisps, salted peanuts and similar snacks, chocolate, confectionary and ice creams
Drinks: full cream milk, alcohol, in particular sweet wines and liqueurs
Fried foods, lard and suet, fatty or greasy foods
Meat soups, broths, juices and similar meat extracts
Peanut butter, jams, yeast extract spreads
Salted meats and fish and other salted products
Sausages, salami and similar meat products, taramasalata
Single and double cream, and non-dairy cream
Spice, pickles, relishes, gravies, sauces, preserved foods
Sugar, treacle, syrups etc.
White flour and flour products, white rice

Eating and Digestion

We need to consider some basic aspects of how our digestive systems work so that we can use this to help us towards a successful diet and good health.

In Chapter 4 you read briefly about the importance of chewing. In fact, the first stage of food digestion is in the mouth. Enzymes in saliva carry out the initial part of carbohydrate digestion; unless the food is properly chewed, saliva and its enzyme, ptyalin, will not be generated, and carbohydrates will pass in to the stomach in a form which cannot be further digested by the body. The body can only use the nutrients found in carbohydrates if these are properly digested – and they cannot go through the next stages of digestion in the stomach and small intestine unless they have already been partly broken down in the mouth.

This brings us to a further, vital point about the digestion of different types of food. Carbohydrates require an alkaline medium for further digestion, and this is stimulated by the action of ptyalin in the mouth. The stomach is naturally acid, but not sufficiently so as to interfere with the level of alkalinity needed in the stomach to further break down the carbohydrates for their final stage of digestion in the small intestine.

However – and it is a big however – proteins require an **acid** medium for digestion. They are unaffected by ptyalin and their first stage of digestion is in the stomach, where the fats are broken up by hydrochloric acid. The enzyme pepsin then acts with the acid to digest the proteins into amino acids. And – as anyone with an elementary knowledge of chemistry might guess – if carbohydrates and protein are eaten **together**, the alkaline and acid mediums required for further effective digestion are interfered with or neutralized.

The effects of this apparently vary considerably from person to person; in some people it makes little difference, whereas it can dominate the lives of others. The main result of inadequate protein digestion is allergies – and of inadequate carbohydrate digestion, flatulence and indigestion. But this imbalance in body chemistry is also associated with constipation, arthritis, diabetes, skin diseases, colds, headaches, tooth decay and obesity.

The rationale for this is that while the body is trying to cope with the digestive chaos caused by eating carbohydrates and proteins together, it cannot also use its natural healing processes to deal with routine health problems. Changing the way that we combine foods is not a cure for the body's ailments: it simply removes the obstacles that prevent the body from healing itself.

This is a further illustration of the need to eat naturally evolved foods: our ancestors ate very little protein, and were certainly unlikely to eat it at the same time as carbohydrates. Nature does combine proteins and starches in the same foods, but high concentrations of protein are never combined with high concentrations of carbohydrate.

Proteins can be defined as foods with more

than a 20 per cent concentration of protein, such as meat, poultry, fish and cheese. Although these do contain some carbohydrates it is in the form of glycogen which requires little digestion and so does not interfere with the acid medium necessary for proper protein digestion. Carbohydrates can similarly be defined as foods with more than a 20 per cent concentration of carbohydrate such as bread, cereals and potatoes. Although these contain some protein, it is in an incomplete, unconcentrated form and so does not interfere with the alkaline medium needed for proper carbohydrate digestion.

The one exception to the rule are the legumes – dried peas, beans, lentils and peanuts – which have high concentrations of both protein and carbohydrate. Anyone who has ever eaten baked beans will appreciate the effects such badly combined foods have! These foods should be avoided, and do not form part of the *Bodyclock* Diet, other than as a baked bean treat on one of the critical menus!

The *Bodyclock* Diet menus and recipes follow the principles of good food combining – the basic rule of not eating concentrated carbohydrate and protein at the same meal in fact expands to the following:

- *Starches and sugars should not be eaten at the same meal as proteins and acid fruits*
- *Vegetables and fats may be eaten with either carbohydrate or protein meals*
- *At least four hours should be left between eating a carbohydrate and a protein meal.*

The chart on the next page shows which foods are compatible, divided between those which are 'safe' and those which are 'concentrated' as defined earlier in the chapter. Any food in the 'Protein' section at the top – safe or concentrated – may be combined with any other protein food or any food in the 'Neutral' section in the middle; although as part of our *Bodyclock* diet and health plan, we will be restricting the amount of concentrated protein foods.

Likewise, any food in the 'Starch' section at the bottom – 'safe' or 'concentrated' – may be combined with any other starch food or any food in the 'Neutral' section in the middle.

If none of this has seemed particularly relevant to you so far, just consider the number of well-known dishes which break the combination guidelines:

> *Meat and potatoes, fish and chips, spaghetti bolognaise, hamburger and bun, salt-beef sandwich, lasagne, meat curry and rice, cheese sandwich, steak pie ...*

Now do you see the point?

You may feel that this is too much of a break from your normal eating habits, but once you have tried the diet plans, you are unlikely to find proper combining a problem. Although you may feel that bad combining has not caused any problems for you, remember the list of ailments it apparently affects and see what it can do for you!

FOOD COMBINING CHART

SAFE

PROTEIN MEALS	FRUIT:	Apples, apricots, blackberries, blueberries, cherries, gooseberries, grapefruit, grapes, kiwis, lemons, limes, loganberries,mangoes, nectarines, oranges, papayas, peaches, pears, pineapples, raspberries, rhubarb, satsumas, strawberries, tangerines.
	PROTEINS:	Low-fat cottage cheese, low-fat fromage frais and low-fat curd cheese.
NEUTRAL FOODS	VEGETABLES:	Asparagus, aubergines, beetroot, broccoli, Brussels Sprouts, cabbage, carrots, cauliflower, celery, celeriac, courgettes, green beans, leeks, marrow, mushrooms, onions, parsnips, peas, spinach, swede, sweetcorn, turnips.
	PROTEINS:	Natural low-fat yogurt
	SALADS:	Chicory, cucumber, endive, fennel, garlic, lettuce, mustard and cress, peppers, radishes, spring onions, sprouted legumes, sprouted seeds, tomatoes, watercress.
	DRINKS:	Filtered water, herbal tea, mineral water.
	FLAVOURINGS:	Herbs, lemon and orange rind.
STARCH MEALS	SWEET FRUIT:	Bananas, papaya, sweet grapes, sweet pears.
	VEGETABLES:	Jerusalem artichokes, potatoes.

FOOD COMBINING CHART

CONCENTRATED

PROTEIN MEALS	FRUIT:	Dried apricots, prunes, ripe currants.
	DRINKS:	Fruit juice.
	ALCOHOL:	IN EXCEPTIONAL CIRCUMSTANCES ONLY! Dry cider, dry red and white wine.
	PROTEINS:	Lean beef, lamb, pork, venison. Chicken, duck, goose, turkey. Grouse, hare, patridge, pheasant. Oily and white fish, shellfish. Free range eggs, cheese.
	LEGUMES:	FOR VEGETARIANS, BUT NOT RECOMMENDED – Butter beans, chick peas, kidney beans, lentils, pinto eans, soya beans.
NEUTRAL FOODS	FATS:	Butter, egg yolks, olive oil.
	SUGARS:	Honey, raisins, raisin juice.
	SEEDS:	Pumpkin, sesame, sunflower.
	PROTEINS:	All nuts except peanuts.
	SALADS:	Avocado
	STARCHES:	Wheat or oat bran, wheatgerm.
	DRINKS:	Filter coffee, skimmed milk, tea.
	ALCOHOL:	IN EXCEPTIONAL CIRCUMSTANCES ONLY! Gin, whiskey.
	FLAVOURINGS:	Freshly ground black pepper, mustard, sea salt.
STARCH MEALS	SWEET FRUIT:	Currants, dates, figs, raisins, sultanas.
	STARCHES:	Oatmeal, wholegrain cereals, wholemeal bread, flour, pasta and rice.
	DRINKS:	Grape juice.
	ALCOHOL:	IN EXCEPTIONAL CIRCUMSTANCES ONLY! Beer, lager.

Appendix III – Setting the Time on Your *Bodyclock*

Setting the Time on Your *Bodyclock*

Your *Bodyclock* is designed to show you your weekly rhythms with a minimum of effort, but first it must be set up to show your individual 'body time'. Since all rhythms start their first positive period on the day of birth, the calculation of your current bodytime is based on the number of days you have been alive. It is possible to calculate your biorhythms with pen, paper and calculator but the following steps use charts to help simplify setting up your *Bodyclock*.

If you experience any difficulty, there is a full example of how to use the charts and set up your *Bodyclock* on pages 230 to 234.

Setting your Bodytime

1. Turn to Chart A on pages 236 and 241. Look down the left hand column until you find your age on your birthday this year. Look across to the columns headed Physical, Emotional and Intellectual and note below the numbers which appear in each column on the same line as your age on your birthday this year, and which are under the heading which includes your birthday. i.e. either 1 January to 29 February or 1 March to 31 December.

Note: 29 February (the leap day that exists

only once every four years) is shown in order to take account of those few people who were born on 29 February even though the year of the chart may not be a leap year.

Physical 1 = Emotional 1 = Intellectual 1 =

2. Now turn to the Physical section of Chart B on pages 242 to 253. Find the page with the month of your birthday. Look down the left hand column until you find the Physical number you noted down above. Next look across on the same line until you are in the column with the day of your birthday along the top line and note down below the value at this point.

Note: if you were born on 29 February, treat 28 February as your birthday – the charts take account of this problem.

Repeat this process with the Emotional section of Chart B on pages 254 to 265 using the Emotional number from above, and with the Intellectual section on pages 266 to 277 using the Intellectual number from above.

Physical 2 = Emotional 2 = Intellectual 2 =

3. Now turn back to the Physical section of Chart B on pages 242 to 253. Find the page with the current month. Find today's date on the top line and move down this column until you find the Physical value noted in 2 above. Note below the value on the same line in the left hand column. Repeat this process with the Emotional section of Chart B on pages 254 to 265 using the Emotional value from above, and with the Intellectual section on pages

266 to 277 using the Intellectual value from above.

Physical 3 =   Emotional 3 =   Intellectual 3 =

Note: **Only** if there is a leap day (a 29th February) between the day of your birthday this year and today's date add 1 to each of the numbers above. However

If Physical becomes 24 change it to 1
If Emotional becomes 29 change it to 1
If Intellectual becomes 34 change it to 1

Now take your *Bodyclock*

Note: Remember to always handle it with care and do not touch the display window.

4. Press the knob on the top – this will release the winding key.

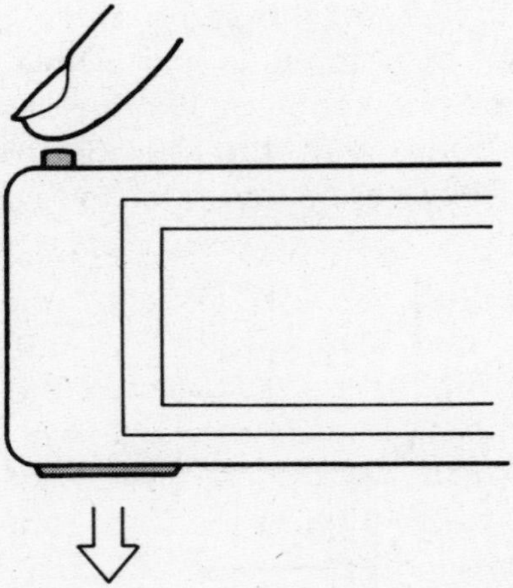

5. Keeping the key grip within a few millimetres of the body, gently turn the key in any direction until the display 'head' with the right number recorded in Intellectual 3 appears under today's day.

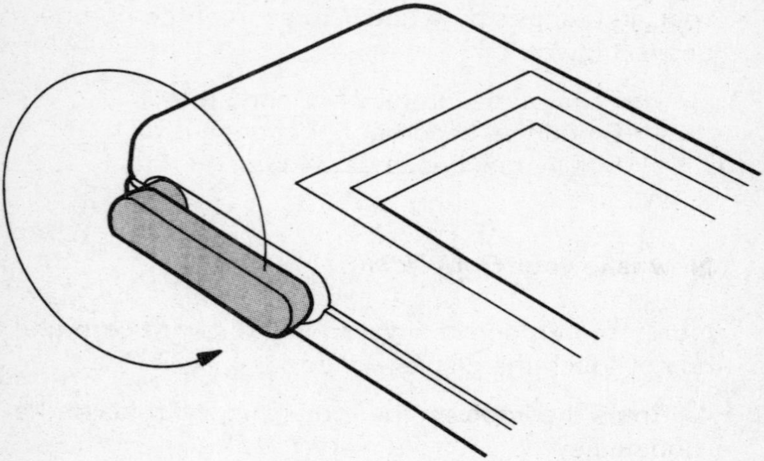

6. Keeping the key at the same angle, pull the key out until a set of notches is just visible on the key shaft. Now turn the knob again in any direction until the display 'body' with the number recorded in Emotional 3 above appears under today's day.

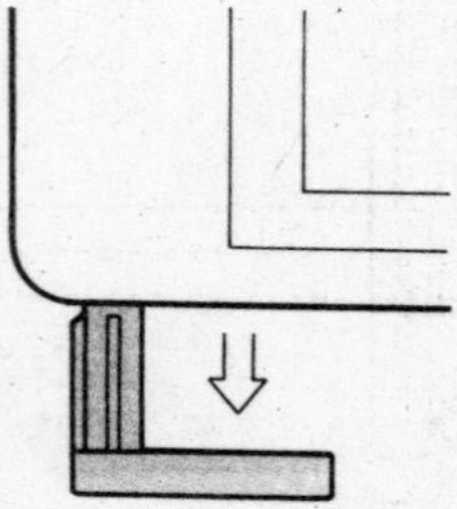

7. Keeping the key at the same angle, pull the key out further until a second set of notches is just visible on the shaft. Now gently turn the key again in any direction until the 'legs' with the number recorded in Physical 3 above is shown under today's day.

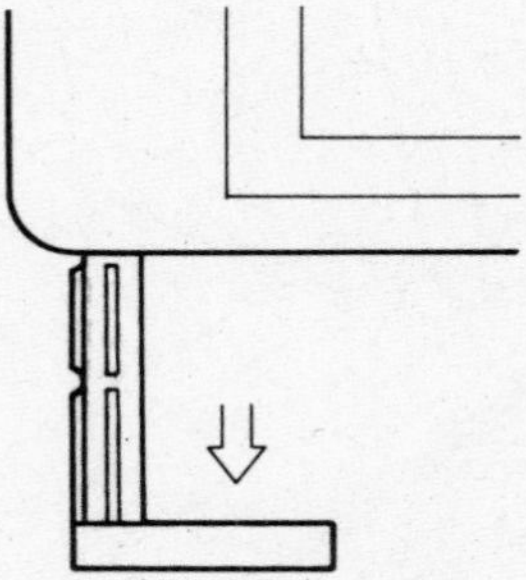

8. Keeping the key at the same angle, pull the key all the way out. Now rotate the key so that the key grip is aligned with the slot in the body and push it all the way back into the body until you feel it click into position.

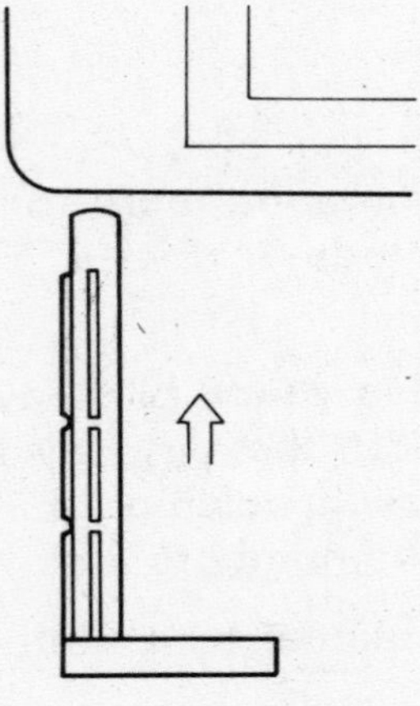

9. Now adjust the week number 1 to 52. by pushing in either direction with a ball point pen or similar instrument in the back of the *Bodyclock*. The week number can be checked in a diary or from the chart on the back of the *Bodyclock*.

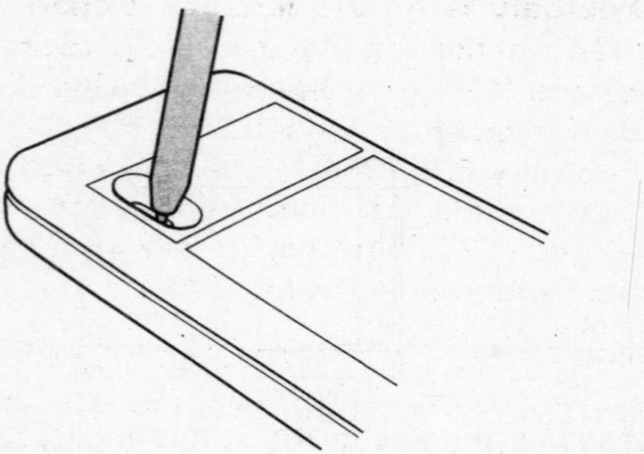

Your *Bodyclock* is now set up to show your body time.

EXAMPLE

Let's go through the steps for setting up the Bodyclock for someone born on 12 February 1951, assuming today's date is 5 May 1992, a Tuesday.

1. The age on this year's birthday is 41, and in Chart A, Page 238, the birthday falls under the first heading in each column i.e. 1 Jan-29 Feb. Reading across, the numbers are:

Physical 1 = 3 Emotional 1 = 24 Intellectual 1 = 27

2. February, the month of the birthday, is on the Physical chart on page 243. '3' in the left hand column (from step 1 above) and '12' along the top row (the day of the birthday) intersect at the letter 'G'.

February is on the Emotional chart on page 255. '24' in the left hand column (from step 1 above) and '12' along the top row (the day of the birthday) intersect at the letter 'J'.

February is on the Intellectual chart on page 267. '27' in the left hand column (from step 1 above) and '12' along the top row (the day of the birthday) intersect at the letter 'R'.

Physical 2 = G Emotional 2 = J Intellectual 2 = R

3. May, the current month, is on the Physical chart on page 246. Looking down from '5' in the top row (the current day of the month), the letter 'G' (from step 2 above) is on the same line as '16' in the lefthand column.

May is on the Emotional chart on page 258. Looking down from '5' in the top row (the current day of the month), the letter 'J' (from step 2 above) is on the same line as '22' in the left hand column.

May is on the intellectual chart on page 270. Looking down from '5' in the top row (the current day of the month), the letter 'R' (from step 2 above) is on the same line as '10' in the left hand column.

Physical 3 = 16 Emotional 3 = 22 Intellectual 3 = 10

As there is a leap day (Feb 29th) between the birthday (12 Feb 1992) and today's date (5 May

1991) we are required to add 1 to each of the above numbers. So this becomes:

Physical 3 = 17 Emotional 3 = 23 Intellectual 3 = 11

4. Taking the *Bodyclock*, the display will look something like this:

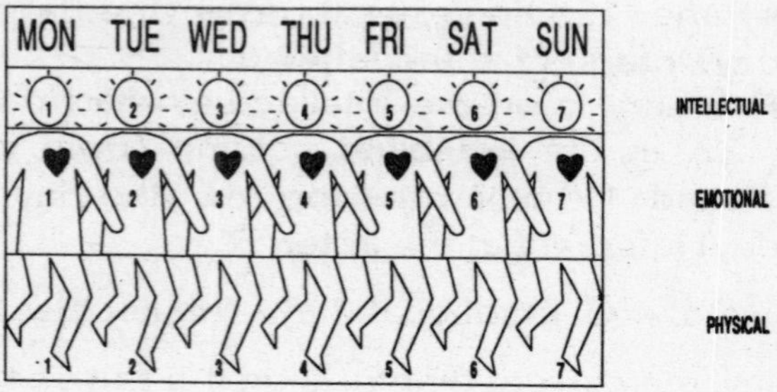

5. The Intellectual value noted in step 3 above was '11' and the current day of the week is Tuesday. The *Bodyclock* display will therefore be changed to:

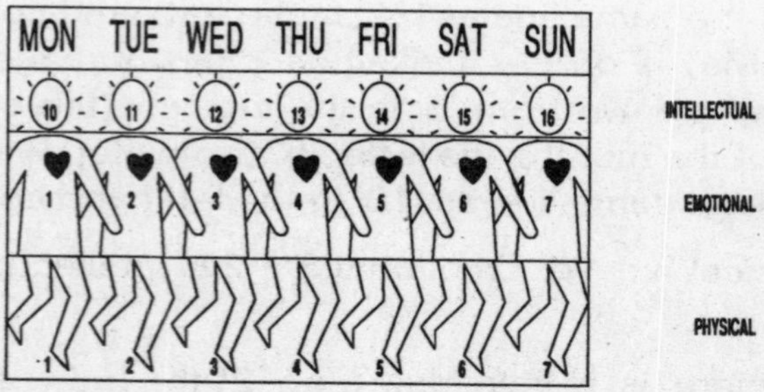

6. The Emotional value noted in step 3 above was '23' and the display will therefore be changed to:

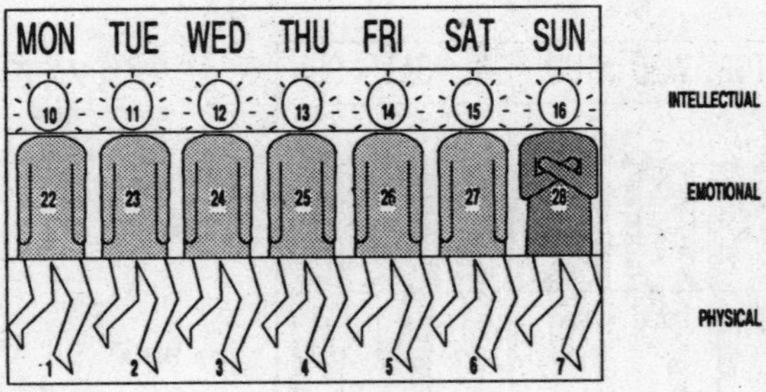

7. The Physical value noted in step 3 above was '17' and the *Bodyclock* should be fully set up as follows:

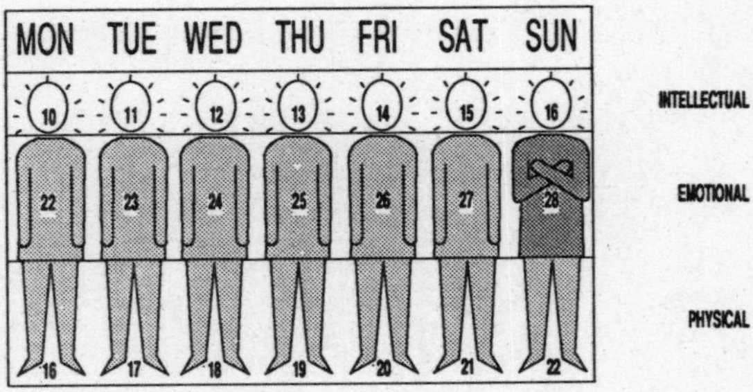

8. The key is realigned.

9. Finally, 5th May 1992 is in week No 19, so the display is set up to look like this:

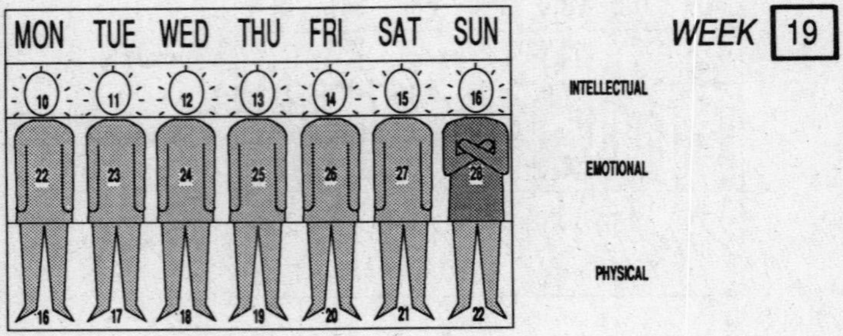

The Bodyclock is now set up correctly.

Appendix IV – Charts A and B

CHART A 1991

AGE ON BIRTHDAY IN 1991	PHYSICAL 1 Jan–29 Feb	PHYSICAL 1 Mar–31 Dec	EMOTIONAL 1 Jan–29 Feb	EMOTIONAL 1 Mar–31 Dec	INTELLECTUAL 1 Jan–29 Feb	INTELLECTUAL 1 Mar–31 Dec
10	18	18	12	12	22	22
11	16	15	14	13	25	24
12	13	13	15	15	27	27
13	10	10	16	16	29	29
14	7	7	17	17	31	31
15	5	4	19	18	1	33
16	2	2	20	20	3	3
17	22	22	21	21	5	5
18	19	19	22	22	7	7
19	17	16	24	23	10	9
20	14	14	25	25	12	12
21	11	11	26	26	14	14
22	8	8	27	27	16	16
23	6	5	1	28	19	18
24	3	3	2	2	21	21
25	23	23	3	3	23	23
26	20	20	4	4	25	25
27	18	17	6	5	28	27
28	15	15	7	7	30	30
29	12	12	8	8	32	32
30	9	9	9	9	1	1
31	7	6	11	10	4	3
32	4	4	12	12	6	6
33	1	1	13	13	8	8
34	21	21	14	14	10	10
35	19	18	16	15	13	12
36	16	16	17	17	15	15
37	13	13	18	18	17	17
38	10	10	19	19	19	19
39	8	7	21	20	22	21
40	5	5	22	22	24	24
41	2	2	23	23	26	26
42	22	22	24	24	28	28
43	20	19	26	25	31	30
44	17	17	27	27	33	33
45	14	14	28	28	2	2

CHART A 1991

AGE ON BIRTHDAY IN 1991	PHYSICAL 1 Jan–29 Feb	PHYSICAL 1 Mar–31 Dec	EMOTIONAL 1 Jan–29 Feb	EMOTIONAL 1 Mar–31 Dec	INTELLECTUAL 1 Jan–29 Feb	INTELLECTUAL 1 Mar–31 Dec
46	11	11	1	1	4	4
47	9	8	3	2	7	6
48	6	6	4	4	9	9
49	3	3	5	5	11	11
50	23	23	6	6	13	13
51	21	20	8	7	16	15
52	18	18	9	9	18	18
53	15	15	10	10	20	20
54	12	12	11	11	22	22
55	10	9	13	12	25	24
56	7	7	14	14	27	27
57	4	4	15	15	29	29
58	1	1	16	16	31	31
59	22	21	18	17	1	33
60	19	19	19	19	3	3
61	16	16	20	20	5	5
62	13	13	21	21	7	7
63	11	10	23	22	10	9
64	8	8	24	24	12	12
65	5	5	25	25	14	14
66	2	2	26	26	16	16
67	23	22	28	27	19	18
68	20	20	1	1	21	21
69	17	17	2	2	23	23
70	14	14	3	3	25	25
71	12	11	5	4	28	27
72	9	9	6	6	30	30
73	6	6	7	7	32	32
74	3	3	8	8	1	1
75	1	23	10	9	4	3
76	21	21	11	11	6	6
77	18	18	12	12	8	8
78	15	15	13	13	10	10
79	13	12	15	14	13	12
80	10	10	16	16	15	15

CHART A 1992

AGE ON BIRTHDAY IN 1992	PHYSICAL 1 Jan–29 Feb	PHYSICAL 1 Mar–31 Dec	EMOTIONAL 1 Jan–29 Feb	EMOTIONAL 1 Mar–31 Dec	INTELLECTUAL 1 Jan–29 Feb	INTELLECTUAL 1 Mar–31 Dec
10	19	19	13	13	23	23
11	16	16	14	14	25	25
12	14	13	16	15	28	27
13	11	11	17	17	30	30
14	8	8	18	18	32	32
15	5	5	19	19	1	1
16	3	2	21	20	4	3
17	23	23	22	22	6	6
18	20	20	23	23	8	8
19	17	17	24	24	10	10
20	15	14	26	25	13	12
21	12	12	27	27	15	15
22	9	9	28	28	17	17
23	6	6	1	1	19	19
24	4	3	3	2	22	21
25	1	1	4	4	24	24
26	21	21	5	5	26	26
27	18	18	6	6	28	28
28	16	15	8	7	31	30
29	13	13	9	9	33	33
30	10	10	10	10	2	2
31	7	7	11	11	4	4
32	5	4	13	12	7	6
33	2	2	14	14	9	9
34	22	22	15	15	11	11
35	19	19	16	16	13	13
36	17	16	18	17	16	15
37	14	14	19	19	18	18
38	11	11	20	20	20	20
39	8	8	21	21	22	22
40	6	5	23	22	25	24
41	3	3	24	24	27	27
42	23	23	25	25	29	29
43	20	20	26	26	31	31
44	18	17	28	27	1	33
45	15	15	1	1	3	3

CHART A 1992

AGE ON BIRTHDAY IN 1992	PHYSICAL 1 Jan–29 Feb	PHYSICAL 1 Mar–31 Dec	EMOTIONAL 1 Jan–29 Feb	EMOTIONAL 1 Mar–31 Dec	INTELLECTUAL 1 Jan–29 Feb	INTELLECTUAL 1 Mar–31 Dec
46	12	12	2	2	5	5
47	9	9	3	3	7	7
48	7	6	5	4	10	9
49	4	4	6	6	12	12
50	1	1	7	7	14	14
51	21	21	8	8	16	16
52	19	18	10	9	19	18
53	16	16	11	11	21	21
54	13	13	12	12	23	23
55	10	10	13	13	25	25
56	8	7	15	14	28	27
57	5	5	16	16	30	30
58	2	2	17	17	32	32
59	22	22	18	18	1	1
60	20	19	20	19	4	3
61	17	17	21	21	6	6
62	14	14	22	22	8	8
63	11	11	23	23	10	10
64	9	8	25	24	13	12
65	6	6	26	26	15	15
66	3	3	27	27	17	17
67	23	23	28	28	19	19
68	21	20	2	1	22	21
69	18	18	3	3	24	24
70	15	15	4	4	26	26
71	12	12	5	5	28	28
72	10	9	7	6	31	30
73	7	7	8	8	33	33
74	4	4	9	9	2	2
75	1	1	10	10	4	4
76	22	21	12	11	7	6
77	19	19	13	13	9	9
78	16	16	14	14	11	11
79	13	13	15	15	13	13
80	11	10	17	16	16	15

CHART A 1993

AGE ON BIRTHDAY IN 1993	PHYSICAL 1 Jan–29 Feb	PHYSICAL 1 Mar–31 Dec	EMOTIONAL 1 Jan–29 Feb	EMOTIONAL 1 Mar–31 Dec	INTELLECTUAL 1 Jan–29 Feb	INTELLECTUAL 1 Mar–31 Dec
10	19	19	13	13	23	23
11	16	16	14	14	25	25
12	13	13	15	15	27	27
13	11	10	17	16	30	29
14	8	8	18	18	32	32
15	5	5	19	19	1	1
16	2	2	20	20	3	3
17	23	22	22	21	6	5
18	20	20	23	23	8	8
19	17	17	24	24	10	10
20	14	14	25	25	12	12
21	12	11	27	26	15	14
22	9	9	28	28	17	17
23	6	6	1	1	19	19
24	3	3	2	2	21	21
25	1	23	4	3	24	23
26	21	21	5	5	26	26
27	18	18	6	6	28	28
28	15	15	7	7	30	30
29	13	12	9	8	33	32
30	10	10	10	10	2	2
31	7	7	11	11	4	4
32	4	4	12	12	6	6
33	2	1	14	13	9	8
34	22	22	15	15	11	11
35	19	19	16	16	13	13
36	16	16	17	17	15	15
37	14	13	19	18	18	17
38	11	11	20	20	20	20
39	8	8	21	21	22	22
40	5	5	22	22	24	24
41	3	2	24	23	27	26
42	23	23	25	25	29	29
43	20	20	26	26	31	31
44	17	17	27	27	33	33
45	15	14	1	28	3	2

CHART A 1993

AGE ON BIRTHDAY IN 1993	PHYSICAL 1 Jan–29 Feb	PHYSICAL 1 Mar–31 Dec	EMOTIONAL 1 Jan–29 Feb	EMOTIONAL 1 Mar–31 Dec	INTELLECTUAL 1 Jan–29 Feb	INTELLECTUAL 1 Mar–31 Dec
46	12	12	2	2	5	5
47	9	9	3	3	7	7
48	6	6	4	4	9	9
49	4	3	6	5	12	11
50	1	1	7	7	14	14
51	21	21	8	8	16	16
52	18	18	9	9	18	18
53	16	15	11	10	21	20
54	13	13	12	12	23	23
55	10	10	13	13	25	25
56	7	7	14	14	27	27
57	5	4	16	15	30	29
58	2	2	17	17	32	32
59	22	22	18	18	1	1
60	19	19	19	19	3	3
61	17	16	21	20	6	5
62	14	14	22	22	8	8
63	11	11	23	23	10	10
64	8	8	24	24	12	12
65	6	5	26	25	15	14
66	3	3	27	27	17	17
67	23	23	28	28	19	19
68	20	20	1	1	21	21
69	18	17	3	2	24	23
70	15	15	4	4	26	26
71	12	12	5	5	28	28
72	9	9	6	6	30	30
73	7	6	8	7	33	32
74	4	4	9	9	2	2
75	1	1	10	10	4	4
76	21	21	11	11	6	6
77	19	18	13	12	9	8
78	16	16	14	14	11	11
79	13	13	15	15	13	13
80	10	10	16	16	15	15

CHART B

PHYSICAL

BIO	JANUARY 1	2	3	4	5	6	7	8	9	10	11	12	13	14	15	16	17	18	19	20	21	22	23	24	25	26	27	28	29	30	31
1	A	W	V	U	T	S	R	Q	P	O	N	M	L	K	J	I	H	G	F	E	D	C	B	A	W	V	U	T	S	R	Q
2	B	A	W	V	U	T	S	R	Q	P	O	N	M	L	K	J	I	H	G	F	E	D	C	B	A	W	V	U	T	S	R
3	C	B	A	W	V	U	T	S	R	Q	P	O	N	M	L	K	J	I	H	G	F	E	D	C	B	A	W	V	U	T	S
4	D	C	B	A	W	V	U	T	S	R	Q	P	O	N	M	L	K	J	I	H	G	F	E	D	C	B	A	W	V	U	T
5	E	D	C	B	A	W	V	U	T	S	R	Q	P	O	N	M	L	K	J	I	H	G	F	E	D	C	B	A	W	V	U
6	F	E	D	C	B	A	W	V	U	T	S	R	Q	P	O	N	M	L	K	J	I	H	G	F	E	D	C	B	A	W	V
7	G	F	E	D	C	B	A	W	V	U	T	S	R	Q	P	O	N	M	L	K	J	I	H	G	F	E	D	C	B	A	W
8	H	G	F	E	D	C	B	A	W	V	U	T	S	R	Q	P	O	N	M	L	K	J	I	H	G	F	E	D	C	B	A
9	I	H	G	F	E	D	C	B	A	W	V	U	T	S	R	Q	P	O	N	M	L	K	J	I	H	G	F	E	D	C	B
10	J	I	H	G	F	E	D	C	B	A	W	V	U	T	S	R	Q	P	O	N	M	L	K	J	I	H	G	F	E	D	C
11	K	J	I	H	G	F	E	D	C	B	A	W	V	U	T	S	R	Q	P	O	N	M	L	K	J	I	H	G	F	E	D
12	L	K	J	I	H	G	F	E	D	C	B	A	W	V	U	T	S	R	Q	P	O	N	M	L	K	J	I	H	G	F	E
13	M	L	K	J	I	H	G	F	E	D	C	B	A	W	V	U	T	S	R	Q	P	O	N	M	L	K	J	I	H	G	F
14	N	M	L	K	J	I	H	G	F	E	D	C	B	A	W	V	U	T	S	R	Q	P	O	N	M	L	K	J	I	H	G
15	O	N	M	L	K	J	I	H	G	F	E	D	C	B	A	W	V	U	T	S	R	Q	P	O	N	M	L	K	J	I	H
16	P	O	N	M	L	K	J	I	H	G	F	E	D	C	B	A	W	V	U	T	S	R	Q	P	O	N	M	L	K	J	I
17	Q	P	O	N	M	L	K	J	I	H	G	F	E	D	C	B	A	W	V	U	T	S	R	Q	P	O	N	M	L	K	J
18	R	Q	P	O	N	M	L	K	J	I	H	G	F	E	D	C	B	A	W	V	U	T	S	R	Q	P	O	N	M	L	K
19	S	R	Q	P	O	N	M	L	K	J	I	H	G	F	E	D	C	B	A	W	V	U	T	S	R	Q	P	O	N	M	L
20	T	S	R	Q	P	O	N	M	L	K	J	I	H	G	F	E	D	C	B	A	W	V	U	T	S	R	Q	P	O	N	M
21	U	T	S	R	Q	P	O	N	M	L	K	J	I	H	G	F	E	D	C	B	A	W	V	U	T	S	R	Q	P	O	N
22	V	U	T	S	R	Q	P	O	N	M	L	K	J	I	H	G	F	E	D	C	B	A	W	V	U	T	S	R	Q	P	O
23	W	V	U	T	S	R	Q	P	O	N	M	L	K	J	I	H	G	F	E	D	C	B	A	W	V	U	T	S	R	Q	P

FEBRUARY

BIO	1	2	3	4	5	6	7	8	9	10	11	12	13	14	15	16	17	18	19	20	21	22	23	24	25	26	27	28
1	P	O	N	M	L	K	J	I	H	G	F	E	D	C	B	A	W	V	U	T	S	R	Q	P	O	N	M	L
2	Q	P	O	N	M	L	K	J	I	H	G	F	E	D	C	B	A	W	V	U	T	S	R	Q	P	O	N	M
3	R	Q	P	O	N	M	L	K	J	I	H	G	F	E	D	C	B	A	W	V	U	T	S	R	Q	P	O	N
4	S	R	Q	P	O	N	M	L	K	J	I	H	G	F	E	D	C	B	A	W	V	U	T	S	R	Q	P	O
5	T	S	R	Q	P	O	N	M	L	K	J	I	H	G	F	E	D	C	B	A	W	V	U	T	S	R	Q	P
6	U	T	S	R	Q	P	O	N	M	L	K	J	I	H	G	F	E	D	C	B	A	W	V	U	T	S	R	Q
7	V	U	T	S	R	Q	P	O	N	M	L	K	J	I	H	G	F	E	D	C	B	A	W	V	U	T	S	R
8	W	V	U	T	S	R	Q	P	O	N	M	L	K	J	I	H	G	F	E	D	C	B	A	W	V	U	T	S
9	A	W	V	U	T	S	R	Q	P	O	N	M	L	K	J	I	H	G	F	E	D	C	B	A	W	V	U	T
10	B	A	W	V	U	T	S	R	Q	P	O	N	M	L	K	J	I	H	G	F	E	D	C	B	A	W	V	U
11	C	B	A	W	V	U	T	S	R	Q	P	O	N	M	L	K	J	I	H	G	F	E	D	C	B	A	W	V
12	D	C	B	A	W	V	U	T	S	R	Q	P	O	N	M	L	K	J	I	H	G	F	E	D	C	B	A	W
13	E	D	C	B	A	W	V	U	T	S	R	Q	P	O	N	M	L	K	J	I	H	G	F	E	D	C	B	A
14	F	E	D	C	B	A	W	V	U	T	S	R	Q	P	O	N	M	L	K	J	I	H	G	F	E	D	C	B
15	G	F	E	D	C	B	A	W	V	U	T	S	R	Q	P	O	N	M	L	K	J	I	H	G	F	E	D	C
16	H	G	F	E	D	C	B	A	W	V	U	T	S	R	Q	P	O	N	M	L	K	J	I	H	G	F	E	D
17	I	H	G	F	E	D	C	B	A	W	V	U	T	S	R	Q	P	O	N	M	L	K	J	I	H	G	F	E
18	J	I	H	G	F	E	D	C	B	A	W	V	U	T	S	R	Q	P	O	N	M	L	K	J	I	H	G	F
19	K	J	I	H	G	F	E	D	C	B	A	W	V	U	T	S	R	Q	P	O	N	M	L	K	J	I	H	G
20	L	K	J	I	H	G	F	E	D	C	B	A	W	V	U	T	S	R	Q	P	O	N	M	L	K	J	I	H
21	M	L	K	J	I	H	G	F	E	D	C	B	A	W	V	U	T	S	R	Q	P	O	N	M	L	K	J	I
22	N	M	L	K	J	I	H	G	F	E	D	C	B	A	W	V	U	T	S	R	Q	P	O	N	M	L	K	J
23	O	N	M	L	K	J	I	H	G	F	E	D	C	B	A	W	V	U	T	S	R	Q	P	O	N	M	L	K

CHART B

PHYSICAL

MARCH

BIO	1	2	3	4	5	6	7	8	9	10	11	12	13	14	15	16	17	18	19	20	21	22	23	24	25	26	27	28	29	30	31
1	K	J	I	H	G	F	E	D	C	B	A	W	V	U	T	S	R	Q	P	O	N	M	L	K	J	I	H	G	F	E	D
2	L	K	J	I	H	G	F	E	D	C	B	A	W	V	U	T	S	R	Q	P	O	N	M	L	K	J	I	H	G	F	E
3	M	L	K	J	I	H	G	F	E	D	C	B	A	W	V	U	T	S	R	Q	P	O	N	M	L	K	J	I	H	G	F
4	N	M	L	K	J	I	H	G	F	E	D	C	B	A	W	V	U	T	S	R	Q	P	O	N	M	L	K	J	I	H	G
5	O	N	M	L	K	J	I	H	G	F	E	D	C	B	A	W	V	U	T	S	R	Q	P	O	N	M	L	K	J	I	H
6	P	O	N	M	L	K	J	I	H	G	F	E	D	C	B	A	W	V	U	T	S	R	Q	P	O	N	M	L	K	J	I
7	Q	P	O	N	M	L	K	J	I	H	G	F	E	D	C	B	A	W	V	U	T	S	R	Q	P	O	N	M	L	K	J
8	R	Q	P	O	N	M	L	K	J	I	H	G	F	E	D	C	B	A	W	V	U	T	S	R	Q	P	O	N	M	L	K
9	S	R	Q	P	O	N	M	L	K	J	I	H	G	F	E	D	C	B	A	W	V	U	T	S	R	Q	P	O	N	M	L
10	T	S	R	Q	P	O	N	M	L	K	J	I	H	G	F	E	D	C	B	A	W	V	U	T	S	R	Q	P	O	N	M
11	U	T	S	R	Q	P	O	N	M	L	K	J	I	H	G	F	E	D	C	B	A	W	V	U	T	S	R	Q	P	O	N
12	V	U	T	S	R	Q	P	O	N	M	L	K	J	I	H	G	F	E	D	C	B	A	W	V	U	T	S	R	Q	P	O
13	W	V	U	T	S	R	Q	P	O	N	M	L	K	J	I	H	G	F	E	D	C	B	A	W	V	U	T	S	R	Q	P
14	A	W	V	U	T	S	R	Q	P	O	N	M	L	K	J	I	H	G	F	E	D	C	B	A	W	V	U	T	S	R	Q
15	B	A	W	V	U	T	S	R	Q	P	O	N	M	L	K	J	I	H	G	F	E	D	C	B	A	W	V	U	T	S	R
16	C	B	A	W	V	U	T	S	R	Q	P	O	N	M	L	K	J	I	H	G	F	E	D	C	B	A	W	V	U	T	S
17	D	C	B	A	W	V	U	T	S	R	Q	P	O	N	M	L	K	J	I	H	G	F	E	D	C	B	A	W	V	U	T
18	E	D	C	B	A	W	V	U	T	S	R	Q	P	O	N	M	L	K	J	I	H	G	F	E	D	C	B	A	W	V	U
19	F	E	D	C	B	A	W	V	U	T	S	R	Q	P	O	N	M	L	K	J	I	H	G	F	E	D	C	B	A	W	V
20	G	F	E	D	C	B	A	W	V	U	T	S	R	Q	P	O	N	M	L	K	J	I	H	G	F	E	D	C	B	A	W
21	H	G	F	E	D	C	B	A	W	V	U	T	S	R	Q	P	O	N	M	L	K	J	I	H	G	F	E	D	C	B	A
22	I	H	G	F	E	D	C	B	A	W	V	U	T	S	R	Q	P	O	N	M	L	K	J	I	H	G	F	E	D	C	B
23	J	I	H	G	F	E	D	C	B	A	W	V	U	T	S	R	Q	P	O	N	M	L	K	J	I	H	G	F	E	D	C

APRIL

BIO	1	2	3	4	5	6	7	8	9	10	11	12	13	14	15	16	17	18	19	20	21	22	23	24	25	26	27	28	29	30
1	C	B	A	W	V	U	T	S	R	Q	P	O	N	M	L	K	J	I	H	G	F	E	D	C	B	A	W	V	U	T
2	D	C	B	A	W	V	U	T	S	R	Q	P	O	N	M	L	K	J	I	H	G	F	E	D	C	B	A	W	V	U
3	E	D	C	B	A	W	V	U	T	S	R	Q	P	O	N	M	L	K	J	I	H	G	F	E	D	C	B	A	W	V
4	F	E	D	C	B	A	W	V	U	T	S	R	Q	P	O	N	M	L	K	J	I	H	G	F	E	D	C	B	A	W
5	G	F	E	D	C	B	A	W	V	U	T	S	R	Q	P	O	N	M	L	K	J	I	H	G	F	E	D	C	B	A
6	H	G	F	E	D	C	B	A	W	V	U	T	S	R	Q	P	O	N	M	L	K	J	I	H	G	F	E	D	C	B
7	I	H	G	F	E	D	C	B	A	W	V	U	T	S	R	Q	P	O	N	M	L	K	J	I	H	G	F	E	D	C
8	J	I	H	G	F	E	D	C	B	A	W	V	U	T	S	R	Q	P	O	N	M	L	K	J	I	H	G	F	E	D
9	K	J	I	H	G	F	E	D	C	B	A	W	V	U	T	S	R	Q	P	O	N	M	L	K	J	I	H	G	F	E
10	L	K	J	I	H	G	F	E	D	C	B	A	W	V	U	T	S	R	Q	P	O	N	M	L	K	J	I	H	G	F
11	M	L	K	J	I	H	G	F	E	D	C	B	A	W	V	U	T	S	R	Q	P	O	N	M	L	K	J	I	H	G
12	N	M	L	K	J	I	H	G	F	E	D	C	B	A	W	V	U	T	S	R	Q	P	O	N	M	L	K	J	I	H
13	O	N	M	L	K	J	I	H	G	F	E	D	C	B	A	W	V	U	T	S	R	Q	P	O	N	M	L	K	J	I
14	P	O	N	M	L	K	J	I	H	G	F	E	D	C	B	A	W	V	U	T	S	R	Q	P	O	N	M	L	K	J
15	Q	P	O	N	M	L	K	J	I	H	G	F	E	D	C	B	A	W	V	U	T	S	R	Q	P	O	N	M	L	K
16	R	Q	P	O	N	M	L	K	J	I	H	G	F	E	D	C	B	A	W	V	U	T	S	R	Q	P	O	N	M	L
17	S	R	Q	P	O	N	M	L	K	J	I	H	G	F	E	D	C	B	A	W	V	U	T	S	R	Q	P	O	N	M
18	T	S	R	Q	P	O	N	M	L	K	J	I	H	G	F	E	D	C	B	A	W	V	U	T	S	R	Q	P	O	N
19	U	T	S	R	Q	P	O	N	M	L	K	J	I	H	G	F	E	D	C	B	A	W	V	U	T	S	R	Q	P	O
20	V	U	T	S	R	Q	P	O	N	M	L	K	J	I	H	G	F	E	D	C	B	A	W	V	U	T	S	R	Q	P
21	W	V	U	T	S	R	Q	P	O	N	M	L	K	J	I	H	G	F	E	D	C	B	A	W	V	U	T	S	R	Q
22	A	W	V	U	T	S	R	Q	P	O	N	M	L	K	J	I	H	G	F	E	D	C	B	A	W	V	U	T	S	R
23	B	A	W	V	U	T	S	R	Q	P	O	N	M	L	K	J	I	H	G	F	E	D	C	B	A	W	V	U	T	S

CHART B

PHYSICAL

MAY

BIO	1	2	3	4	5	6	7	8	9	10	11	12	13	14	15	16	17	18	19	20	21	22	23	24	25	26	27	28	29	30	31
1	S	R	Q	P	O	N	M	L	K	J	I	H	G	F	E	D	C	B	A	W	V	U	T	S	R	Q	P	O	N	M	L
2	T	S	R	Q	P	O	N	M	L	K	J	I	H	G	F	E	D	C	B	A	W	V	U	T	S	R	Q	P	O	N	M
3	U	T	S	R	Q	P	O	N	M	L	K	J	I	H	G	F	E	D	C	B	A	W	V	U	T	S	R	Q	P	O	N
4	V	U	T	S	R	Q	P	O	N	M	L	K	J	I	H	G	F	E	D	C	B	A	W	V	U	T	S	R	Q	P	O
5	W	V	U	T	S	R	Q	P	O	N	M	L	K	J	I	H	G	F	E	D	C	B	A	W	V	U	T	S	R	Q	P
6	A	W	V	U	T	S	R	Q	P	O	N	M	L	K	J	I	H	G	F	E	D	C	B	A	W	V	U	T	S	R	Q
7	B	A	W	V	U	T	S	R	Q	P	O	N	M	L	K	J	I	H	G	F	E	D	C	B	A	W	V	U	T	S	R
8	C	B	A	W	V	U	T	S	R	Q	P	O	N	M	L	K	J	I	H	G	F	E	D	C	B	A	W	V	U	T	S
9	D	C	B	A	W	V	U	T	S	R	Q	P	O	N	M	L	K	J	I	H	G	F	E	D	C	B	A	W	V	U	T
10	E	D	C	B	A	W	V	U	T	S	R	Q	P	O	N	M	L	K	J	I	H	G	F	E	D	C	B	A	W	V	U
11	F	E	D	C	B	A	W	V	U	T	S	R	Q	P	O	N	M	L	K	J	I	H	G	F	E	D	C	B	A	W	V
12	G	F	E	D	C	B	A	W	V	U	T	S	R	Q	P	O	N	M	L	K	J	I	H	G	F	E	D	C	B	A	W
13	H	G	F	E	D	C	B	A	W	V	U	T	S	R	Q	P	O	N	M	L	K	J	I	H	G	F	E	D	C	B	A
14	I	H	G	F	E	D	C	B	A	W	V	U	T	S	R	Q	P	O	N	M	L	K	J	I	H	G	F	E	D	C	B
15	J	I	H	G	F	E	D	C	B	A	W	V	U	T	S	R	Q	P	O	N	M	L	K	J	I	H	G	F	E	D	C
16	K	J	I	H	G	F	E	D	C	B	A	W	V	U	T	S	R	Q	P	O	N	M	L	K	J	I	H	G	F	E	D
17	L	K	J	I	H	G	F	E	D	C	B	A	W	V	U	T	S	R	Q	P	O	N	M	L	K	J	I	H	G	F	E
18	M	L	K	J	I	H	G	F	E	D	C	B	A	W	V	U	T	S	R	Q	P	O	N	M	L	K	J	I	H	G	F
19	N	M	L	K	J	I	H	G	F	E	D	C	B	A	W	V	U	T	S	R	Q	P	O	N	M	L	K	J	I	H	G
20	O	N	M	L	K	J	I	H	G	F	E	D	C	B	A	W	V	U	T	S	R	Q	P	O	N	M	L	K	J	I	H
21	P	O	N	M	L	K	J	I	H	G	F	E	D	C	B	A	W	V	U	T	S	R	Q	P	O	N	M	L	K	J	I
22	Q	P	O	N	M	L	K	J	I	H	G	F	E	D	C	B	A	W	V	U	T	S	R	Q	P	O	N	M	L	K	J
23	R	Q	P	O	N	M	L	K	J	I	H	G	F	E	D	C	B	A	W	V	U	T	S	R	Q	P	O	N	M	L	K

JUNE

BIO	1	2	3	4	5	6	7	8	9	10	11	12	13	14	15	16	17	18	19	20	21	22	23	24	25	26	27	28	29	30
1	K	J	I	H	G	F	E	D	C	B	A	W	V	U	T	S	R	Q	P	O	N	M	L	K	J	I	H	G	F	E
2	L	K	J	I	H	G	F	E	D	C	B	A	W	V	U	T	S	R	Q	P	O	N	M	L	K	J	I	H	G	F
3	M	L	K	J	I	H	G	F	E	D	C	B	A	W	V	U	T	S	R	Q	P	O	N	M	L	K	J	I	H	G
4	N	M	L	K	J	I	H	G	F	E	D	C	B	A	W	V	U	T	S	R	Q	P	O	N	M	L	K	J	I	H
5	O	N	M	L	K	J	I	H	G	F	E	D	C	B	A	W	V	U	T	S	R	Q	P	O	N	M	L	K	J	I
6	P	O	N	M	L	K	J	I	H	G	F	E	D	C	B	A	W	V	U	T	S	R	Q	P	O	N	M	L	K	J
7	Q	P	O	N	M	L	K	J	I	H	G	F	E	D	C	B	A	W	V	U	T	S	R	Q	P	O	N	M	L	K
8	R	Q	P	O	N	M	L	K	J	I	H	G	F	E	D	C	B	A	W	V	U	T	S	R	Q	P	O	N	M	L
9	S	R	Q	P	O	N	M	L	K	J	I	H	G	F	E	D	C	B	A	W	V	U	T	S	R	Q	P	O	N	M
10	T	S	R	Q	P	O	N	M	L	K	J	I	H	G	F	E	D	C	B	A	W	V	U	T	S	R	Q	P	O	N
11	U	T	S	R	Q	P	O	N	M	L	K	J	I	H	G	F	E	D	C	B	A	W	V	U	T	S	R	Q	P	O
12	V	U	T	S	R	Q	P	O	N	M	L	K	J	I	H	G	F	E	D	C	B	A	W	V	U	T	S	R	Q	P
13	W	V	U	T	S	R	Q	P	O	N	M	L	K	J	I	H	G	F	E	D	C	B	A	W	V	U	T	S	R	Q
14	A	W	V	U	T	S	R	Q	P	O	N	M	L	K	J	I	H	G	F	E	D	C	B	A	W	V	U	T	S	R
15	B	A	W	V	U	T	S	R	Q	P	O	N	M	L	K	J	I	H	G	F	E	D	C	B	A	W	V	U	T	S
16	C	B	A	W	V	U	T	S	R	Q	P	O	N	M	L	K	J	I	H	G	F	E	D	C	B	A	W	V	U	T
17	D	C	B	A	W	V	U	T	S	R	Q	P	O	N	M	L	K	J	I	H	G	F	E	D	C	B	A	W	V	U
18	E	D	C	B	A	W	V	U	T	S	R	Q	P	O	N	M	L	K	J	I	H	G	F	E	D	C	B	A	W	V
19	F	E	D	C	B	A	W	V	U	T	S	R	Q	P	O	N	M	L	K	J	I	H	G	F	E	D	C	B	A	W
20	G	F	E	D	C	B	A	W	V	U	T	S	R	Q	P	O	N	M	L	K	J	I	H	G	F	E	D	C	B	A
21	H	G	F	E	D	C	B	A	W	V	U	T	S	R	Q	P	O	N	M	L	K	J	I	H	G	F	E	D	C	B
22	I	H	G	F	E	D	C	B	A	W	V	U	T	S	R	Q	P	O	N	M	L	K	J	I	H	G	F	E	D	C
23	J	I	H	G	F	E	D	C	B	A	W	V	U	T	S	R	Q	P	O	N	M	L	K	J	I	H	G	F	E	D

CHART B

PHYSICAL

JULY

BIO	1	2	3	4	5	6	7	8	9	10	11	12	13	14	15	16	17	18	19	20	21	22	23	24	25	26	27	28	29	30	31
1	D	C	B	A	W	V	U	T	S	R	Q	P	O	N	M	L	K	J	I	H	G	F	E	D	C	B	A	W	V	U	T
2	E	D	C	B	A	W	V	U	T	S	R	Q	P	O	N	M	L	K	J	I	H	G	F	E	D	C	B	A	W	V	U
3	F	E	D	C	B	A	W	V	U	T	S	R	Q	P	O	N	M	L	K	J	I	H	G	F	E	D	C	B	A	W	V
4	G	F	E	D	C	B	A	W	V	U	T	S	R	Q	P	O	N	M	L	K	J	I	H	G	F	E	D	C	B	A	W
5	H	G	F	E	D	C	B	A	W	V	U	T	S	R	Q	P	O	N	M	L	K	J	I	H	G	F	E	D	C	B	A
6	I	H	G	F	E	D	C	B	A	W	V	U	T	S	R	Q	P	O	N	M	L	K	J	I	H	G	F	E	D	C	B
7	J	I	H	G	F	E	D	C	B	A	W	V	U	T	S	R	Q	P	O	N	M	L	K	J	I	H	G	F	E	D	C
8	K	J	I	H	G	F	E	D	C	B	A	W	V	U	T	S	R	Q	P	O	N	M	L	K	J	I	H	G	F	E	D
9	L	K	J	I	H	G	F	E	D	C	B	A	W	V	U	T	S	R	Q	P	O	N	M	L	K	J	I	H	G	F	E
10	M	L	K	J	I	H	G	F	E	D	C	B	A	W	V	U	T	S	R	Q	P	O	N	M	L	K	J	I	H	G	F
11	N	M	L	K	J	I	H	G	F	E	D	C	B	A	W	V	U	T	S	R	Q	P	O	N	M	L	K	J	I	H	G
12	O	N	M	L	K	J	I	H	G	F	E	D	C	B	A	W	V	U	T	S	R	Q	P	O	N	M	L	K	J	I	H
13	P	O	N	M	L	K	J	I	H	G	F	E	D	C	B	A	W	V	U	T	S	R	Q	P	O	N	M	L	K	J	I
14	Q	P	O	N	M	L	K	J	I	H	G	F	E	D	C	B	A	W	V	U	T	S	R	Q	P	O	N	M	L	K	J
15	R	Q	P	O	N	M	L	K	J	I	H	G	F	E	D	C	B	A	W	V	U	T	S	R	Q	P	O	N	M	L	K
16	S	R	Q	P	O	N	M	L	K	J	I	H	G	F	E	D	C	B	A	W	V	U	T	S	R	Q	P	O	N	M	L
17	T	S	R	Q	P	O	N	M	L	K	J	I	H	G	F	E	D	C	B	A	W	V	U	T	S	R	Q	P	O	N	M
18	U	T	S	R	Q	P	O	N	M	L	K	J	I	H	G	F	E	D	C	B	A	W	V	U	T	S	R	Q	P	O	N
19	V	U	T	S	R	Q	P	O	N	M	L	K	J	I	H	G	F	E	D	C	B	A	W	V	U	T	S	R	Q	P	O
20	W	V	U	T	S	R	Q	P	O	N	M	L	K	J	I	H	G	F	E	D	C	B	A	W	V	U	T	S	R	Q	P
21	A	W	V	U	T	S	R	Q	P	O	N	M	L	K	J	I	H	G	F	E	D	C	B	A	W	V	U	T	S	R	Q
22	B	A	W	V	U	T	S	R	Q	P	O	N	M	L	K	J	I	H	G	F	E	D	C	B	A	W	V	U	T	S	R
23	C	B	A	W	V	U	T	S	R	Q	P	O	N	M	L	K	J	I	H	G	F	E	D	C	B	A	W	V	U	T	S

AUGUST

BIO	1	2	3	4	5	6	7	8	9	10	11	12	13	14	15	16	17	18	19	20	21	22	23	24	25	26	27	28	29	30	31
1	S	R	Q	P	O	N	M	L	K	J	I	H	G	F	E	D	C	B	A	W	V	U	T	S	R	Q	P	O	N	M	L
2	T	S	R	Q	P	O	N	M	L	K	J	I	H	G	F	E	D	C	B	A	W	V	U	T	S	R	Q	P	O	N	M
3	U	T	S	R	Q	P	O	N	M	L	K	J	I	H	G	F	E	D	C	B	A	W	V	U	T	S	R	Q	P	O	N
4	V	U	T	S	R	Q	P	O	N	M	L	K	J	I	H	G	F	E	D	C	B	A	W	V	U	T	S	R	Q	P	O
5	W	V	U	T	S	R	Q	P	O	N	M	L	K	J	I	H	G	F	E	D	C	B	A	W	V	U	T	S	R	Q	P
6	A	W	V	U	T	S	R	Q	P	O	N	M	L	K	J	I	H	G	F	E	D	C	B	A	W	V	U	T	S	R	Q
7	B	A	W	V	U	T	S	R	Q	P	O	N	M	L	K	J	I	H	G	F	E	D	C	B	A	W	V	U	T	S	R
8	C	B	A	W	V	U	T	S	R	Q	P	O	N	M	L	K	J	I	H	G	F	E	D	C	B	A	W	V	U	T	S
9	D	C	B	A	W	V	U	T	S	R	Q	P	O	N	M	L	K	J	I	H	G	F	E	D	C	B	A	W	V	U	T
10	E	D	C	B	A	W	V	U	T	S	R	Q	P	O	N	M	L	K	J	I	H	G	F	E	D	C	B	A	W	V	U
11	F	E	D	C	B	A	W	V	U	T	S	R	Q	P	O	N	M	L	K	J	I	H	G	F	E	D	C	B	A	W	V
12	G	F	E	D	C	B	A	W	V	U	T	S	R	Q	P	O	N	M	L	K	J	I	H	G	F	E	D	C	B	A	W
13	H	G	F	E	D	C	B	A	W	V	U	T	S	R	Q	P	O	N	M	L	K	J	I	H	G	F	E	D	C	B	A
14	I	H	G	F	E	D	C	B	A	W	V	U	T	S	R	Q	P	O	N	M	L	K	J	I	H	G	F	E	D	C	B
15	J	I	H	G	F	E	D	C	B	A	W	V	U	T	S	R	Q	P	O	N	M	L	K	J	I	H	G	F	E	D	C
16	K	J	I	H	G	F	E	D	C	B	A	W	V	U	T	S	R	Q	P	O	N	M	L	K	J	I	H	G	F	E	D
17	L	K	J	I	H	G	F	E	D	C	B	A	W	V	U	T	S	R	Q	P	O	N	M	L	K	J	I	H	G	F	E
18	M	L	K	J	I	H	G	F	E	D	C	B	A	W	V	U	T	S	R	Q	P	O	N	M	L	K	J	I	H	G	F
19	N	M	L	K	J	I	H	G	F	E	D	C	B	A	W	V	U	T	S	R	Q	P	O	N	M	L	K	J	I	H	G
20	O	N	M	L	K	J	I	H	G	F	E	D	C	B	A	W	V	U	T	S	R	Q	P	O	N	M	L	K	J	I	H
21	P	O	N	M	L	K	J	I	H	G	F	E	D	C	B	A	W	V	U	T	S	R	Q	P	O	N	M	L	K	J	I
22	Q	P	O	N	M	L	K	J	I	H	G	F	E	D	C	B	A	W	V	U	T	S	R	Q	P	O	N	M	L	K	J
23	R	Q	P	O	N	M	L	K	J	I	H	G	F	E	D	C	B	A	W	V	U	T	S	R	Q	P	O	N	M	L	K

CHART B

PHYSICAL

BIO	SEPTEMBER 1	2	3	4	5	6	7	8	9	10	11	12	13	14	15	16	17	18	19	20	21	22	23	24	25	26	27	28	29	30
1	K	J	I	H	G	F	E	D	C	B	A	W	V	U	T	S	R	Q	P	O	N	M	L	K	J	I	H	G	F	E
2	L	K	J	I	H	G	F	E	D	C	B	A	W	V	U	T	S	R	Q	P	O	N	M	L	K	J	I	H	G	F
3	M	L	K	J	I	H	G	F	E	D	C	B	A	W	V	U	T	S	R	Q	P	O	N	M	L	K	J	I	H	G
4	N	M	L	K	J	I	H	G	F	E	D	C	B	A	W	V	U	T	S	R	Q	P	O	N	M	L	K	J	I	H
5	O	N	M	L	K	J	I	H	G	F	E	D	C	B	A	W	V	U	T	S	R	Q	P	O	N	M	L	K	J	I
6	P	O	N	M	L	K	J	I	H	G	F	E	D	C	B	A	W	V	U	T	S	R	Q	P	O	N	M	L	K	J
7	Q	P	O	N	M	L	K	J	I	H	G	F	E	D	C	B	A	W	V	U	T	S	R	Q	P	O	N	M	L	K
8	R	Q	P	O	N	M	L	K	J	I	H	G	F	E	D	C	B	A	W	V	U	T	S	R	Q	P	O	N	M	L
9	S	R	Q	P	O	N	M	L	K	J	I	H	G	F	E	D	C	B	A	W	V	U	T	S	R	Q	P	O	N	M
10	T	S	R	Q	P	O	N	M	L	K	J	I	H	G	F	E	D	C	B	A	W	V	U	T	S	R	Q	P	O	N
11	U	T	S	R	Q	P	O	N	M	L	K	J	I	H	G	F	E	D	C	B	A	W	V	U	T	S	R	Q	P	O
12	V	U	T	S	R	Q	P	O	N	M	L	K	J	I	H	G	F	E	D	C	B	A	W	V	U	T	S	R	Q	P
13	W	V	U	T	S	R	Q	P	O	N	M	L	K	J	I	H	G	F	E	D	C	B	A	W	V	U	T	S	R	Q
14	A	W	V	U	T	S	R	Q	P	O	N	M	L	K	J	I	H	G	F	E	D	C	B	A	W	V	U	T	S	R
15	B	A	W	V	U	T	S	R	Q	P	O	N	M	L	K	J	I	H	G	F	E	D	C	B	A	W	V	U	T	S
16	C	B	A	W	V	U	T	S	R	Q	P	O	N	M	L	K	J	I	H	G	F	E	D	C	B	A	W	V	U	T
17	D	C	B	A	W	V	U	T	S	R	Q	P	O	N	M	L	K	J	I	H	G	F	E	D	C	B	A	W	V	U
18	E	D	C	B	A	W	V	U	T	S	R	Q	P	O	N	M	L	K	J	I	H	G	F	E	D	C	B	A	W	V
19	F	E	D	C	B	A	W	V	U	T	S	R	Q	P	O	N	M	L	K	J	I	H	G	F	E	D	C	B	A	W
20	G	F	E	D	C	B	A	W	V	U	T	S	R	Q	P	O	N	M	L	K	J	I	H	G	F	E	D	C	B	A
21	H	G	F	E	D	C	B	A	W	V	U	T	S	R	Q	P	O	N	M	L	K	J	I	H	G	F	E	D	C	B
22	I	H	G	F	E	D	C	B	A	W	V	U	T	S	R	Q	P	O	N	M	L	K	J	I	H	G	F	E	D	C
23	J	I	H	G	F	E	D	C	B	A	W	V	U	T	S	R	Q	P	O	N	M	L	K	J	I	H	G	F	E	D

OCTOBER

BIO	1	2	3	4	5	6	7	8	9	10	11	12	13	14	15	16	17	18	19	20	21	22	23	24	25	26	27	28	29	30	31
1	D	C	B	A	W	V	U	T	S	R	Q	P	O	N	M	L	K	J	I	H	G	F	E	D	C	B	A	W	V	U	T
2	E	D	C	B	A	W	V	U	T	S	R	Q	P	O	N	M	L	K	J	I	H	G	F	E	D	C	B	A	W	V	U
3	F	E	D	C	B	A	W	V	U	T	S	R	Q	P	O	N	M	L	K	J	I	H	G	F	E	D	C	B	A	W	V
4	G	F	E	D	C	B	A	W	V	U	T	S	R	Q	P	O	N	M	L	K	J	I	H	G	F	E	D	C	B	A	W
5	H	G	F	E	D	C	B	A	W	V	U	T	S	R	Q	P	O	N	M	L	K	J	I	H	G	F	E	D	C	B	A
6	I	H	G	F	E	D	C	B	A	W	V	U	T	S	R	Q	P	O	N	M	L	K	J	I	H	G	F	E	D	C	B
7	J	I	H	G	F	E	D	C	B	A	W	V	U	T	S	R	Q	P	O	N	M	L	K	J	I	H	G	F	E	D	C
8	K	J	I	H	G	F	E	D	C	B	A	W	V	U	T	S	R	Q	P	O	N	M	L	K	J	I	H	G	F	E	D
9	L	K	J	I	H	G	F	E	D	C	B	A	W	V	U	T	S	R	Q	P	O	N	M	L	K	J	I	H	G	F	E
10	M	L	K	J	I	H	G	F	E	D	C	B	A	W	V	U	T	S	R	Q	P	O	N	M	L	K	J	I	H	G	F
11	N	M	L	K	J	I	H	G	F	E	D	C	B	A	W	V	U	T	S	R	Q	P	O	N	M	L	K	J	I	H	G
12	O	N	M	L	K	J	I	H	G	F	E	D	C	B	A	W	V	U	T	S	R	Q	P	O	N	M	L	K	J	I	H
13	P	O	N	M	L	K	J	I	H	G	F	E	D	C	B	A	W	V	U	T	S	R	Q	P	O	N	M	L	K	J	I
14	Q	P	O	N	M	L	K	J	I	H	G	F	E	D	C	B	A	W	V	U	T	S	R	Q	P	O	N	M	L	K	J
15	R	Q	P	O	N	M	L	K	J	I	H	G	F	E	D	C	B	A	W	V	U	T	S	R	Q	P	O	N	M	L	K
16	S	R	Q	P	O	N	M	L	K	J	I	H	G	F	E	D	C	B	A	W	V	U	T	S	R	Q	P	O	N	M	L
17	T	S	R	Q	P	O	N	M	L	K	J	I	H	G	F	E	D	C	B	A	W	V	U	T	S	R	Q	P	O	N	M
18	U	T	S	R	Q	P	O	N	M	L	K	J	I	H	G	F	E	D	C	B	A	W	V	U	T	S	R	Q	P	O	N
19	V	U	T	S	R	Q	P	O	N	M	L	K	J	I	H	G	F	E	D	C	B	A	W	V	U	T	S	R	Q	P	O
20	W	V	U	T	S	R	Q	P	O	N	M	L	K	J	I	H	G	F	E	D	C	B	A	W	V	U	T	S	R	Q	P
21	A	W	V	U	T	S	R	Q	P	O	N	M	L	K	J	I	H	G	F	E	D	C	B	A	W	V	U	T	S	R	Q
22	B	A	W	V	U	T	S	R	Q	P	O	N	M	L	K	J	I	H	G	F	E	D	C	B	A	W	V	U	T	S	R
23	C	B	A	W	V	U	T	S	R	Q	P	O	N	M	L	K	J	I	H	G	F	E	D	C	B	A	W	V	U	T	S

CHART B

PHYSICAL

NOVEMBER

BIO	1	2	3	4	5	6	7	8	9	10	11	12	13	14	15	16	17	18	19	20	21	22	23	24	25	26	27	28	29	30
1	S	R	Q	P	O	N	M	L	K	J	I	H	G	F	E	D	C	B	A	W	V	U	T	S	R	Q	P	O	N	M
2	T	S	R	Q	P	O	N	M	L	K	J	I	H	G	F	E	D	C	B	A	W	V	U	T	S	R	Q	P	O	N
3	U	T	S	R	Q	P	O	N	M	L	K	J	I	H	G	F	E	D	C	B	A	W	V	U	T	S	R	Q	P	O
4	V	U	T	S	R	Q	P	O	N	M	L	K	J	I	H	G	F	E	D	C	B	A	W	V	U	T	S	R	Q	P
5	W	V	U	T	S	R	Q	P	O	N	M	L	K	J	I	H	G	F	E	D	C	B	A	W	V	U	T	S	R	Q
6	A	W	V	U	T	S	R	Q	P	O	N	M	L	K	J	I	H	G	F	E	D	C	B	A	W	V	U	T	S	R
7	B	A	W	V	U	T	S	R	Q	P	O	N	M	L	K	J	I	H	G	F	E	D	C	B	A	W	V	U	T	S
8	C	B	A	W	V	U	T	S	R	Q	P	O	N	M	L	K	J	I	H	G	F	E	D	C	B	A	W	V	U	T
9	D	C	B	A	W	V	U	T	S	R	Q	P	O	N	M	L	K	J	I	H	G	F	E	D	C	B	A	W	V	U
10	E	D	C	B	A	W	V	U	T	S	R	Q	P	O	N	M	L	K	J	I	H	G	F	E	D	C	B	A	W	V
11	F	E	D	C	B	A	W	V	U	T	S	R	Q	P	O	N	M	L	K	J	I	H	G	F	E	D	C	B	A	W
12	G	F	E	D	C	B	A	W	V	U	T	S	R	Q	P	O	N	M	L	K	J	I	H	G	F	E	D	C	B	A
13	H	G	F	E	D	C	B	A	W	V	U	T	S	R	Q	P	O	N	M	L	K	J	I	H	G	F	E	D	C	B
14	I	H	G	F	E	D	C	B	A	W	V	U	T	S	R	Q	P	O	N	M	L	K	J	I	H	G	F	E	D	C
15	J	I	H	G	F	E	D	C	B	A	W	V	U	T	S	R	Q	P	O	N	M	L	K	J	I	H	G	F	E	D
16	K	J	I	H	G	F	E	D	C	B	A	W	V	U	T	S	R	Q	P	O	N	M	L	K	J	I	H	G	F	E
17	L	K	J	I	H	G	F	E	D	C	B	A	W	V	U	T	S	R	Q	P	O	N	M	L	K	J	I	H	G	F
18	M	L	K	J	I	H	G	F	E	D	C	B	A	W	V	U	T	S	R	Q	P	O	N	M	L	K	J	I	H	G
19	N	M	L	K	J	I	H	G	F	E	D	C	B	A	W	V	U	T	S	R	Q	P	O	N	M	L	K	J	I	H
20	O	N	M	L	K	J	I	H	G	F	E	D	C	B	A	W	V	U	T	S	R	Q	P	O	N	M	L	K	J	I
21	P	O	N	M	L	K	J	I	H	G	F	E	D	C	B	A	W	V	U	T	S	R	Q	P	O	N	M	L	K	J
22	Q	P	O	N	M	L	K	J	I	H	G	F	E	D	C	B	A	W	V	U	T	S	R	Q	P	O	N	M	L	K
23	R	Q	P	O	N	M	L	K	J	I	H	G	F	E	D	C	B	A	W	V	U	T	S	R	Q	P	O	N	M	L

DECEMBER

BIO	1	2	3	4	5	6	7	8	9	10	11	12	13	14	15	16	17	18	19	20	21	22	23	24	25	26	27	28	29	30	31
1	L	K	J	I	H	G	F	E	D	C	B	A	W	V	U	T	S	R	Q	P	O	N	M	L	K	J	I	H	G	F	E
2	M	L	K	J	I	H	G	F	E	D	C	B	A	W	V	U	T	S	R	Q	P	O	N	M	L	K	J	I	H	G	F
3	N	M	L	K	J	I	H	G	F	E	D	C	B	A	W	V	U	T	S	R	Q	P	O	N	M	L	K	J	I	H	G
4	O	N	M	L	K	J	I	H	G	F	E	D	C	B	A	W	V	U	T	S	R	Q	P	O	N	M	L	K	J	I	H
5	P	O	N	M	L	K	J	I	H	G	F	E	D	C	B	A	W	V	U	T	S	R	Q	P	O	N	M	L	K	J	I
6	Q	P	O	N	M	L	K	J	I	H	G	F	E	D	C	B	A	W	V	U	T	S	R	Q	P	O	N	M	L	K	J
7	R	Q	P	O	N	M	L	K	J	I	H	G	F	E	D	C	B	A	W	V	U	T	S	R	Q	P	O	N	M	L	K
8	S	R	Q	P	O	N	M	L	K	J	I	H	G	F	E	D	C	B	A	W	V	U	T	S	R	Q	P	O	N	M	L
9	T	S	R	Q	P	O	N	M	L	K	J	I	H	G	F	E	D	C	B	A	W	V	U	T	S	R	Q	P	O	N	M
10	U	T	S	R	Q	P	O	N	M	L	K	J	I	H	G	F	E	D	C	B	A	W	V	U	T	S	R	Q	P	O	N
11	V	U	T	S	R	Q	P	O	N	M	L	K	J	I	H	G	F	E	D	C	B	A	W	V	U	T	S	R	Q	P	O
12	W	V	U	T	S	R	Q	P	O	N	M	L	K	J	I	H	G	F	E	D	C	B	A	W	V	U	T	S	R	Q	P
13	A	W	V	U	T	S	R	Q	P	O	N	M	L	K	J	I	H	G	F	E	D	C	B	A	W	V	U	T	S	R	Q
14	B	A	W	V	U	T	S	R	Q	P	O	N	M	L	K	J	I	H	G	F	E	D	C	B	A	W	V	U	T	S	R
15	C	B	A	W	V	U	T	S	R	Q	P	O	N	M	L	K	J	I	H	G	F	E	D	C	B	A	W	V	U	T	S
16	D	C	B	A	W	V	U	T	S	R	Q	P	O	N	M	L	K	J	I	H	G	F	E	D	C	B	A	W	V	U	T
17	E	D	C	B	A	W	V	U	T	S	R	Q	P	O	N	M	L	K	J	I	H	G	F	E	D	C	B	A	W	V	U
18	F	E	D	C	B	A	W	V	U	T	S	R	Q	P	O	N	M	L	K	J	I	H	G	F	E	D	C	B	A	W	V
19	G	F	E	D	C	B	A	W	V	U	T	S	R	Q	P	O	N	M	L	K	J	I	H	G	F	E	D	C	B	A	W
20	H	G	F	E	D	C	B	A	W	V	U	T	S	R	Q	P	O	N	M	L	K	J	I	H	G	F	E	D	C	B	A
21	I	H	G	F	E	D	C	B	A	W	V	U	T	S	R	Q	P	O	N	M	L	K	J	I	H	G	F	E	D	C	B
22	J	I	H	G	F	E	D	C	B	A	W	V	U	T	S	R	Q	P	O	N	M	L	K	J	I	H	G	F	E	D	C
23	K	J	I	H	G	F	E	D	C	B	A	W	V	U	T	S	R	Q	P	O	N	M	L	K	J	I	H	G	F	E	D

CHART B

EMOTIONAL

JANUARY

BIO	1	2	3	4	5	6	7	8	9	10	11	12	13	14	15	16	17	18	19	20	21	22	23	24	25	26	27	28	29	30	31
1	A	>	@	Z	Y	X	W	V	U	T	S	R	Q	P	O	N	M	L	K	J	I	H	G	F	E	D	C	B	A	>	@
2	B	A	>	@	Z	Y	X	W	V	U	T	S	R	Q	P	O	N	M	L	K	J	I	H	G	F	E	D	C	B	A	>
3	C	B	A	>	@	Z	Y	X	W	V	U	T	S	R	Q	P	O	N	M	L	K	J	I	H	G	F	E	D	C	B	A
4	D	C	B	A	>	@	Z	Y	X	W	V	U	T	S	R	Q	P	O	N	M	L	K	J	I	H	G	F	E	D	C	B
5	E	D	C	B	A	>	@	Z	Y	X	W	V	U	T	S	R	Q	P	O	N	M	L	K	J	I	H	G	F	E	D	C
6	F	E	D	C	B	A	>	@	Z	Y	X	W	V	U	T	S	R	Q	P	O	N	M	L	K	J	I	H	G	F	E	D
7	G	F	E	D	C	B	A	>	@	Z	Y	X	W	V	U	T	S	R	Q	P	O	N	M	L	K	J	I	H	G	F	E
8	H	G	F	E	D	C	B	A	>	@	Z	Y	X	W	V	U	T	S	R	Q	P	O	N	M	L	K	J	I	H	G	F
9	I	H	G	F	E	D	C	B	A	>	@	Z	Y	X	W	V	U	T	S	R	Q	P	O	N	M	L	K	J	I	H	G
10	J	I	H	G	F	E	D	C	B	A	>	@	Z	Y	X	W	V	U	T	S	R	Q	P	O	N	M	L	K	J	I	H
11	K	J	I	H	G	F	E	D	C	B	A	>	@	Z	Y	X	W	V	U	T	S	R	Q	P	O	N	M	L	K	J	I
12	L	K	J	I	H	G	F	E	D	C	B	A	>	@	Z	Y	X	W	V	U	T	S	R	Q	P	O	N	M	L	K	J
13	M	L	K	J	I	H	G	F	E	D	C	B	A	>	@	Z	Y	X	W	V	U	T	S	R	Q	P	O	N	M	L	K
14	N	M	L	K	J	I	H	G	F	E	D	C	B	A	>	@	Z	Y	X	W	V	U	T	S	R	Q	P	O	N	M	L
15	O	N	M	L	K	J	I	H	G	F	E	D	C	B	A	>	@	Z	Y	X	W	V	U	T	S	R	Q	P	O	N	M
16	P	O	N	M	L	K	J	I	H	G	F	E	D	C	B	A	>	@	Z	Y	X	W	V	U	T	S	R	Q	P	O	N
17	Q	P	O	N	M	L	K	J	I	H	G	F	E	D	C	B	A	>	@	Z	Y	X	W	V	U	T	S	R	Q	P	O
18	R	Q	P	O	N	M	L	K	J	I	H	G	F	E	D	C	B	A	>	@	Z	Y	X	W	V	U	T	S	R	Q	P
19	S	R	Q	P	O	N	M	L	K	J	I	H	G	F	E	D	C	B	A	>	@	Z	Y	X	W	V	U	T	S	R	Q
20	T	S	R	Q	P	O	N	M	L	K	J	I	H	G	F	E	D	C	B	A	>	@	Z	Y	X	W	V	U	T	S	R
21	U	T	S	R	Q	P	O	N	M	L	K	J	I	H	G	F	E	D	C	B	A	>	@	Z	Y	X	W	V	U	T	S
22	V	U	T	S	R	Q	P	O	N	M	L	K	J	I	H	G	F	E	D	C	B	A	>	@	Z	Y	X	W	V	U	T
23	W	V	U	T	S	R	Q	P	O	N	M	L	K	J	I	H	G	F	E	D	C	B	A	>	@	Z	Y	X	W	V	U
24	X	W	V	U	T	S	R	Q	P	O	N	M	L	K	J	I	H	G	F	E	D	C	B	A	>	@	Z	Y	X	W	V
25	Y	X	W	V	U	T	S	R	Q	P	O	N	M	L	K	J	I	H	G	F	E	D	C	B	A	>	@	Z	Y	X	W
26	Z	Y	X	W	V	U	T	S	R	Q	P	O	N	M	L	K	J	I	H	G	F	E	D	C	B	A	>	@	Z	Y	X
27	@	Z	Y	X	W	V	U	T	S	R	Q	P	O	N	M	L	K	J	I	H	G	F	E	D	C	B	A	>	@	Z	Y
28	>	@	Z	Y	X	W	V	U	T	S	R	Q	P	O	N	M	L	K	J	I	H	G	F	E	D	C	B	A	>	@	Z

FEBRUARY

BIO	1	2	3	4	5	6	7	8	9	10	11	12	13	14	15	16	17	18	19	20	21	22	23	24	25	26	27	28
1	Z	Y	X	W	V	U	T	S	R	Q	P	O	N	M	L	K	J	I	H	G	F	E	D	C	B	A	>	@
2	@	Z	Y	X	W	V	U	T	S	R	Q	P	O	N	M	L	K	J	I	H	G	F	E	D	C	B	A	>
3	>	@	Z	Y	X	W	V	U	T	S	R	Q	P	O	N	M	L	K	J	I	H	G	F	E	D	C	B	A
4	A	>	@	Z	Y	X	W	V	U	T	S	R	Q	P	O	N	M	L	K	J	I	H	G	F	E	D	C	B
5	B	A	>	@	Z	Y	X	W	V	U	T	S	R	Q	P	O	N	M	L	K	J	I	H	G	F	E	D	C
6	C	B	A	>	@	Z	Y	X	W	V	U	T	S	R	Q	P	O	N	M	L	K	J	I	H	G	F	E	D
7	D	C	B	A	>	@	Z	Y	X	W	V	U	T	S	R	Q	P	O	N	M	L	K	J	I	H	G	F	E
8	E	D	C	B	A	>	@	Z	Y	X	W	V	U	T	S	R	Q	P	O	N	M	L	K	J	I	H	G	F
9	F	E	D	C	B	A	>	@	Z	Y	X	W	V	U	T	S	R	Q	P	O	N	M	L	K	J	I	H	G
10	G	F	E	D	C	B	A	>	@	Z	Y	X	W	V	U	T	S	R	Q	P	O	N	M	L	K	J	I	H
11	H	G	F	E	D	C	B	A	>	@	Z	Y	X	W	V	U	T	S	R	Q	P	O	N	M	L	K	J	I
12	I	H	G	F	E	D	C	B	A	>	@	Z	Y	X	W	V	U	T	S	R	Q	P	O	N	M	L	K	J
13	J	I	H	G	F	E	D	C	B	A	>	@	Z	Y	X	W	V	U	T	S	R	Q	P	O	N	M	L	K
14	K	J	I	H	G	F	E	D	C	B	A	>	@	Z	Y	X	W	V	U	T	S	R	Q	P	O	N	M	L
15	L	K	J	I	H	G	F	E	D	C	B	A	>	@	Z	Y	X	W	V	U	T	S	R	Q	P	O	N	M
16	M	L	K	J	I	H	G	F	E	D	C	B	A	>	@	Z	Y	X	W	V	U	T	S	R	Q	P	O	N
17	N	M	L	K	J	I	H	G	F	E	D	C	B	A	>	@	Z	Y	X	W	V	U	T	S	R	Q	P	O
18	O	N	M	L	K	J	I	H	G	F	E	D	C	B	A	>	@	Z	Y	X	W	V	U	T	S	R	Q	P
19	P	O	N	M	L	K	J	I	H	G	F	E	D	C	B	A	>	@	Z	Y	X	W	V	U	T	S	R	Q
20	Q	P	O	N	M	L	K	J	I	H	G	F	E	D	C	B	A	>	@	Z	Y	X	W	V	U	T	S	R
21	R	Q	P	O	N	M	L	K	J	I	H	G	F	E	D	C	B	A	>	@	Z	Y	X	W	V	U	T	S
22	S	R	Q	P	O	N	M	L	K	J	I	H	G	F	E	D	C	B	A	>	@	Z	Y	X	W	V	U	T
23	T	S	R	Q	P	O	N	M	L	K	J	I	H	G	F	E	D	C	B	A	>	@	Z	Y	X	W	V	U
24	U	T	S	R	Q	P	O	N	M	L	K	J	I	H	G	F	E	D	C	B	A	>	@	Z	Y	X	W	V
25	V	U	T	S	R	Q	P	O	N	M	L	K	J	I	H	G	F	E	D	C	B	A	>	@	Z	Y	X	W
26	W	V	U	T	S	R	Q	P	O	N	M	L	K	J	I	H	G	F	E	D	C	B	A	>	@	Z	Y	X
27	X	W	V	U	T	S	R	Q	P	O	N	M	L	K	J	I	H	G	F	E	D	C	B	A	>	@	Z	Y
28	Y	X	W	V	U	T	S	R	Q	P	O	N	M	L	K	J	I	H	G	F	E	D	C	B	A	>	@	Z

CHART B

EMOTIONAL

BIO \ MARCH	1	2	3	4	5	6	7	8	9	10	11	12	13	14	15	16	17	18	19	20	21	22	23	24	25	26	27	28	29	30	31
1	Z	Y	X	W	V	U	T	S	R	Q	P	O	N	M	L	K	J	I	H	G	F	E	D	C	B	A	>	@	Z	Y	X
2	@	Z	Y	X	W	V	U	T	S	R	Q	P	O	N	M	L	K	J	I	H	G	F	E	D	C	B	A	>	@	Z	Y
3	>	@	Z	Y	X	W	V	U	T	S	R	Q	P	O	N	M	L	K	J	I	H	G	F	E	D	C	B	A	>	@	Z
4	A	>	@	Z	Y	X	W	V	U	T	S	R	Q	P	O	N	M	L	K	J	I	H	G	F	E	D	C	B	A	>	@
5	B	A	>	@	Z	Y	X	W	V	U	T	S	R	Q	P	O	N	M	L	K	J	I	H	G	F	E	D	C	B	A	>
6	C	B	A	>	@	Z	Y	X	W	V	U	T	S	R	Q	P	O	N	M	L	K	J	I	H	G	F	E	D	C	B	A
7	D	C	B	A	>	@	Z	Y	X	W	V	U	T	S	R	Q	P	O	N	M	L	K	J	I	H	G	F	E	D	C	B
8	E	D	C	B	A	>	@	Z	Y	X	W	V	U	T	S	R	Q	P	O	N	M	L	K	J	I	H	G	F	E	D	C
9	F	E	D	C	B	A	>	@	Z	Y	X	W	V	U	T	S	R	Q	P	O	N	M	L	K	J	I	H	G	F	E	D
10	G	F	E	D	C	B	A	>	@	Z	Y	X	W	V	U	T	S	R	Q	P	O	N	M	L	K	J	I	H	G	F	E
11	H	G	F	E	D	C	B	A	>	@	Z	Y	X	W	V	U	T	S	R	Q	P	O	N	M	L	K	J	I	H	G	F
12	I	H	G	F	E	D	C	B	A	>	@	Z	Y	X	W	V	U	T	S	R	Q	P	O	N	M	L	K	J	I	H	G
13	J	I	H	G	F	E	D	C	B	A	>	@	Z	Y	X	W	V	U	T	S	R	Q	P	O	N	M	L	K	J	I	H
14	K	J	I	H	G	F	E	D	C	B	A	>	@	Z	Y	X	W	V	U	T	S	R	Q	P	O	N	M	L	K	J	I
15	L	K	J	I	H	G	F	E	D	C	B	A	>	@	Z	Y	X	W	V	U	T	S	R	Q	P	O	N	M	L	K	J
16	M	L	K	J	I	H	G	F	E	D	C	B	A	>	@	Z	Y	X	W	V	U	T	S	R	Q	P	O	N	M	L	K
17	N	M	L	K	J	I	H	G	F	E	D	C	B	A	>	@	Z	Y	X	W	V	U	T	S	R	Q	P	O	N	M	L
18	O	N	M	L	K	J	I	H	G	F	E	D	C	B	A	>	@	Z	Y	X	W	V	U	T	S	R	Q	P	O	N	M
19	P	O	N	M	L	K	J	I	H	G	F	E	D	C	B	A	>	@	Z	Y	X	W	V	U	T	S	R	Q	P	O	N
20	Q	P	O	N	M	L	K	J	I	H	G	F	E	D	C	B	A	>	@	Z	Y	X	W	V	U	T	S	R	Q	P	O
21	R	Q	P	O	N	M	L	K	J	I	H	G	F	E	D	C	B	A	>	@	Z	Y	X	W	V	U	T	S	R	Q	P
22	S	R	Q	P	O	N	M	L	K	J	I	H	G	F	E	D	C	B	A	>	@	Z	Y	X	W	V	U	T	S	R	Q
23	T	S	R	Q	P	O	N	M	L	K	J	I	H	G	F	E	D	C	B	A	>	@	Z	Y	X	W	V	U	T	S	R
24	U	T	S	R	Q	P	O	N	M	L	K	J	I	H	G	F	E	D	C	B	A	>	@	Z	Y	X	W	V	U	T	S
25	V	U	T	S	R	Q	P	O	N	M	L	K	J	I	H	G	F	E	D	C	B	A	>	@	Z	Y	X	W	V	U	T
26	W	V	U	T	S	R	Q	P	O	N	M	L	K	J	I	H	G	F	E	D	C	B	A	>	@	Z	Y	X	W	V	U
27	X	W	V	U	T	S	R	Q	P	O	N	M	L	K	J	I	H	G	F	E	D	C	B	A	>	@	Z	Y	X	W	V
28	Y	X	W	V	U	T	S	R	Q	P	O	N	M	L	K	J	I	H	G	F	E	D	C	B	A	>	@	Z	Y	X	W

APRIL

BIO	1	2	3	4	5	6	7	8	9	10	11	12	13	14	15	16	17	18	19	20	21	22	23	24	25	26	27	28	29	30
1	W	V	U	T	S	R	Q	P	O	N	M	L	K	J	I	H	G	F	E	D	C	B	A	>	@	Z	Y	X	W	V
2	X	W	V	U	T	S	R	Q	P	O	N	M	L	K	J	I	H	G	F	E	D	C	B	A	>	@	Z	Y	X	W
3	Y	X	W	V	U	T	S	R	Q	P	O	N	M	L	K	J	I	H	G	F	E	D	C	B	A	>	@	Z	Y	X
4	Z	Y	X	W	V	U	T	S	R	Q	P	O	N	M	L	K	J	I	H	G	F	E	D	C	B	A	>	@	Z	Y
5	@	Z	Y	X	W	V	U	T	S	R	Q	P	O	N	M	L	K	J	I	H	G	F	E	D	C	B	A	>	@	Z
6	>	@	Z	Y	X	W	V	U	T	S	R	Q	P	O	N	M	L	K	J	I	H	G	F	E	D	C	B	A	>	@
7	A	>	@	Z	Y	X	W	V	U	T	S	R	Q	P	O	N	M	L	K	J	I	H	G	F	E	D	C	B	A	>
8	B	A	>	@	Z	Y	X	W	V	U	T	S	R	Q	P	O	N	M	L	K	J	I	H	G	F	E	D	C	B	A
9	C	B	A	>	@	Z	Y	X	W	V	U	T	S	R	Q	P	O	N	M	L	K	J	I	H	G	F	E	D	C	B
10	D	C	B	A	>	@	Z	Y	X	W	V	U	T	S	R	Q	P	O	N	M	L	K	J	I	H	G	F	E	D	C
11	E	D	C	B	A	>	@	Z	Y	X	W	V	U	T	S	R	Q	P	O	N	M	L	K	J	I	H	G	F	E	D
12	F	E	D	C	B	A	>	@	Z	Y	X	W	V	U	T	S	R	Q	P	O	N	M	L	K	J	I	H	G	F	E
13	G	F	E	D	C	B	A	>	@	Z	Y	X	W	V	U	T	S	R	Q	P	O	N	M	L	K	J	I	H	G	F
14	H	G	F	E	D	C	B	A	>	@	Z	Y	X	W	V	U	T	S	R	Q	P	O	N	M	L	K	J	I	H	G
15	I	H	G	F	E	D	C	B	A	>	@	Z	Y	X	W	V	U	T	S	R	Q	P	O	N	M	L	K	J	I	H
16	J	I	H	G	F	E	D	C	B	A	>	@	Z	Y	X	W	V	U	T	S	R	Q	P	O	N	M	L	K	J	I
17	K	J	I	H	G	F	E	D	C	B	A	>	@	Z	Y	X	W	V	U	T	S	R	Q	P	O	N	M	L	K	J
18	L	K	J	I	H	G	F	E	D	C	B	A	>	@	Z	Y	X	W	V	U	T	S	R	Q	P	O	N	M	L	K
19	M	L	K	J	I	H	G	F	E	D	C	B	A	>	@	Z	Y	X	W	V	U	T	S	R	Q	P	O	N	M	L
20	N	M	L	K	J	I	H	G	F	E	D	C	B	A	>	@	Z	Y	X	W	V	U	T	S	R	Q	P	O	N	M
21	O	N	M	L	K	J	I	H	G	F	E	D	C	B	A	>	@	Z	Y	X	W	V	U	T	S	R	Q	P	O	N
22	P	O	N	M	L	K	J	I	H	G	F	E	D	C	B	A	>	@	Z	Y	X	W	V	U	T	S	R	Q	P	O
23	Q	P	O	N	M	L	K	J	I	H	G	F	E	D	C	B	A	>	@	Z	Y	X	W	V	U	T	S	R	Q	P
24	R	Q	P	O	N	M	L	K	J	I	H	G	F	E	D	C	B	A	>	@	Z	Y	X	W	V	U	T	S	R	Q
25	S	R	Q	P	O	N	M	L	K	J	I	H	G	F	E	D	C	B	A	>	@	Z	Y	X	W	V	U	T	S	R
26	T	S	R	Q	P	O	N	M	L	K	J	I	H	G	F	E	D	C	B	A	>	@	Z	Y	X	W	V	U	T	S
27	U	T	S	R	Q	P	O	N	M	L	K	J	I	H	G	F	E	D	C	B	A	>	@	Z	Y	X	W	V	U	T
28	V	U	T	S	R	Q	P	O	N	M	L	K	J	I	H	G	F	E	D	C	B	A	>	@	Z	Y	X	W	V	U

CHART B

EMOTIONAL

BIO	MAY 1	2	3	4	5	6	7	8	9	10	11	12	13	14	15	16	17	18	19	20	21	22	23	24	25	26	27	28	29	30	31
1	U	T	S	R	Q	P	O	N	M	L	K	J	I	H	G	F	E	D	C	B	A	>	@	Z	Y	X	W	V	U	T	S
2	V	U	T	S	R	Q	P	O	N	M	L	K	J	I	H	G	F	E	D	C	B	A	>	@	Z	Y	X	W	V	U	T
3	W	V	U	T	S	R	Q	P	O	N	M	L	K	J	I	H	G	F	E	D	C	B	A	>	@	Z	Y	X	W	V	U
4	X	W	V	U	T	S	R	Q	P	O	N	M	L	K	J	I	H	G	F	E	D	C	B	A	>	@	Z	Y	X	W	V
5	Y	X	W	V	U	T	S	R	Q	P	O	N	M	L	K	J	I	H	G	F	E	D	C	B	A	>	@	Z	Y	X	W
6	Z	Y	X	W	V	U	T	S	R	Q	P	O	N	M	L	K	J	I	H	G	F	E	D	C	B	A	>	@	Z	Y	X
7	@	Z	Y	X	W	V	U	T	S	R	Q	P	O	N	M	L	K	J	I	H	G	F	E	D	C	B	A	>	@	Z	Y
8	>	@	Z	Y	X	W	V	U	T	S	R	Q	P	O	N	M	L	K	J	I	H	G	F	E	D	C	B	A	>	@	Z
9	A	>	@	Z	Y	X	W	V	U	T	S	R	Q	P	O	N	M	L	K	J	I	H	G	F	E	D	C	B	A	>	@
10	B	A	>	@	Z	Y	X	W	V	U	T	S	R	Q	P	O	N	M	L	K	J	I	H	G	F	E	D	C	B	A	>
11	C	B	A	>	@	Z	Y	X	W	V	U	T	S	R	Q	P	O	N	M	L	K	J	I	H	G	F	E	D	C	B	A
12	D	C	B	A	>	@	Z	Y	X	W	V	U	T	S	R	Q	P	O	N	M	L	K	J	I	H	G	F	E	D	C	B
13	E	D	C	B	A	>	@	Z	Y	X	W	V	U	T	S	R	Q	P	O	N	M	L	K	J	I	H	G	F	E	D	C
14	F	E	D	C	B	A	>	@	Z	Y	X	W	V	U	T	S	R	Q	P	O	N	M	L	K	J	I	H	G	F	E	D
15	G	F	E	D	C	B	A	>	@	Z	Y	X	W	V	U	T	S	R	Q	P	O	N	M	L	K	J	I	H	G	F	E
16	H	G	F	E	D	C	B	A	>	@	Z	Y	X	W	V	U	T	S	R	Q	P	O	N	M	L	K	J	I	H	G	F
17	I	H	G	F	E	D	C	B	A	>	@	Z	Y	X	W	V	U	T	S	R	Q	P	O	N	M	L	K	J	I	H	G
18	J	I	H	G	F	E	D	C	B	A	>	@	Z	Y	X	W	V	U	T	S	R	Q	P	O	N	M	L	K	J	I	H
19	K	J	I	H	G	F	E	D	C	B	A	>	@	Z	Y	X	W	V	U	T	S	R	Q	P	O	N	M	L	K	J	I
20	L	K	J	I	H	G	F	E	D	C	B	A	>	@	Z	Y	X	W	V	U	T	S	R	Q	P	O	N	M	L	K	J
21	M	L	K	J	I	H	G	F	E	D	C	B	A	>	@	Z	Y	X	W	V	U	T	S	R	Q	P	O	N	M	L	K
22	N	M	L	K	J	I	H	G	F	E	D	C	B	A	>	@	Z	Y	X	W	V	U	T	S	R	Q	P	O	N	M	L
23	O	N	M	L	K	J	I	H	G	F	E	D	C	B	A	>	@	Z	Y	X	W	V	U	T	S	R	Q	P	O	N	M
24	P	O	N	M	L	K	J	I	H	G	F	E	D	C	B	A	>	@	Z	Y	X	W	V	U	T	S	R	Q	P	O	N
25	Q	P	O	N	M	L	K	J	I	H	G	F	E	D	C	B	A	>	@	Z	Y	X	W	V	U	T	S	R	Q	P	O
26	R	Q	P	O	N	M	L	K	J	I	H	G	F	E	D	C	B	A	>	@	Z	Y	X	W	V	U	T	S	R	Q	P
27	S	R	Q	P	O	N	M	L	K	J	I	H	G	F	E	D	C	B	A	>	@	Z	Y	X	W	V	U	T	S	R	Q
28	T	S	R	Q	P	O	N	M	L	K	J	I	H	G	F	E	D	C	B	A	>	@	Z	Y	X	W	V	U	T	S	R

JUNE

BIO	1	2	3	4	5	6	7	8	9	10	11	12	13	14	15	16	17	18	19	20	21	22	23	24	25	26	27	28	29	30
1	R	Q	P	O	N	M	L	K	J	I	H	G	F	E	D	C	B	A	>	@	Z	Y	X	W	V	U	T	S	R	Q
2	S	R	Q	P	O	N	M	L	K	J	I	H	G	F	E	D	C	B	A	>	@	Z	Y	X	W	V	U	T	S	R
3	T	S	R	Q	P	O	N	M	L	K	J	I	H	G	F	E	D	C	B	A	>	@	Z	Y	X	W	V	U	T	S
4	U	T	S	R	Q	P	O	N	M	L	K	J	I	H	G	F	E	D	C	B	A	>	@	Z	Y	X	W	V	U	T
5	V	U	T	S	R	Q	P	O	N	M	L	K	J	I	H	G	F	E	D	C	B	A	>	@	Z	Y	X	W	V	U
6	W	V	U	T	S	R	Q	P	O	N	M	L	K	J	I	H	G	F	E	D	C	B	A	>	@	Z	Y	X	W	V
7	X	W	V	U	T	S	R	Q	P	O	N	M	L	K	J	I	H	G	F	E	D	C	B	A	>	@	Z	Y	X	W
8	Y	X	W	V	U	T	S	R	Q	P	O	N	M	L	K	J	I	H	G	F	E	D	C	B	A	>	@	Z	Y	X
9	Z	Y	X	W	V	U	T	S	R	Q	P	O	N	M	L	K	J	I	H	G	F	E	D	C	B	A	>	@	Z	Y
10	@	Z	Y	X	W	V	U	T	S	R	Q	P	O	N	M	L	K	J	I	H	G	F	E	D	C	B	A	>	@	Z
11	>	@	Z	Y	X	W	V	U	T	S	R	Q	P	O	N	M	L	K	J	I	H	G	F	E	D	C	B	A	>	@
12	A	>	@	Z	Y	X	W	V	U	T	S	R	Q	P	O	N	M	L	K	J	I	H	G	F	E	D	C	B	A	>
13	B	A	>	@	Z	Y	X	W	V	U	T	S	R	Q	P	O	N	M	L	K	J	I	H	G	F	E	D	C	B	A
14	C	B	A	>	@	Z	Y	X	W	V	U	T	S	R	Q	P	O	N	M	L	K	J	I	H	G	F	E	D	C	B
15	D	C	B	A	>	@	Z	Y	X	W	V	U	T	S	R	Q	P	O	N	M	L	K	J	I	H	G	F	E	D	C
16	E	D	C	B	A	>	@	Z	Y	X	W	V	U	T	S	R	Q	P	O	N	M	L	K	J	I	H	G	F	E	D
17	F	E	D	C	B	A	>	@	Z	Y	X	W	V	U	T	S	R	Q	P	O	N	M	L	K	J	I	H	G	F	E
18	G	F	E	D	C	B	A	>	@	Z	Y	X	W	V	U	T	S	R	Q	P	O	N	M	L	K	J	I	H	G	F
19	H	G	F	E	D	C	B	A	>	@	Z	Y	X	W	V	U	T	S	R	Q	P	O	N	M	L	K	J	I	H	G
20	I	H	G	F	E	D	C	B	A	>	@	Z	Y	X	W	V	U	T	S	R	Q	P	O	N	M	L	K	J	I	H
21	J	I	H	G	F	E	D	C	B	A	>	@	Z	Y	X	W	V	U	T	S	R	Q	P	O	N	M	L	K	J	I
22	K	J	I	H	G	F	E	D	C	B	A	>	@	Z	Y	X	W	V	U	T	S	R	Q	P	O	N	M	L	K	J
23	L	K	J	I	H	G	F	E	D	C	B	A	>	@	Z	Y	X	W	V	U	T	S	R	Q	P	O	N	M	L	K
24	M	L	K	J	I	H	G	F	E	D	C	B	A	>	@	Z	Y	X	W	V	U	T	S	R	Q	P	O	N	M	L
25	N	M	L	K	J	I	H	G	F	E	D	C	B	A	>	@	Z	Y	X	W	V	U	T	S	R	Q	P	O	N	M
26	O	N	M	L	K	J	I	H	G	F	E	D	C	B	A	>	@	Z	Y	X	W	V	U	T	S	R	Q	P	O	N
27	P	O	N	M	L	K	J	I	H	G	F	E	D	C	B	A	>	@	Z	Y	X	W	V	U	T	S	R	Q	P	O
28	Q	P	O	N	M	L	K	J	I	H	G	F	E	D	C	B	A	>	@	Z	Y	X	W	V	U	T	S	R	Q	P

CHART B

EMOTIONAL

BIO \ JULY	1	2	3	4	5	6	7	8	9	10	11	12	13	14	15	16	17	18	19	20	21	22	23	24	25	26	27	28	29	30	31
1	P	O	N	M	L	K	J	I	H	G	F	E	D	C	B	A	>	@	Z	Y	X	W	V	U	T	S	R	Q	P	O	N
2	Q	P	O	N	M	L	K	J	I	H	G	F	E	D	C	B	A	>	@	Z	Y	X	W	V	U	T	S	R	Q	P	O
3	R	Q	P	O	N	M	L	K	J	I	H	G	F	E	D	C	B	A	>	@	Z	Y	X	W	V	U	T	S	R	Q	P
4	S	R	Q	P	O	N	M	L	K	J	I	H	G	F	E	D	C	B	A	>	@	Z	Y	X	W	V	U	T	S	R	Q
5	T	S	R	Q	P	O	N	M	L	K	J	I	H	G	F	E	D	C	B	A	>	@	Z	Y	X	W	V	U	T	S	R
6	U	T	S	R	Q	P	O	N	M	L	K	J	I	H	G	F	E	D	C	B	A	>	@	Z	Y	X	W	V	U	T	S
7	V	U	T	S	R	Q	P	O	N	M	L	K	J	I	H	G	F	E	D	C	B	A	>	@	Z	Y	X	W	V	U	T
8	W	V	U	T	S	R	Q	P	O	N	M	L	K	J	I	H	G	F	E	D	C	B	A	>	@	Z	Y	X	W	V	U
9	X	W	V	U	T	S	R	Q	P	O	N	M	L	K	J	I	H	G	F	E	D	C	B	A	>	@	Z	Y	X	W	V
10	Y	X	W	V	U	T	S	R	Q	P	O	N	M	L	K	J	I	H	G	F	E	D	C	B	A	>	@	Z	Y	X	W
11	Z	Y	X	W	V	U	T	S	R	Q	P	O	N	M	L	K	J	I	H	G	F	E	D	C	B	A	>	@	Z	Y	X
12	@	Z	Y	X	W	V	U	T	S	R	Q	P	O	N	M	L	K	J	I	H	G	F	E	D	C	B	A	>	@	Z	Y
13	>	@	Z	Y	X	W	V	U	T	S	R	Q	P	O	N	M	L	K	J	I	H	G	F	E	D	C	B	A	>	@	Z
14	A	>	@	Z	Y	X	W	V	U	T	S	R	Q	P	O	N	M	L	K	J	I	H	G	F	E	D	C	B	A	>	@
15	B	A	>	@	Z	Y	X	W	V	U	T	S	R	Q	P	O	N	M	L	K	J	I	H	G	F	E	D	C	B	A	>
16	C	B	A	>	@	Z	Y	X	W	V	U	T	S	R	Q	P	O	N	M	L	K	J	I	H	G	F	E	D	C	B	A
17	D	C	B	A	>	@	Z	Y	X	W	V	U	T	S	R	Q	P	O	N	M	L	K	J	I	H	G	F	E	D	C	B
18	E	D	C	B	A	>	@	Z	Y	X	W	V	U	T	S	R	Q	P	O	N	M	L	K	J	I	H	G	F	E	D	C
19	F	E	D	C	B	A	>	@	Z	Y	X	W	V	U	T	S	R	Q	P	O	N	M	L	K	J	I	H	G	F	E	D
20	G	F	E	D	C	B	A	>	@	Z	Y	X	W	V	U	T	S	R	Q	P	O	N	M	L	K	J	I	H	G	F	E
21	H	G	F	E	D	C	B	A	>	@	Z	Y	X	W	V	U	T	S	R	Q	P	O	N	M	L	K	J	I	H	G	F
22	I	H	G	F	E	D	C	B	A	>	@	Z	Y	X	W	V	U	T	S	R	Q	P	O	N	M	L	K	J	I	H	G
23	J	I	H	G	F	E	D	C	B	A	>	@	Z	Y	X	W	V	U	T	S	R	Q	P	O	N	M	L	K	J	I	H
24	K	J	I	H	G	F	E	D	C	B	A	>	@	Z	Y	X	W	V	U	T	S	R	Q	P	O	N	M	L	K	J	I
25	L	K	J	I	H	G	F	E	D	C	B	A	>	@	Z	Y	X	W	V	U	T	S	R	Q	P	O	N	M	L	K	J
26	M	L	K	J	I	H	G	F	E	D	C	B	A	>	@	Z	Y	X	W	V	U	T	S	R	Q	P	O	N	M	L	K
27	N	M	L	K	J	I	H	G	F	E	D	C	B	A	>	@	Z	Y	X	W	V	U	T	S	R	Q	P	O	N	M	L
28	O	N	M	L	K	J	I	H	G	F	E	D	C	B	A	>	@	Z	Y	X	W	V	U	T	S	R	Q	P	O	N	M

AUGUST

BIO	1	2	3	4	5	6	7	8	9	10	11	12	13	14	15	16	17	18	19	20	21	22	23	24	25	26	27	28	29	30	31
1	M	L	K	J	I	H	G	F	E	D	C	B	A	>	@	Z	Y	X	W	V	U	T	S	R	Q	P	O	N	M	L	K
2	N	M	L	K	J	I	H	G	F	E	D	C	B	A	>	@	Z	Y	X	W	V	U	T	S	R	Q	P	O	N	M	L
3	O	N	M	L	K	J	I	H	G	F	E	D	C	B	A	>	@	Z	Y	X	W	V	U	T	S	R	Q	P	O	N	M
4	P	O	N	M	L	K	J	I	H	G	F	E	D	C	B	A	>	@	Z	Y	X	W	V	U	T	S	R	Q	P	O	N
5	Q	P	O	N	M	L	K	J	I	H	G	F	E	D	C	B	A	>	@	Z	Y	X	W	V	U	T	S	R	Q	P	O
6	R	Q	P	O	N	M	L	K	J	I	H	G	F	E	D	C	B	A	>	@	Z	Y	X	W	V	U	T	S	R	Q	P
7	S	R	Q	P	O	N	M	L	K	J	I	H	G	F	E	D	C	B	A	>	@	Z	Y	X	W	V	U	T	S	R	Q
8	T	S	R	Q	P	O	N	M	L	K	J	I	H	G	F	E	D	C	B	A	>	@	Z	Y	X	W	V	U	T	S	R
9	U	T	S	R	Q	P	O	N	M	L	K	J	I	H	G	F	E	D	C	B	A	>	@	Z	Y	X	W	V	U	T	S
10	V	U	T	S	R	Q	P	O	N	M	L	K	J	I	H	G	F	E	D	C	B	A	>	@	Z	Y	X	W	V	U	T
11	W	V	U	T	S	R	Q	P	O	N	M	L	K	J	I	H	G	F	E	D	C	B	A	>	@	Z	Y	X	W	V	U
12	X	W	V	U	T	S	R	Q	P	O	N	M	L	K	J	I	H	G	F	E	D	C	B	A	>	@	Z	Y	X	W	V
13	Y	X	W	V	U	T	S	R	Q	P	O	N	M	L	K	J	I	H	G	F	E	D	C	B	A	>	@	Z	Y	X	W
14	Z	Y	X	W	V	U	T	S	R	Q	P	O	N	M	L	K	J	I	H	G	F	E	D	C	B	A	>	@	Z	Y	X
15	@	Z	Y	X	W	V	U	T	S	R	Q	P	O	N	M	L	K	J	I	H	G	F	E	D	C	B	A	>	@	Z	Y
16	>	@	Z	Y	X	W	V	U	T	S	R	Q	P	O	N	M	L	K	J	I	H	G	F	E	D	C	B	A	>	@	Z
17	A	>	@	Z	Y	X	W	V	U	T	S	R	Q	P	O	N	M	L	K	J	I	H	G	F	E	D	C	B	A	>	@
18	B	A	>	@	Z	Y	X	W	V	U	T	S	R	Q	P	O	N	M	L	K	J	I	H	G	F	E	D	C	B	A	>
19	C	B	A	>	@	Z	Y	X	W	V	U	T	S	R	Q	P	O	N	M	L	K	J	I	H	G	F	E	D	C	B	A
20	D	C	B	A	>	@	Z	Y	X	W	V	U	T	S	R	Q	P	O	N	M	L	K	J	I	H	G	F	E	D	C	B
21	E	D	C	B	A	>	@	Z	Y	X	W	V	U	T	S	R	Q	P	O	N	M	L	K	J	I	H	G	F	E	D	C
22	F	E	D	C	B	A	>	@	Z	Y	X	W	V	U	T	S	R	Q	P	O	N	M	L	K	J	I	H	G	F	E	D
23	G	F	E	D	C	B	A	>	@	Z	Y	X	W	V	U	T	S	R	Q	P	O	N	M	L	K	J	I	H	G	F	E
24	H	G	F	E	D	C	B	A	>	@	Z	Y	X	W	V	U	T	S	R	Q	P	O	N	M	L	K	J	I	H	G	F
25	I	H	G	F	E	D	C	B	A	>	@	Z	Y	X	W	V	U	T	S	R	Q	P	O	N	M	L	K	J	I	H	G
26	J	I	H	G	F	E	D	C	B	A	>	@	Z	Y	X	W	V	U	T	S	R	Q	P	O	N	M	L	K	J	I	H
27	K	J	I	H	G	F	E	D	C	B	A	>	@	Z	Y	X	W	V	U	T	S	R	Q	P	O	N	M	L	K	J	I
28	L	K	J	I	H	G	F	E	D	C	B	A	>	@	Z	Y	X	W	V	U	T	S	R	Q	P	O	N	M	L	K	J

CHART B

EMOTIONAL

SEPTEMBER

BIO	1	2	3	4	5	6	7	8	9	10	11	12	13	14	15	16	17	18	19	20	21	22	23	24	25	26	27	28	29	30
1	J	I	H	G	F	E	D	C	B	A	>	@	Z	Y	X	W	V	U	T	S	R	Q	P	O	N	M	L	K	J	I
2	K	J	I	H	G	F	E	D	C	B	A	>	@	Z	Y	X	W	V	U	T	S	R	Q	P	O	N	M	L	K	J
3	L	K	J	I	H	G	F	E	D	C	B	A	>	@	Z	Y	X	W	V	U	T	S	R	Q	P	O	N	M	L	K
4	M	L	K	J	I	H	G	F	E	D	C	B	A	>	@	Z	Y	X	W	V	U	T	S	R	Q	P	O	N	M	L
5	N	M	L	K	J	I	H	G	F	E	D	C	B	A	>	@	Z	Y	X	W	V	U	T	S	R	Q	P	O	N	M
6	O	N	M	L	K	J	I	H	G	F	E	D	C	B	A	>	@	Z	Y	X	W	V	U	T	S	R	Q	P	O	N
7	P	O	N	M	L	K	J	I	H	G	F	E	D	C	B	A	>	@	Z	Y	X	W	V	U	T	S	R	Q	P	O
8	Q	P	O	N	M	L	K	J	I	H	G	F	E	D	C	B	A	>	@	Z	Y	X	W	V	U	T	S	R	Q	P
9	R	Q	P	O	N	M	L	K	J	I	H	G	F	E	D	C	B	A	>	@	Z	Y	X	W	V	U	T	S	R	Q
10	S	R	Q	P	O	N	M	L	K	J	I	H	G	F	E	D	C	B	A	>	@	Z	Y	X	W	V	U	T	S	R
11	T	S	R	Q	P	O	N	M	L	K	J	I	H	G	F	E	D	C	B	A	>	@	Z	Y	X	W	V	U	T	S
12	U	T	S	R	Q	P	O	N	M	L	K	J	I	H	G	F	E	D	C	B	A	>	@	Z	Y	X	W	V	U	T
13	V	U	T	S	R	Q	P	O	N	M	L	K	J	I	H	G	F	E	D	C	B	A	>	@	Z	Y	X	W	V	U
14	W	V	U	T	S	R	Q	P	O	N	M	L	K	J	I	H	G	F	E	D	C	B	A	>	@	Z	Y	X	W	V
15	X	W	V	U	T	S	R	Q	P	O	N	M	L	K	J	I	H	G	F	E	D	C	B	A	>	@	Z	Y	X	W
16	Y	X	W	V	U	T	S	R	Q	P	O	N	M	L	K	J	I	H	G	F	E	D	C	B	A	>	@	Z	Y	X
17	Z	Y	X	W	V	U	T	S	R	Q	P	O	N	M	L	K	J	I	H	G	F	E	D	C	B	A	>	@	Z	Y
18	@	Z	Y	X	W	V	U	T	S	R	Q	P	O	N	M	L	K	J	I	H	G	F	E	D	C	B	A	>	@	Z
19	>	@	Z	Y	X	W	V	U	T	S	R	Q	P	O	N	M	L	K	J	I	H	G	F	E	D	C	B	A	>	@
20	A	>	@	Z	Y	X	W	V	U	T	S	R	Q	P	O	N	M	L	K	J	I	H	G	F	E	D	C	B	A	>
21	B	A	>	@	Z	Y	X	W	V	U	T	S	R	Q	P	O	N	M	L	K	J	I	H	G	F	E	D	C	B	A
22	C	B	A	>	@	Z	Y	X	W	V	U	T	S	R	Q	P	O	N	M	L	K	J	I	H	G	F	E	D	C	B
23	D	C	B	A	>	@	Z	Y	X	W	V	U	T	S	R	Q	P	O	N	M	L	K	J	I	H	G	F	E	D	C
24	E	D	C	B	A	>	@	Z	Y	X	W	V	U	T	S	R	Q	P	O	N	M	L	K	J	I	H	G	F	E	D
25	F	E	D	C	B	A	>	@	Z	Y	X	W	V	U	T	S	R	Q	P	O	N	M	L	K	J	I	H	G	F	E
26	G	F	E	D	C	B	A	>	@	Z	Y	X	W	V	U	T	S	R	Q	P	O	N	M	L	K	J	I	H	G	F
27	H	G	F	E	D	C	B	A	>	@	Z	Y	X	W	V	U	T	S	R	Q	P	O	N	M	L	K	J	I	H	G
28	I	H	G	F	E	D	C	B	A	>	@	Z	Y	X	W	V	U	T	S	R	Q	P	O	N	M	L	K	J	I	H

OCTOBER

BIO	1	2	3	4	5	6	7	8	9	10	11	12	13	14	15	16	17	18	19	20	21	22	23	24	25	26	27	28	29	30	31
1	H	G	F	E	D	C	B	A	>	@	Z	Y	X	W	V	U	T	S	R	Q	P	O	N	M	L	K	J	I	H	G	F
2	I	H	G	F	E	D	C	B	A	>	@	Z	Y	X	W	V	U	T	S	R	Q	P	O	N	M	L	K	J	I	H	G
3	J	I	H	G	F	E	D	C	B	A	>	@	Z	Y	X	W	V	U	T	S	R	Q	P	O	N	M	L	K	J	I	H
4	K	J	I	H	G	F	E	D	C	B	A	>	@	Z	Y	X	W	V	U	T	S	R	Q	P	O	N	M	L	K	J	I
5	L	K	J	I	H	G	F	E	D	C	B	A	>	@	Z	Y	X	W	V	U	T	S	R	Q	P	O	N	M	L	K	J
6	M	L	K	J	I	H	G	F	E	D	C	B	A	>	@	Z	Y	X	W	V	U	T	S	R	Q	P	O	N	M	L	K
7	N	M	L	K	J	I	H	G	F	E	D	C	B	A	>	@	Z	Y	X	W	V	U	T	S	R	Q	P	O	N	M	L
8	O	N	M	L	K	J	I	H	G	F	E	D	C	B	A	>	@	Z	Y	X	W	V	U	T	S	R	Q	P	O	N	M
9	P	O	N	M	L	K	J	I	H	G	F	E	D	C	B	A	>	@	Z	Y	X	W	V	U	T	S	R	Q	P	O	N
10	Q	P	O	N	M	L	K	J	I	H	G	F	E	D	C	B	A	>	@	Z	Y	X	W	V	U	T	S	R	Q	P	O
11	R	Q	P	O	N	M	L	K	J	I	H	G	F	E	D	C	B	A	>	@	Z	Y	X	W	V	U	T	S	R	Q	P
12	S	R	Q	P	O	N	M	L	K	J	I	H	G	F	E	D	C	B	A	>	@	Z	Y	X	W	V	U	T	S	R	Q
13	T	S	R	Q	P	O	N	M	L	K	J	I	H	G	F	E	D	C	B	A	>	@	Z	Y	X	W	V	U	T	S	R
14	U	T	S	R	Q	P	O	N	M	L	K	J	I	H	G	F	E	D	C	B	A	>	@	Z	Y	X	W	V	U	T	S
15	V	U	T	S	R	Q	P	O	N	M	L	K	J	I	H	G	F	E	D	C	B	A	>	@	Z	Y	X	W	V	U	T
16	W	V	U	T	S	R	Q	P	O	N	M	L	K	J	I	H	G	F	E	D	C	B	A	>	@	Z	Y	X	W	V	U
17	X	W	V	U	T	S	R	Q	P	O	N	M	L	K	J	I	H	G	F	E	D	C	B	A	>	@	Z	Y	X	W	V
18	Y	X	W	V	U	T	S	R	Q	P	O	N	M	L	K	J	I	H	G	F	E	D	C	B	A	>	@	Z	Y	X	W
19	Z	Y	X	W	V	U	T	S	R	Q	P	O	N	M	L	K	J	I	H	G	F	E	D	C	B	A	>	@	Z	Y	X
20	@	Z	Y	X	W	V	U	T	S	R	Q	P	O	N	M	L	K	J	I	H	G	F	E	D	C	B	A	>	@	Z	Y
21	>	@	Z	Y	X	W	V	U	T	S	R	Q	P	O	N	M	L	K	J	I	H	G	F	E	D	C	B	A	>	@	Z
22	A	>	@	Z	Y	X	W	V	U	T	S	R	Q	P	O	N	M	L	K	J	I	H	G	F	E	D	C	B	A	>	@
23	B	A	>	@	Z	Y	X	W	V	U	T	S	R	Q	P	O	N	M	L	K	J	I	H	G	F	E	D	C	B	A	>
24	C	B	A	>	@	Z	Y	X	W	V	U	T	S	R	Q	P	O	N	M	L	K	J	I	H	G	F	E	D	C	B	A
25	D	C	B	A	>	@	Z	Y	X	W	V	U	T	S	R	Q	P	O	N	M	L	K	J	I	H	G	F	E	D	C	B
26	E	D	C	B	A	>	@	Z	Y	X	W	V	U	T	S	R	Q	P	O	N	M	L	K	J	I	H	G	F	E	D	C
27	F	E	D	C	B	A	>	@	Z	Y	X	W	V	U	T	S	R	Q	P	O	N	M	L	K	J	I	H	G	F	E	D
28	G	F	E	D	C	B	A	>	@	Z	Y	X	W	V	U	T	S	R	Q	P	O	N	M	L	K	J	I	H	G	F	E

CHART B

EMOTIONAL

NOVEMBER

BIO	1	2	3	4	5	6	7	8	9	10	11	12	13	14	15	16	17	18	19	20	21	22	23	24	25	26	27	28	29	30
1	E	D	C	B	A	>	@	Z	Y	X	W	V	U	T	S	R	Q	P	O	N	M	L	K	J	I	H	G	F	E	D
2	F	E	D	C	B	A	>	@	Z	Y	X	W	V	U	T	S	R	Q	P	O	N	M	L	K	J	I	H	G	F	E
3	G	F	E	D	C	B	A	>	@	Z	Y	X	W	V	U	T	S	R	Q	P	O	N	M	L	K	J	I	H	G	F
4	H	G	F	E	D	C	B	A	>	@	Z	Y	X	W	V	U	T	S	R	Q	P	O	N	M	L	K	J	I	H	G
5	I	H	G	F	E	D	C	B	A	>	@	Z	Y	X	W	V	U	T	S	R	Q	P	O	N	M	L	K	J	I	H
6	J	I	H	G	F	E	D	C	B	A	>	@	Z	Y	X	W	V	U	T	S	R	Q	P	O	N	M	L	K	J	I
7	K	J	I	H	G	F	E	D	C	B	A	>	@	Z	Y	X	W	V	U	T	S	R	Q	P	O	N	M	L	K	J
8	L	K	J	I	H	G	F	E	D	C	B	A	>	@	Z	Y	X	W	V	U	T	S	R	Q	P	O	N	M	L	K
9	M	L	K	J	I	H	G	F	E	D	C	B	A	>	@	Z	Y	X	W	V	U	T	S	R	Q	P	O	N	M	L
10	N	M	L	K	J	I	H	G	F	E	D	C	B	A	>	@	Z	Y	X	W	V	U	T	S	R	Q	P	O	N	M
11	O	N	M	L	K	J	I	H	G	F	E	D	C	B	A	>	@	Z	Y	X	W	V	U	T	S	R	Q	P	O	N
12	P	O	N	M	L	K	J	I	H	G	F	E	D	C	B	A	>	@	Z	Y	X	W	V	U	T	S	R	Q	P	O
13	Q	P	O	N	M	L	K	J	I	H	G	F	E	D	C	B	A	>	@	Z	Y	X	W	V	U	T	S	R	Q	P
14	R	Q	P	O	N	M	L	K	J	I	H	G	F	E	D	C	B	A	>	@	Z	Y	X	W	V	U	T	S	R	Q
15	S	R	Q	P	O	N	M	L	K	J	I	H	G	F	E	D	C	B	A	>	@	Z	Y	X	W	V	U	T	S	R
16	T	S	R	Q	P	O	N	M	L	K	J	I	H	G	F	E	D	C	B	A	>	@	Z	Y	X	W	V	U	T	S
17	U	T	S	R	Q	P	O	N	M	L	K	J	I	H	G	F	E	D	C	B	A	>	@	Z	Y	X	W	V	U	T
18	V	U	T	S	R	Q	P	O	N	M	L	K	J	I	H	G	F	E	D	C	B	A	>	@	Z	Y	X	W	V	U
19	W	V	U	T	S	R	Q	P	O	N	M	L	K	J	I	H	G	F	E	D	C	B	A	>	@	Z	Y	X	W	V
20	X	W	V	U	T	S	R	Q	P	O	N	M	L	K	J	I	H	G	F	E	D	C	B	A	>	@	Z	Y	X	W
21	Y	X	W	V	U	T	S	R	Q	P	O	N	M	L	K	J	I	H	G	F	E	D	C	B	A	>	@	Z	Y	X
22	Z	Y	X	W	V	U	T	S	R	Q	P	O	N	M	L	K	J	I	H	G	F	E	D	C	B	A	>	@	Z	Y
23	@	Z	Y	X	W	V	U	T	S	R	Q	P	O	N	M	L	K	J	I	H	G	F	E	D	C	B	A	>	@	Z
24	>	@	Z	Y	X	W	V	U	T	S	R	Q	P	O	N	M	L	K	J	I	H	G	F	E	D	C	B	A	>	@
25	A	>	@	Z	Y	X	W	V	U	T	S	R	Q	P	O	N	M	L	K	J	I	H	G	F	E	D	C	B	A	>
26	B	A	>	@	Z	Y	X	W	V	U	T	S	R	Q	P	O	N	M	L	K	J	I	H	G	F	E	D	C	B	A
27	C	B	A	>	@	Z	Y	X	W	V	U	T	S	R	Q	P	O	N	M	L	K	J	I	H	G	F	E	D	C	B
28	D	C	B	A	>	@	Z	Y	X	W	V	U	T	S	R	Q	P	O	N	M	L	K	J	I	H	G	F	E	D	C

BIO DECEMBER

BIO	1	2	3	4	5	6	7	8	9	10	11	12	13	14	15	16	17	18	19	20	21	22	23	24	25	26	27	28	29	30	31
1	C	B	A	>	@	Z	Y	X	W	V	U	T	S	R	Q	P	O	N	M	L	K	J	I	H	G	F	E	D	C	B	A
2	D	C	B	A	>	@	Z	Y	X	W	V	U	T	S	R	Q	P	O	N	M	L	K	J	I	H	G	F	E	D	C	B
3	E	D	C	B	A	>	@	Z	Y	X	W	V	U	T	S	R	Q	P	O	N	M	L	K	J	I	H	G	F	E	D	C
4	F	E	D	C	B	A	>	@	Z	Y	X	W	V	U	T	S	R	Q	P	O	N	M	L	K	J	I	H	G	F	E	D
5	G	F	E	D	C	B	A	>	@	Z	Y	X	W	V	U	T	S	R	Q	P	O	N	M	L	K	J	I	H	G	F	E
6	H	G	F	E	D	C	B	A	>	@	Z	Y	X	W	V	U	T	S	R	Q	P	O	N	M	L	K	J	I	H	G	F
7	I	H	G	F	E	D	C	B	A	>	@	Z	Y	X	W	V	U	T	S	R	Q	P	O	N	M	L	K	J	I	H	G
8	J	I	H	G	F	E	D	C	B	A	>	@	Z	Y	X	W	V	U	T	S	R	Q	P	O	N	M	L	K	J	I	H
9	K	J	I	H	G	F	E	D	C	B	A	>	@	Z	Y	X	W	V	U	T	S	R	Q	P	O	N	M	L	K	J	I
10	L	K	J	I	H	G	F	E	D	C	B	A	>	@	Z	Y	X	W	V	U	T	S	R	Q	P	O	N	M	L	K	J
11	M	L	K	J	I	H	G	F	E	D	C	B	A	>	@	Z	Y	X	W	V	U	T	S	R	Q	P	O	N	M	L	K
12	N	M	L	K	J	I	H	G	F	E	D	C	B	A	>	@	Z	Y	X	W	V	U	T	S	R	Q	P	O	N	M	L
13	O	N	M	L	K	J	I	H	G	F	E	D	C	B	A	>	@	Z	Y	X	W	V	U	T	S	R	Q	P	O	N	M
14	P	O	N	M	L	K	J	I	H	G	F	E	D	C	B	A	>	@	Z	Y	X	W	V	U	T	S	R	Q	P	O	N
15	Q	P	O	N	M	L	K	J	I	H	G	F	E	D	C	B	A	>	@	Z	Y	X	W	V	U	T	S	R	Q	P	O
16	R	Q	P	O	N	M	L	K	J	I	H	G	F	E	D	C	B	A	>	@	Z	Y	X	W	V	U	T	S	R	Q	P
17	S	R	Q	P	O	N	M	L	K	J	I	H	G	F	E	D	C	B	A	>	@	Z	Y	X	W	V	U	T	S	R	Q
18	T	S	R	Q	P	O	N	M	L	K	J	I	H	G	F	E	D	C	B	A	>	@	Z	Y	X	W	V	U	T	S	R
19	U	T	S	R	Q	P	O	N	M	L	K	J	I	H	G	F	E	D	C	B	A	>	@	Z	Y	X	W	V	U	T	S
20	V	U	T	S	R	Q	P	O	N	M	L	K	J	I	H	G	F	E	D	C	B	A	>	@	Z	Y	X	W	V	U	T
21	W	V	U	T	S	R	Q	P	O	N	M	L	K	J	I	H	G	F	E	D	C	B	A	>	@	Z	Y	X	W	V	U
22	X	W	V	U	T	S	R	Q	P	O	N	M	L	K	J	I	H	G	F	E	D	C	B	A	>	@	Z	Y	X	W	V
23	Y	X	W	V	U	T	S	R	Q	P	O	N	M	L	K	J	I	H	G	F	E	D	C	B	A	>	@	Z	Y	X	W
24	Z	Y	X	W	V	U	T	S	R	Q	P	O	N	M	L	K	J	I	H	G	F	E	D	C	B	A	>	@	Z	Y	X
25	@	Z	Y	X	W	V	U	T	S	R	Q	P	O	N	M	L	K	J	I	H	G	F	E	D	C	B	A	>	@	Z	Y
26	>	@	Z	Y	X	W	V	U	T	S	R	Q	P	O	N	M	L	K	J	I	H	G	F	E	D	C	B	A	>	@	Z
27	A	>	@	Z	Y	X	W	V	U	T	S	R	Q	P	O	N	M	L	K	J	I	H	G	F	E	D	C	B	A	>	@
28	B	A	>	@	Z	Y	X	W	V	U	T	S	R	Q	P	O	N	M	L	K	J	I	H	G	F	E	D	C	B	A	>

CHART B

INTELLECTUAL

JANUARY

BIO	1	2	3	4	5	6	7	8	9	10	11	12	13	14	15	16	17	18	19	20	21	22	23	24	25	26	27	28	29	30	31
1	A	•	&	I	%	#	>	@	Z	Y	X	W	V	U	T	S	R	Q	P	O	N	M	L	K	J	I	H	G	F	E	D
2	B	A	•	&	I	%	#	>	@	Z	Y	X	W	V	U	T	S	R	Q	P	O	N	M	L	K	J	I	H	G	F	E
3	C	B	A	•	&	I	%	#	>	@	Z	Y	X	W	V	U	T	S	R	Q	P	O	N	M	L	K	J	I	H	G	F
4	D	C	B	A	•	&	I	%	#	>	@	Z	Y	X	W	V	U	T	S	R	Q	P	O	N	M	L	K	J	I	H	G
5	E	D	C	B	A	•	&	I	%	#	>	@	Z	Y	X	W	V	U	T	S	R	Q	P	O	N	M	L	K	J	I	H
6	F	E	D	C	B	A	•	&	I	%	#	>	@	Z	Y	X	W	V	U	T	S	R	Q	P	O	N	M	L	K	J	I
7	G	F	E	D	C	B	A	•	&	I	%	#	>	@	Z	Y	X	W	V	U	T	S	R	Q	P	O	N	M	L	K	J
8	H	G	F	E	D	C	B	A	•	&	I	%	#	>	@	Z	Y	X	W	V	U	T	S	R	Q	P	O	N	M	L	K
9	I	H	G	F	E	D	C	B	A	•	&	I	%	#	>	@	Z	Y	X	W	V	U	T	S	R	Q	P	O	N	M	L
10	J	I	H	G	F	E	D	C	B	A	•	&	I	%	#	>	@	Z	Y	X	W	V	U	T	S	R	Q	P	O	N	M
11	K	J	I	H	G	F	E	D	C	B	A	•	&	I	%	#	>	@	Z	Y	X	W	V	U	T	S	R	Q	P	O	N
12	L	K	J	I	H	G	F	E	D	C	B	A	•	&	I	%	#	>	@	Z	Y	X	W	V	U	T	S	R	Q	P	O
13	M	L	K	J	I	H	G	F	E	D	C	B	A	•	&	I	%	#	>	@	Z	Y	X	W	V	U	T	S	R	Q	P
14	N	M	L	K	J	I	H	G	F	E	D	C	B	A	•	&	I	%	#	>	@	Z	Y	X	W	V	U	T	S	R	Q
15	O	N	M	L	K	J	I	H	G	F	E	D	C	B	A	•	&	I	%	#	>	@	Z	Y	X	W	V	U	T	S	R
16	P	O	N	M	L	K	J	I	H	G	F	E	D	C	B	A	•	&	I	%	#	>	@	Z	Y	X	W	V	U	T	S
17	Q	P	O	N	M	L	K	J	I	H	G	F	E	D	C	B	A	•	&	I	%	#	>	@	Z	Y	X	W	V	U	T
18	R	Q	P	O	N	M	L	K	J	I	H	G	F	E	D	C	B	A	•	&	I	%	#	>	@	Z	Y	X	W	V	U
19	S	R	Q	P	O	N	M	L	K	J	I	H	G	F	E	D	C	B	A	•	&	I	%	#	>	@	Z	Y	X	W	V
20	T	S	R	Q	P	O	N	M	L	K	J	I	H	G	F	E	D	C	B	A	•	&	I	%	#	>	@	Z	Y	X	W
21	U	T	S	R	Q	P	O	N	M	L	K	J	I	H	G	F	E	D	C	B	A	•	&	I	%	#	>	@	Z	Y	X
22	V	U	T	S	R	Q	P	O	N	M	L	K	J	I	H	G	F	E	D	C	B	A	•	&	I	%	#	>	@	Z	Y
23	W	V	U	T	S	R	Q	P	O	N	M	L	K	J	I	H	G	F	E	D	C	B	A	•	&	I	%	#	>	@	Z
24	X	W	V	U	T	S	R	Q	P	O	N	M	L	K	J	I	H	G	F	E	D	C	B	A	•	&	I	%	#	>	@
25	Y	X	W	V	U	T	S	R	Q	P	O	N	M	L	K	J	I	H	G	F	E	D	C	B	A	•	&	I	%	#	>
26	Z	Y	X	W	V	U	T	S	R	Q	P	O	N	M	L	K	J	I	H	G	F	E	D	C	B	A	•	&	I	%	#
27	@	Z	Y	X	W	V	U	T	S	R	Q	P	O	N	M	L	K	J	I	H	G	F	E	D	C	B	A	•	&	I	%
28	>	@	Z	Y	X	W	V	U	T	S	R	Q	P	O	N	M	L	K	J	I	H	G	F	E	D	C	B	A	•	&	I
29	#	>	@	Z	Y	X	W	V	U	T	S	R	Q	P	O	N	M	L	K	J	I	H	G	F	E	D	C	B	A	•	&
30	%	#	>	@	Z	Y	X	W	V	U	T	S	R	Q	P	O	N	M	L	K	J	I	H	G	F	E	D	C	B	A	•
31	I	%	#	>	@	Z	Y	X	W	V	U	T	S	R	Q	P	O	N	M	L	K	J	I	H	G	F	E	D	C	B	A
32	&	I	%	#	>	@	Z	Y	X	W	V	U	T	S	R	Q	P	O	N	M	L	K	J	I	H	G	F	E	D	C	B
33	•	&	I	%	#	>	@	Z	Y	X	W	V	U	T	S	R	Q	P	O	N	M	L	K	J	I	H	G	F	E	D	C

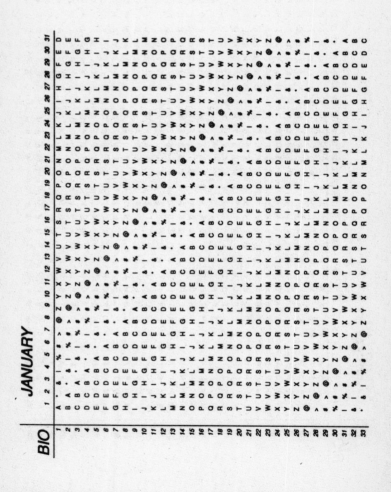

BIO FEBRUARY

BIO	1	2	3	4	5	6	7	8	9	10	11	12	13	14	15	16	17	18	19	20	21	22	23	24	25	26	27	28
1	C	B	A	•	&	I	%	#	>	@	Z	Y	X	W	V	U	T	S	R	Q	P	O	N	M	L	K	J	I
2	D	C	B	A	•	&	I	%	#	>	@	Z	Y	X	W	V	U	T	S	R	Q	P	O	N	M	L	K	J
3	E	D	C	B	A	•	&	I	%	#	>	@	Z	Y	X	W	V	U	T	S	R	Q	P	O	N	M	L	K
4	F	E	D	C	B	A	•	&	I	%	#	>	@	Z	Y	X	W	V	U	T	S	R	Q	P	O	N	M	L
5	G	F	E	D	C	B	A	•	&	I	%	#	>	@	Z	Y	X	W	V	U	T	S	R	Q	P	O	N	M
6	H	G	F	E	D	C	B	A	•	&	I	%	#	>	@	Z	Y	X	W	V	U	T	S	R	Q	P	O	N
7	I	H	G	F	E	D	C	B	A	•	&	I	%	#	>	@	Z	Y	X	W	V	U	T	S	R	Q	P	O
8	J	I	H	G	F	E	D	C	B	A	•	&	I	%	#	>	@	Z	Y	X	W	V	U	T	S	R	Q	P
9	K	J	I	H	G	F	E	D	C	B	A	•	&	I	%	#	>	@	Z	Y	X	W	V	U	T	S	R	Q
10	L	K	J	I	H	G	F	E	D	C	B	A	•	&	I	%	#	>	@	Z	Y	X	W	V	U	T	S	R
11	M	L	K	J	I	H	G	F	E	D	C	B	A	•	&	I	%	#	>	@	Z	Y	X	W	V	U	T	S
12	N	M	L	K	J	I	H	G	F	E	D	C	B	A	•	&	I	%	#	>	@	Z	Y	X	W	V	U	T
13	O	N	M	L	K	J	I	H	G	F	E	D	C	B	A	•	&	I	%	#	>	@	Z	Y	X	W	V	U
14	P	O	N	M	L	K	J	I	H	G	F	E	D	C	B	A	•	&	I	%	#	>	@	Z	Y	X	W	V
15	Q	P	O	N	M	L	K	J	I	H	G	F	E	D	C	B	A	•	&	I	%	#	>	@	Z	Y	X	W
16	R	Q	P	O	N	M	L	K	J	I	H	G	F	E	D	C	B	A	•	&	I	%	#	>	@	Z	Y	X
17	S	R	Q	P	O	N	M	L	K	J	I	H	G	F	E	D	C	B	A	•	&	I	%	#	>	@	Z	Y
18	T	S	R	Q	P	O	N	M	L	K	J	I	H	G	F	E	D	C	B	A	•	&	I	%	#	>	@	Z
19	U	T	S	R	Q	P	O	N	M	L	K	J	I	H	G	F	E	D	C	B	A	•	&	I	%	#	>	@
20	V	U	T	S	R	Q	P	O	N	M	L	K	J	I	H	G	F	E	D	C	B	A	•	&	I	%	#	>
21	W	V	U	T	S	R	Q	P	O	N	M	L	K	J	I	H	G	F	E	D	C	B	A	•	&	I	%	#
22	X	W	V	U	T	S	R	Q	P	O	N	M	L	K	J	I	H	G	F	E	D	C	B	A	•	&	I	%
23	Y	X	W	V	U	T	S	R	Q	P	O	N	M	L	K	J	I	H	G	F	E	D	C	B	A	•	&	I
24	Z	Y	X	W	V	U	T	S	R	Q	P	O	N	M	L	K	J	I	H	G	F	E	D	C	B	A	•	&
25	@	Z	Y	X	W	V	U	T	S	R	Q	P	O	N	M	L	K	J	I	H	G	F	E	D	C	B	A	•
26	>	@	Z	Y	X	W	V	U	T	S	R	Q	P	O	N	M	L	K	J	I	H	G	F	E	D	C	B	A
27	#	>	@	Z	Y	X	W	V	U	T	S	R	Q	P	O	N	M	L	K	J	I	H	G	F	E	D	C	B
28	%	#	>	@	Z	Y	X	W	V	U	T	S	R	Q	P	O	N	M	L	K	J	I	H	G	F	E	D	C
29	I	%	#	>	@	Z	Y	X	W	V	U	T	S	R	Q	P	O	N	M	L	K	J	I	H	G	F	E	D
30	&	I	%	#	>	@	Z	Y	X	W	V	U	T	S	R	Q	P	O	N	M	L	K	J	I	H	G	F	E
31	•	&	I	%	#	>	@	Z	Y	X	W	V	U	T	S	R	Q	P	O	N	M	L	K	J	I	H	G	F
32	A	•	&	I	%	#	>	@	Z	Y	X	W	V	U	T	S	R	Q	P	O	N	M	L	K	J	I	H	G
33	B	A	•	&	I	%	#	>	@	Z	Y	X	W	V	U	T	S	R	Q	P	O	N	M	L	K	J	I	H

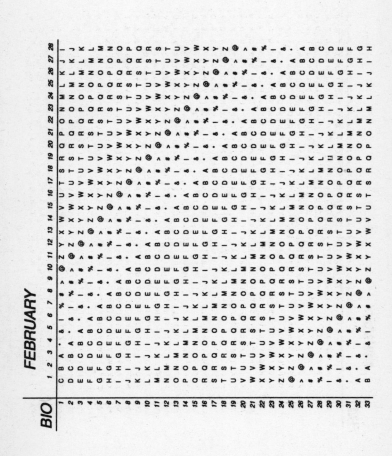

CHART B

INTELLECTUAL

BIO	MARCH 1	2	3	4	5	6	7	8	9	10	11	12	13	14	15	16	17	18	19	20	21	22	23	24	25	26	27	28	29	30	31
1	H	G	F	E	D	C	B	A	•	&	I	%	#	>	@	Z	Y	X	W	V	U	T	S	R	Q	P	O	N	M	L	K
2	I	H	G	F	E	D	C	B	A	•	&	I	%	#	>	@	Z	Y	X	W	V	U	T	S	R	Q	P	O	N	M	L
3	J	I	H	G	F	E	D	C	B	A	•	&	I	%	#	>	@	Z	Y	X	W	V	U	T	S	R	Q	P	O	N	M
4	K	J	I	H	G	F	E	D	C	B	A	•	&	I	%	#	>	@	Z	Y	X	W	V	U	T	S	R	Q	P	O	N
5	L	K	J	I	H	G	F	E	D	C	B	A	•	&	I	%	#	>	@	Z	Y	X	W	V	U	T	S	R	Q	P	O
6	M	L	K	J	I	H	G	F	E	D	C	B	A	•	&	I	%	#	>	@	Z	Y	X	W	V	U	T	S	R	Q	P
7	N	M	L	K	J	I	H	G	F	E	D	C	B	A	•	&	I	%	#	>	@	Z	Y	X	W	V	U	T	S	R	Q
8	O	N	M	L	K	J	I	H	G	F	E	D	C	B	A	•	&	I	%	#	>	@	Z	Y	X	W	V	U	T	S	R
9	P	O	N	M	L	K	J	I	H	G	F	E	D	C	B	A	•	&	I	%	#	>	@	Z	Y	X	W	V	U	T	S
10	Q	P	O	N	M	L	K	J	I	H	G	F	E	D	C	B	A	•	&	I	%	#	>	@	Z	Y	X	W	V	U	T
11	R	Q	P	O	N	M	L	K	J	I	H	G	F	E	D	C	B	A	•	&	I	%	#	>	@	Z	Y	X	W	V	U
12	S	R	Q	P	O	N	M	L	K	J	I	H	G	F	E	D	C	B	A	•	&	I	%	#	>	@	Z	Y	X	W	V
13	T	S	R	Q	P	O	N	M	L	K	J	I	H	G	F	E	D	C	B	A	•	&	I	%	#	>	@	Z	Y	X	W
14	U	T	S	R	Q	P	O	N	M	L	K	J	I	H	G	F	E	D	C	B	A	•	&	I	%	#	>	@	Z	Y	X
15	V	U	T	S	R	Q	P	O	N	M	L	K	J	I	H	G	F	E	D	C	B	A	•	&	I	%	#	>	@	Z	Y
16	W	V	U	T	S	R	Q	P	O	N	M	L	K	J	I	H	G	F	E	D	C	B	A	•	&	I	%	#	>	@	Z
17	X	W	V	U	T	S	R	Q	P	O	N	M	L	K	J	I	H	G	F	E	D	C	B	A	•	&	I	%	#	>	@
18	Y	X	W	V	U	T	S	R	Q	P	O	N	M	L	K	J	I	H	G	F	E	D	C	B	A	•	&	I	%	#	>
19	Z	Y	X	W	V	U	T	S	R	Q	P	O	N	M	L	K	J	I	H	G	F	E	D	C	B	A	•	&	I	%	#
20	@	Z	Y	X	W	V	U	T	S	R	Q	P	O	N	M	L	K	J	I	H	G	F	E	D	C	B	A	•	&	I	%
21	>	@	Z	Y	X	W	V	U	T	S	R	Q	P	O	N	M	L	K	J	I	H	G	F	E	D	C	B	A	•	&	I
22	#	>	@	Z	Y	X	W	V	U	T	S	R	Q	P	O	N	M	L	K	J	I	H	G	F	E	D	C	B	A	•	&
23	%	#	>	@	Z	Y	X	W	V	U	T	S	R	Q	P	O	N	M	L	K	J	I	H	G	F	E	D	C	B	A	•
24	I	%	#	>	@	Z	Y	X	W	V	U	T	S	R	Q	P	O	N	M	L	K	J	I	H	G	F	E	D	C	B	A
25	&	I	%	#	>	@	Z	Y	X	W	V	U	T	S	R	Q	P	O	N	M	L	K	J	I	H	G	F	E	D	C	B
26	•	&	I	%	#	>	@	Z	Y	X	W	V	U	T	S	R	Q	P	O	N	M	L	K	J	I	H	G	F	E	D	C
27	A	•	&	I	%	#	>	@	Z	Y	X	W	V	U	T	S	R	Q	P	O	N	M	L	K	J	I	H	G	F	E	D
28	B	A	•	&	I	%	#	>	@	Z	Y	X	W	V	U	T	S	R	Q	P	O	N	M	L	K	J	I	H	G	F	E
29	C	B	A	•	&	I	%	#	>	@	Z	Y	X	W	V	U	T	S	R	Q	P	O	N	M	L	K	J	I	H	G	F
30	D	C	B	A	•	&	I	%	#	>	@	Z	Y	X	W	V	U	T	S	R	Q	P	O	N	M	L	K	J	I	H	G
31	E	D	C	B	A	•	&	I	%	#	>	@	Z	Y	X	W	V	U	T	S	R	Q	P	O	N	M	L	K	J	I	H
32	F	E	D	C	B	A	•	&	I	%	#	>	@	Z	Y	X	W	V	U	T	S	R	Q	P	O	N	M	L	K	J	I
33	G	F	E	D	C	B	A	•	&	I	%	#	>	@	Z	Y	X	W	V	U	T	S	R	Q	P	O	N	M	L	K	J

BIO APRIL

BIO	1	2	3	4	5	6	7	8	9	10	11	12	13	14	15	16	17	18	19	20	21	22	23	24	25	26	27	28	29	30
1	J	I	H	G	F	E	D	C	B	A	•	&	I	%	#	>	@	Z	Y	X	W	V	U	T	S	R	Q	P	O	N
2	K	J	I	H	G	F	E	D	C	B	A	•	&	I	%	#	>	@	Z	Y	X	W	V	U	T	S	R	Q	P	O
3	L	K	J	I	H	G	F	E	D	C	B	A	•	&	I	%	#	>	@	Z	Y	X	W	V	U	T	S	R	Q	P
4	M	L	K	J	I	H	G	F	E	D	C	B	A	•	&	I	%	#	>	@	Z	Y	X	W	V	U	T	S	R	Q
5	N	M	L	K	J	I	H	G	F	E	D	C	B	A	•	&	I	%	#	>	@	Z	Y	X	W	V	U	T	S	R
6	O	N	M	L	K	J	I	H	G	F	E	D	C	B	A	•	&	I	%	#	>	@	Z	Y	X	W	V	U	T	S
7	P	O	N	M	L	K	J	I	H	G	F	E	D	C	B	A	•	&	I	%	#	>	@	Z	Y	X	W	V	U	T
8	Q	P	O	N	M	L	K	J	I	H	G	F	E	D	C	B	A	•	&	I	%	#	>	@	Z	Y	X	W	V	U
9	R	Q	P	O	N	M	L	K	J	I	H	G	F	E	D	C	B	A	•	&	I	%	#	>	@	Z	Y	X	W	V
10	S	R	Q	P	O	N	M	L	K	J	I	H	G	F	E	D	C	B	A	•	&	I	%	#	>	@	Z	Y	X	W
11	T	S	R	Q	P	O	N	M	L	K	J	I	H	G	F	E	D	C	B	A	•	&	I	%	#	>	@	Z	Y	X
12	U	T	S	R	Q	P	O	N	M	L	K	J	I	H	G	F	E	D	C	B	A	•	&	I	%	#	>	@	Z	Y
13	V	U	T	S	R	Q	P	O	N	M	L	K	J	I	H	G	F	E	D	C	B	A	•	&	I	%	#	>	@	Z
14	W	V	U	T	S	R	Q	P	O	N	M	L	K	J	I	H	G	F	E	D	C	B	A	•	&	I	%	#	>	@
15	X	W	V	U	T	S	R	Q	P	O	N	M	L	K	J	I	H	G	F	E	D	C	B	A	•	&	I	%	#	>
16	Y	X	W	V	U	T	S	R	Q	P	O	N	M	L	K	J	I	H	G	F	E	D	C	B	A	•	&	I	%	#
17	Z	Y	X	W	V	U	T	S	R	Q	P	O	N	M	L	K	J	I	H	G	F	E	D	C	B	A	•	&	I	%
18	@	Z	Y	X	W	V	U	T	S	R	Q	P	O	N	M	L	K	J	I	H	G	F	E	D	C	B	A	•	&	I
19	>	@	Z	Y	X	W	V	U	T	S	R	Q	P	O	N	M	L	K	J	I	H	G	F	E	D	C	B	A	•	&
20	#	>	@	Z	Y	X	W	V	U	T	S	R	Q	P	O	N	M	L	K	J	I	H	G	F	E	D	C	B	A	•
21	%	#	>	@	Z	Y	X	W	V	U	T	S	R	Q	P	O	N	M	L	K	J	I	H	G	F	E	D	C	B	A
22	I	%	#	>	@	Z	Y	X	W	V	U	T	S	R	Q	P	O	N	M	L	K	J	I	H	G	F	E	D	C	B
23	&	I	%	#	>	@	Z	Y	X	W	V	U	T	S	R	Q	P	O	N	M	L	K	J	I	H	G	F	E	D	C
24	•	&	I	%	#	>	@	Z	Y	X	W	V	U	T	S	R	Q	P	O	N	M	L	K	J	I	H	G	F	E	D
25	A	•	&	I	%	#	>	@	Z	Y	X	W	V	U	T	S	R	Q	P	O	N	M	L	K	J	I	H	G	F	E
26	B	A	•	&	I	%	#	>	@	Z	Y	X	W	V	U	T	S	R	Q	P	O	N	M	L	K	J	I	H	G	F
27	C	B	A	•	&	I	%	#	>	@	Z	Y	X	W	V	U	T	S	R	Q	P	O	N	M	L	K	J	I	H	G
28	D	C	B	A	•	&	I	%	#	>	@	Z	Y	X	W	V	U	T	S	R	Q	P	O	N	M	L	K	J	I	H
29	E	D	C	B	A	•	&	I	%	#	>	@	Z	Y	X	W	V	U	T	S	R	Q	P	O	N	M	L	K	J	I
30	F	E	D	C	B	A	•	&	I	%	#	>	@	Z	Y	X	W	V	U	T	S	R	Q	P	O	N	M	L	K	J
31	G	F	E	D	C	B	A	•	&	I	%	#	>	@	Z	Y	X	W	V	U	T	S	R	Q	P	O	N	M	L	K
32	H	G	F	E	D	C	B	A	•	&	I	%	#	>	@	Z	Y	X	W	V	U	T	S	R	Q	P	O	N	M	L
33	I	H	G	F	E	D	C	B	A	•	&	I	%	#	>	@	Z	Y	X	W	V	U	T	S	R	Q	P	O	N	M

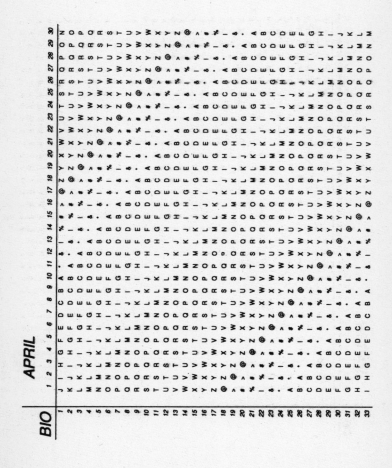

CHART B

INTELLECTUAL

BIO	1	2	3	4	5	6	7	8	9	10	11	12	13	14	15	16	17	18	19	20	21	22	23	24	25	26	27	28	29	30	31
1	M	L	K	J	I	H	G	F	E	D	C	B	A	·	&	I	%	#	>	@	Z	Y	X	W	V	U	T	S	R	Q	P
2	N	M	L	K	J	I	H	G	F	E	D	C	B	A	·	&	I	%	#	>	@	Z	Y	X	W	V	U	T	S	R	Q
3	O	N	M	L	K	J	I	H	G	F	E	D	C	B	A	·	&	I	%	#	>	@	Z	Y	X	W	V	U	T	S	R
4	P	O	N	M	L	K	J	I	H	G	F	E	D	C	B	A	·	&	I	%	#	>	@	Z	Y	X	W	V	U	T	S
5	Q	P	O	N	M	L	K	J	I	H	G	F	E	D	C	B	A	·	&	I	%	#	>	@	Z	Y	X	W	V	U	T
6	R	Q	P	O	N	M	L	K	J	I	H	G	F	E	D	C	B	A	·	&	I	%	#	>	@	Z	Y	X	W	V	U
7	S	R	Q	P	O	N	M	L	K	J	I	H	G	F	E	D	C	B	A	·	&	I	%	#	>	@	Z	Y	X	W	V
8	T	S	R	Q	P	O	N	M	L	K	J	I	H	G	F	E	D	C	B	A	·	&	I	%	#	>	@	Z	Y	X	W
9	U	T	S	R	Q	P	O	N	M	L	K	J	I	H	G	F	E	D	C	B	A	·	&	I	%	#	>	@	Z	Y	X
10	V	U	T	S	R	Q	P	O	N	M	L	K	J	I	H	G	F	E	D	C	B	A	·	&	I	%	#	>	@	Z	Y
11	W	V	U	T	S	R	Q	P	O	N	M	L	K	J	I	H	G	F	E	D	C	B	A	·	&	I	%	#	>	@	Z
12	X	W	V	U	T	S	R	Q	P	O	N	M	L	K	J	I	H	G	F	E	D	C	B	A	·	&	I	%	#	>	@
13	Y	X	W	V	U	T	S	R	Q	P	O	N	M	L	K	J	I	H	G	F	E	D	C	B	A	·	&	I	%	#	>
14	Z	Y	X	W	V	U	T	S	R	Q	P	O	N	M	L	K	J	I	H	G	F	E	D	C	B	A	·	&	I	%	#
15	@	Z	Y	X	W	V	U	T	S	R	Q	P	O	N	M	L	K	J	I	H	G	F	E	D	C	B	A	·	&	I	%
16	>	@	Z	Y	X	W	V	U	T	S	R	Q	P	O	N	M	L	K	J	I	H	G	F	E	D	C	B	A	·	&	I
17	#	>	@	Z	Y	X	W	V	U	T	S	R	Q	P	O	N	M	L	K	J	I	H	G	F	E	D	C	B	A	·	&
18	%	#	>	@	Z	Y	X	W	V	U	T	S	R	Q	P	O	N	M	L	K	J	I	H	G	F	E	D	C	B	A	·
19	I	%	#	>	@	Z	Y	X	W	V	U	T	S	R	Q	P	O	N	M	L	K	J	I	H	G	F	E	D	C	B	A
20	&	I	%	#	>	@	Z	Y	X	W	V	U	T	S	R	Q	P	O	N	M	L	K	J	I	H	G	F	E	D	C	B
21	·	&	I	%	#	>	@	Z	Y	X	W	V	U	T	S	R	Q	P	O	N	M	L	K	J	I	H	G	F	E	D	C
22	A	·	&	I	%	#	>	@	Z	Y	X	W	V	U	T	S	R	Q	P	O	N	M	L	K	J	I	H	G	F	E	D
23	B	A	·	&	I	%	#	>	@	Z	Y	X	W	V	U	T	S	R	Q	P	O	N	M	L	K	J	I	H	G	F	E
24	C	B	A	·	&	I	%	#	>	@	Z	Y	X	W	V	U	T	S	R	Q	P	O	N	M	L	K	J	I	H	G	F
25	D	C	B	A	·	&	I	%	#	>	@	Z	Y	X	W	V	U	T	S	R	Q	P	O	N	M	L	K	J	I	H	G
26	E	D	C	B	A	·	&	I	%	#	>	@	Z	Y	X	W	V	U	T	S	R	Q	P	O	N	M	L	K	J	I	H
27	F	E	D	C	B	A	·	&	I	%	#	>	@	Z	Y	X	W	V	U	T	S	R	Q	P	O	N	M	L	K	J	I
28	G	F	E	D	C	B	A	·	&	I	%	#	>	@	Z	Y	X	W	V	U	T	S	R	Q	P	O	N	M	L	K	J
29	H	G	F	E	D	C	B	A	·	&	I	%	#	>	@	Z	Y	X	W	V	U	T	S	R	Q	P	O	N	M	L	K
30	I	H	G	F	E	D	C	B	A	·	&	I	%	#	>	@	Z	Y	X	W	V	U	T	S	R	Q	P	O	N	M	L
31	J	I	H	G	F	E	D	C	B	A	·	&	I	%	#	>	@	Z	Y	X	W	V	U	T	S	R	Q	P	O	N	M
32	K	J	I	H	G	F	E	D	C	B	A	·	&	I	%	#	>	@	Z	Y	X	W	V	U	T	S	R	Q	P	O	N
33	L	K	J	I	H	G	F	E	D	C	B	A	·	&	I	%	#	>	@	Z	Y	X	W	V	U	T	S	R	Q	P	O

Column heading: MAY

JUNE

BIO	1	2	3	4	5	6	7	8	9	10	11	12	13	14	15	16	17	18	19	20	21	22	23	24	25	26	27	28	29	30
1	O	N	M	L	K	J	I	H	G	F	E	D	C	B	A	•	&	I	%	#	>	@	Z	Y	X	W	V	U	T	S
2	P	O	N	M	L	K	J	I	H	G	F	E	D	C	B	A	•	&	I	%	#	>	@	Z	Y	X	W	V	U	T
3	Q	P	O	N	M	L	K	J	I	H	G	F	E	D	C	B	A	•	&	I	%	#	>	@	Z	Y	X	W	V	U
4	R	Q	P	O	N	M	L	K	J	I	H	G	F	E	D	C	B	A	•	&	I	%	#	>	@	Z	Y	X	W	V
5	S	R	Q	P	O	N	M	L	K	J	I	H	G	F	E	D	C	B	A	•	&	I	%	#	>	@	Z	Y	X	W
6	T	S	R	Q	P	O	N	M	L	K	J	I	H	G	F	E	D	C	B	A	•	&	I	%	#	>	@	Z	Y	X
7	U	T	S	R	Q	P	O	N	M	L	K	J	I	H	G	F	E	D	C	B	A	•	&	I	%	#	>	@	Z	Y
8	V	U	T	S	R	Q	P	O	N	M	L	K	J	I	H	G	F	E	D	C	B	A	•	&	I	%	#	>	@	Z
9	W	V	U	T	S	R	Q	P	O	N	M	L	K	J	I	H	G	F	E	D	C	B	A	•	&	I	%	#	>	@
10	X	W	V	U	T	S	R	Q	P	O	N	M	L	K	J	I	H	G	F	E	D	C	B	A	•	&	I	%	#	>
11	Y	X	W	V	U	T	S	R	Q	P	O	N	M	L	K	J	I	H	G	F	E	D	C	B	A	•	&	I	%	#
12	Z	Y	X	W	V	U	T	S	R	Q	P	O	N	M	L	K	J	I	H	G	F	E	D	C	B	A	•	&	I	%
13	@	Z	Y	X	W	V	U	T	S	R	Q	P	O	N	M	L	K	J	I	H	G	F	E	D	C	B	A	•	&	I
14	>	@	Z	Y	X	W	V	U	T	S	R	Q	P	O	N	M	L	K	J	I	H	G	F	E	D	C	B	A	•	&
15	#	>	@	Z	Y	X	W	V	U	T	S	R	Q	P	O	N	M	L	K	J	I	H	G	F	E	D	C	B	A	•
16	%	#	>	@	Z	Y	X	W	V	U	T	S	R	Q	P	O	N	M	L	K	J	I	H	G	F	E	D	C	B	A
17	I	%	#	>	@	Z	Y	X	W	V	U	T	S	R	Q	P	O	N	M	L	K	J	I	H	G	F	E	D	C	B
18	&	I	%	#	>	@	Z	Y	X	W	V	U	T	S	R	Q	P	O	N	M	L	K	J	I	H	G	F	E	D	C
19	•	&	I	%	#	>	@	Z	Y	X	W	V	U	T	S	R	Q	P	O	N	M	L	K	J	I	H	G	F	E	D
20	A	•	&	I	%	#	>	@	Z	Y	X	W	V	U	T	S	R	Q	P	O	N	M	L	K	J	I	H	G	F	E
21	B	A	•	&	I	%	#	>	@	Z	Y	X	W	V	U	T	S	R	Q	P	O	N	M	L	K	J	I	H	G	F
22	C	B	A	•	&	I	%	#	>	@	Z	Y	X	W	V	U	T	S	R	Q	P	O	N	M	L	K	J	I	H	G
23	D	C	B	A	•	&	I	%	#	>	@	Z	Y	X	W	V	U	T	S	R	Q	P	O	N	M	L	K	J	I	H
24	E	D	C	B	A	•	&	I	%	#	>	@	Z	Y	X	W	V	U	T	S	R	Q	P	O	N	M	L	K	J	I
25	F	E	D	C	B	A	•	&	I	%	#	>	@	Z	Y	X	W	V	U	T	S	R	Q	P	O	N	M	L	K	J
26	G	F	E	D	C	B	A	•	&	I	%	#	>	@	Z	Y	X	W	V	U	T	S	R	Q	P	O	N	M	L	K
27	H	G	F	E	D	C	B	A	•	&	I	%	#	>	@	Z	Y	X	W	V	U	T	S	R	Q	P	O	N	M	L
28	I	H	G	F	E	D	C	B	A	•	&	I	%	#	>	@	Z	Y	X	W	V	U	T	S	R	Q	P	O	N	M
29	J	I	H	G	F	E	D	C	B	A	•	&	I	%	#	>	@	Z	Y	X	W	V	U	T	S	R	Q	P	O	N
30	K	J	I	H	G	F	E	D	C	B	A	•	&	I	%	#	>	@	Z	Y	X	W	V	U	T	S	R	Q	P	O
31	L	K	J	I	H	G	F	E	D	C	B	A	•	&	I	%	#	>	@	Z	Y	X	W	V	U	T	S	R	Q	P
32	M	L	K	J	I	H	G	F	E	D	C	B	A	•	&	I	%	#	>	@	Z	Y	X	W	V	U	T	S	R	Q
33	N	M	L	K	J	I	H	G	F	E	D	C	B	A	•	&	I	%	#	>	@	Z	Y	X	W	V	U	T	S	R

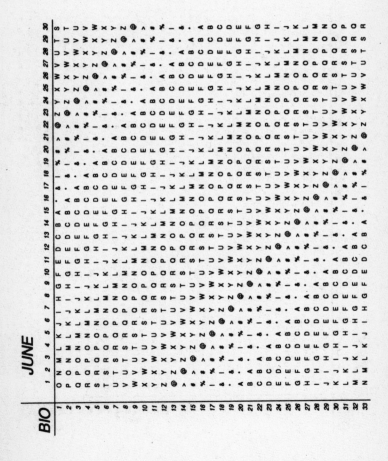

CHART B

INTELLECTUAL

JULY

BIO	1	2	3	4	5	6	7	8	9	10	11	12	13	14	15	16	17	18	19	20	21	22	23	24	25	26	27	28	29	30	31
1	R	Q	P	O	N	M	L	K	J	I	H	G	F	E	D	C	B	A	•	&	|	%	#	>	@	Z	Y	X	W	V	U
2	S	R	Q	P	O	N	M	L	K	J	I	H	G	F	E	D	C	B	A	•	&	|	%	#	>	@	Z	Y	X	W	V
3	T	S	R	Q	P	O	N	M	L	K	J	I	H	G	F	E	D	C	B	A	•	&	|	%	#	>	@	Z	Y	X	W
4	U	T	S	R	Q	P	O	N	M	L	K	J	I	H	G	F	E	D	C	B	A	•	&	|	%	#	>	@	Z	Y	X
5	V	U	T	S	R	Q	P	O	N	M	L	K	J	I	H	G	F	E	D	C	B	A	•	&	|	%	#	>	@	Z	Y
6	W	V	U	T	S	R	Q	P	O	N	M	L	K	J	I	H	G	F	E	D	C	B	A	•	&	|	%	#	>	@	Z
7	X	W	V	U	T	S	R	Q	P	O	N	M	L	K	J	I	H	G	F	E	D	C	B	A	•	&	|	%	#	>	@
8	Y	X	W	V	U	T	S	R	Q	P	O	N	M	L	K	J	I	H	G	F	E	D	C	B	A	•	&	|	%	#	>
9	Z	Y	X	W	V	U	T	S	R	Q	P	O	N	M	L	K	J	I	H	G	F	E	D	C	B	A	•	&	|	%	#
10	@	Z	Y	X	W	V	U	T	S	R	Q	P	O	N	M	L	K	J	I	H	G	F	E	D	C	B	A	•	&	|	%
11	>	@	Z	Y	X	W	V	U	T	S	R	Q	P	O	N	M	L	K	J	I	H	G	F	E	D	C	B	A	•	&	|
12	#	>	@	Z	Y	X	W	V	U	T	S	R	Q	P	O	N	M	L	K	J	I	H	G	F	E	D	C	B	A	•	&
13	%	#	>	@	Z	Y	X	W	V	U	T	S	R	Q	P	O	N	M	L	K	J	I	H	G	F	E	D	C	B	A	•
14	|	%	#	>	@	Z	Y	X	W	V	U	T	S	R	Q	P	O	N	M	L	K	J	I	H	G	F	E	D	C	B	A
15	&	|	%	#	>	@	Z	Y	X	W	V	U	T	S	R	Q	P	O	N	M	L	K	J	I	H	G	F	E	D	C	B
16	•	&	|	%	#	>	@	Z	Y	X	W	V	U	T	S	R	Q	P	O	N	M	L	K	J	I	H	G	F	E	D	C
17	A	•	&	|	%	#	>	@	Z	Y	X	W	V	U	T	S	R	Q	P	O	N	M	L	K	J	I	H	G	F	E	D
18	B	A	•	&	|	%	#	>	@	Z	Y	X	W	V	U	T	S	R	Q	P	O	N	M	L	K	J	I	H	G	F	E
19	C	B	A	•	&	|	%	#	>	@	Z	Y	X	W	V	U	T	S	R	Q	P	O	N	M	L	K	J	I	H	G	F
20	D	C	B	A	•	&	|	%	#	>	@	Z	Y	X	W	V	U	T	S	R	Q	P	O	N	M	L	K	J	I	H	G
21	E	D	C	B	A	•	&	|	%	#	>	@	Z	Y	X	W	V	U	T	S	R	Q	P	O	N	M	L	K	J	I	H
22	F	E	D	C	B	A	•	&	|	%	#	>	@	Z	Y	X	W	V	U	T	S	R	Q	P	O	N	M	L	K	J	I
23	G	F	E	D	C	B	A	•	&	|	%	#	>	@	Z	Y	X	W	V	U	T	S	R	Q	P	O	N	M	L	K	J
24	H	G	F	E	D	C	B	A	•	&	|	%	#	>	@	Z	Y	X	W	V	U	T	S	R	Q	P	O	N	M	L	K
25	I	H	G	F	E	D	C	B	A	•	&	|	%	#	>	@	Z	Y	X	W	V	U	T	S	R	Q	P	O	N	M	L
26	J	I	H	G	F	E	D	C	B	A	•	&	|	%	#	>	@	Z	Y	X	W	V	U	T	S	R	Q	P	O	N	M
27	K	J	I	H	G	F	E	D	C	B	A	•	&	|	%	#	>	@	Z	Y	X	W	V	U	T	S	R	Q	P	O	N
28	L	K	J	I	H	G	F	E	D	C	B	A	•	&	|	%	#	>	@	Z	Y	X	W	V	U	T	S	R	Q	P	O
29	M	L	K	J	I	H	G	F	E	D	C	B	A	•	&	|	%	#	>	@	Z	Y	X	W	V	U	T	S	R	Q	P
30	N	M	L	K	J	I	H	G	F	E	D	C	B	A	•	&	|	%	#	>	@	Z	Y	X	W	V	U	T	S	R	Q
31	O	N	M	L	K	J	I	H	G	F	E	D	C	B	A	•	&	|	%	#	>	@	Z	Y	X	W	V	U	T	S	R
32	P	O	N	M	L	K	J	I	H	G	F	E	D	C	B	A	•	&	|	%	#	>	@	Z	Y	X	W	V	U	T	S
33	Q	P	O	N	M	L	K	J	I	H	G	F	E	D	C	B	A	•	&	|	%	#	>	@	Z	Y	X	W	V	U	T

BIO AUGUST

BIO	1	2	3	4	5	6	7	8	9	10	11	12	13	14	15	16	17	18	19	20	21	22	23	24	25	26	27	28	29	30	31
1	T	S	R	Q	P	O	N	M	L	K	J	I	H	G	F	E	D	C	B	A	•	&	I	%	#	>	@	Z	Y	X	W
2	U	T	S	R	Q	P	O	N	M	L	K	J	I	H	G	F	E	D	C	B	A	•	&	I	%	#	>	@	Z	Y	X
3	V	U	T	S	R	Q	P	O	N	M	L	K	J	I	H	G	F	E	D	C	B	A	•	&	I	%	#	>	@	Z	Y
4	W	V	U	T	S	R	Q	P	O	N	M	L	K	J	I	H	G	F	E	D	C	B	A	•	&	I	%	#	>	@	Z
5	X	W	V	U	T	S	R	Q	P	O	N	M	L	K	J	I	H	G	F	E	D	C	B	A	•	&	I	%	#	>	@
6	Y	X	W	V	U	T	S	R	Q	P	O	N	M	L	K	J	I	H	G	F	E	D	C	B	A	•	&	I	%	#	>
7	Z	Y	X	W	V	U	T	S	R	Q	P	O	N	M	L	K	J	I	H	G	F	E	D	C	B	A	•	&	I	%	#
8	@	Z	Y	X	W	V	U	T	S	R	Q	P	O	N	M	L	K	J	I	H	G	F	E	D	C	B	A	•	&	I	%
9	>	@	Z	Y	X	W	V	U	T	S	R	Q	P	O	N	M	L	K	J	I	H	G	F	E	D	C	B	A	•	&	I
10	#	>	@	Z	Y	X	W	V	U	T	S	R	Q	P	O	N	M	L	K	J	I	H	G	F	E	D	C	B	A	•	&
11	%	#	>	@	Z	Y	X	W	V	U	T	S	R	Q	P	O	N	M	L	K	J	I	H	G	F	E	D	C	B	A	•
12	I	%	#	>	@	Z	Y	X	W	V	U	T	S	R	Q	P	O	N	M	L	K	J	I	H	G	F	E	D	C	B	A
13	&	I	%	#	>	@	Z	Y	X	W	V	U	T	S	R	Q	P	O	N	M	L	K	J	I	H	G	F	E	D	C	B
14	•	&	I	%	#	>	@	Z	Y	X	W	V	U	T	S	R	Q	P	O	N	M	L	K	J	I	H	G	F	E	D	C
15	A	•	&	I	%	#	>	@	Z	Y	X	W	V	U	T	S	R	Q	P	O	N	M	L	K	J	I	H	G	F	E	D
16	B	A	•	&	I	%	#	>	@	Z	Y	X	W	V	U	T	S	R	Q	P	O	N	M	L	K	J	I	H	G	F	E
17	C	B	A	•	&	I	%	#	>	@	Z	Y	X	W	V	U	T	S	R	Q	P	O	N	M	L	K	J	I	H	G	F
18	D	C	B	A	•	&	I	%	#	>	@	Z	Y	X	W	V	U	T	S	R	Q	P	O	N	M	L	K	J	I	H	G
19	E	D	C	B	A	•	&	I	%	#	>	@	Z	Y	X	W	V	U	T	S	R	Q	P	O	N	M	L	K	J	I	H
20	F	E	D	C	B	A	•	&	I	%	#	>	@	Z	Y	X	W	V	U	T	S	R	Q	P	O	N	M	L	K	J	I
21	G	F	E	D	C	B	A	•	&	I	%	#	>	@	Z	Y	X	W	V	U	T	S	R	Q	P	O	N	M	L	K	J
22	H	G	F	E	D	C	B	A	•	&	I	%	#	>	@	Z	Y	X	W	V	U	T	S	R	Q	P	O	N	M	L	K
23	I	H	G	F	E	D	C	B	A	•	&	I	%	#	>	@	Z	Y	X	W	V	U	T	S	R	Q	P	O	N	M	L
24	J	I	H	G	F	E	D	C	B	A	•	&	I	%	#	>	@	Z	Y	X	W	V	U	T	S	R	Q	P	O	N	M
25	K	J	I	H	G	F	E	D	C	B	A	•	&	I	%	#	>	@	Z	Y	X	W	V	U	T	S	R	Q	P	O	N
26	L	K	J	I	H	G	F	E	D	C	B	A	•	&	I	%	#	>	@	Z	Y	X	W	V	U	T	S	R	Q	P	O
27	M	L	K	J	I	H	G	F	E	D	C	B	A	•	&	I	%	#	>	@	Z	Y	X	W	V	U	T	S	R	Q	P
28	N	M	L	K	J	I	H	G	F	E	D	C	B	A	•	&	I	%	#	>	@	Z	Y	X	W	V	U	T	S	R	Q
29	O	N	M	L	K	J	I	H	G	F	E	D	C	B	A	•	&	I	%	#	>	@	Z	Y	X	W	V	U	T	S	R
30	P	O	N	M	L	K	J	I	H	G	F	E	D	C	B	A	•	&	I	%	#	>	@	Z	Y	X	W	V	U	T	S
31	Q	P	O	N	M	L	K	J	I	H	G	F	E	D	C	B	A	•	&	I	%	#	>	@	Z	Y	X	W	V	U	T
32	R	Q	P	O	N	M	L	K	J	I	H	G	F	E	D	C	B	A	•	&	I	%	#	>	@	Z	Y	X	W	V	U
33	S	R	Q	P	O	N	M	L	K	J	I	H	G	F	E	D	C	B	A	•	&	I	%	#	>	@	Z	Y	X	W	V

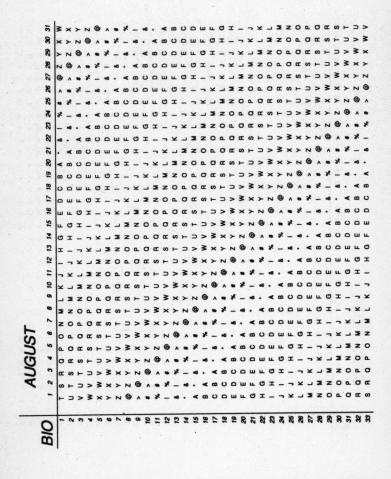

CHART B

INTELLECTUAL

SEPTEMBER

BIO	1	2	3	4	5	6	7	8	9	10	11	12	13	14	15	16	17	18	19	20	21	22	23	24	25	26	27	28	29	30
1	V	U	T	S	R	Q	P	O	N	M	L	K	J	I	H	G	F	E	D	C	B	A	·	&	I	%	#	>	@	Z
2	W	V	U	T	S	R	Q	P	O	N	M	L	K	J	I	H	G	F	E	D	C	B	A	·	&	I	%	#	>	@
3	X	W	V	U	T	S	R	Q	P	O	N	M	L	K	J	I	H	G	F	E	D	C	B	A	·	&	I	%	#	>
4	Y	X	W	V	U	T	S	R	Q	P	O	N	M	L	K	J	I	H	G	F	E	D	C	B	A	·	&	I	%	#
5	Z	Y	X	W	V	U	T	S	R	Q	P	O	N	M	L	K	J	I	H	G	F	E	D	C	B	A	·	&	I	%
6	@	Z	Y	X	W	V	U	T	S	R	Q	P	O	N	M	L	K	J	I	H	G	F	E	D	C	B	A	·	&	I
7	>	@	Z	Y	X	W	V	U	T	S	R	Q	P	O	N	M	L	K	J	I	H	G	F	E	D	C	B	A	·	&
8	#	>	@	Z	Y	X	W	V	U	T	S	R	Q	P	O	N	M	L	K	J	I	H	G	F	E	D	C	B	A	·
9	%	#	>	@	Z	Y	X	W	V	U	T	S	R	Q	P	O	N	M	L	K	J	I	H	G	F	E	D	C	B	A
10	I	%	#	>	@	Z	Y	X	W	V	U	T	S	R	Q	P	O	N	M	L	K	J	I	H	G	F	E	D	C	B
11	&	I	%	#	>	@	Z	Y	X	W	V	U	T	S	R	Q	P	O	N	M	L	K	J	I	H	G	F	E	D	C
12	·	&	I	%	#	>	@	Z	Y	X	W	V	U	T	S	R	Q	P	O	N	M	L	K	J	I	H	G	F	E	D
13	A	·	&	I	%	#	>	@	Z	Y	X	W	V	U	T	S	R	Q	P	O	N	M	L	K	J	I	H	G	F	E
14	B	A	·	&	I	%	#	>	@	Z	Y	X	W	V	U	T	S	R	Q	P	O	N	M	L	K	J	I	H	G	F
15	C	B	A	·	&	I	%	#	>	@	Z	Y	X	W	V	U	T	S	R	Q	P	O	N	M	L	K	J	I	H	G
16	D	C	B	A	·	&	I	%	#	>	@	Z	Y	X	W	V	U	T	S	R	Q	P	O	N	M	L	K	J	I	H
17	E	D	C	B	A	·	&	I	%	#	>	@	Z	Y	X	W	V	U	T	S	R	Q	P	O	N	M	L	K	J	I
18	F	E	D	C	B	A	·	&	I	%	#	>	@	Z	Y	X	W	V	U	T	S	R	Q	P	O	N	M	L	K	J
19	G	F	E	D	C	B	A	·	&	I	%	#	>	@	Z	Y	X	W	V	U	T	S	R	Q	P	O	N	M	L	K
20	H	G	F	E	D	C	B	A	·	&	I	%	#	>	@	Z	Y	X	W	V	U	T	S	R	Q	P	O	N	M	L
21	I	H	G	F	E	D	C	B	A	·	&	I	%	#	>	@	Z	Y	X	W	V	U	T	S	R	Q	P	O	N	M
22	J	I	H	G	F	E	D	C	B	A	·	&	I	%	#	>	@	Z	Y	X	W	V	U	T	S	R	Q	P	O	N
23	K	J	I	H	G	F	E	D	C	B	A	·	&	I	%	#	>	@	Z	Y	X	W	V	U	T	S	R	Q	P	O
24	L	K	J	I	H	G	F	E	D	C	B	A	·	&	I	%	#	>	@	Z	Y	X	W	V	U	T	S	R	Q	P
25	M	L	K	J	I	H	G	F	E	D	C	B	A	·	&	I	%	#	>	@	Z	Y	X	W	V	U	T	S	R	Q
26	N	M	L	K	J	I	H	G	F	E	D	C	B	A	·	&	I	%	#	>	@	Z	Y	X	W	V	U	T	S	R
27	O	N	M	L	K	J	I	H	G	F	E	D	C	B	A	·	&	I	%	#	>	@	Z	Y	X	W	V	U	T	S
28	P	O	N	M	L	K	J	I	H	G	F	E	D	C	B	A	·	&	I	%	#	>	@	Z	Y	X	W	V	U	T
29	Q	P	O	N	M	L	K	J	I	H	G	F	E	D	C	B	A	·	&	I	%	#	>	@	Z	Y	X	W	V	U
30	R	Q	P	O	N	M	L	K	J	I	H	G	F	E	D	C	B	A	·	&	I	%	#	>	@	Z	Y	X	W	V
31	S	R	Q	P	O	N	M	L	K	J	I	H	G	F	E	D	C	B	A	·	&	I	%	#	>	@	Z	Y	X	W
32	T	S	R	Q	P	O	N	M	L	K	J	I	H	G	F	E	D	C	B	A	·	&	I	%	#	>	@	Z	Y	X
33	U	T	S	R	Q	P	O	N	M	L	K	J	I	H	G	F	E	D	C	B	A	·	&	I	%	#	>	@	Z	Y

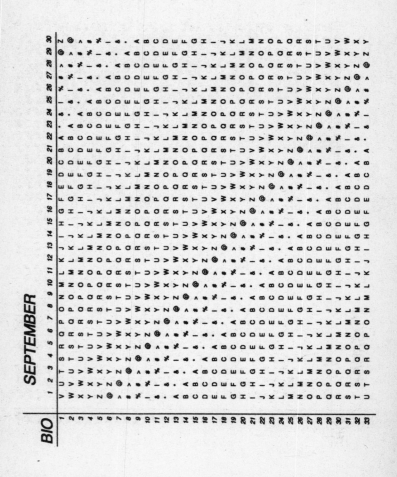

OCTOBER

BIO	1	2	3	4	5	6	7	8	9	10	11	12	13	14	15	16	17	18	19	20	21	22	23	24	25	26	27	28	29	30	31
1	Y	X	W	V	U	T	S	R	Q	P	O	N	M	L	K	J	I	H	G	F	E	D	C	B	A	•	&	I	%	#	>
2	Z	Y	X	W	V	U	T	S	R	Q	P	O	N	M	L	K	J	I	H	G	F	E	D	C	B	A	•	&	I	%	#
3	@	Z	Y	X	W	V	U	T	S	R	Q	P	O	N	M	L	K	J	I	H	G	F	E	D	C	B	A	•	&	I	%
4	>	@	Z	Y	X	W	V	U	T	S	R	Q	P	O	N	M	L	K	J	I	H	G	F	E	D	C	B	A	•	&	I
5	#	>	@	Z	Y	X	W	V	U	T	S	R	Q	P	O	N	M	L	K	J	I	H	G	F	E	D	C	B	A	•	&
6	%	#	>	@	Z	Y	X	W	V	U	T	S	R	Q	P	O	N	M	L	K	J	I	H	G	F	E	D	C	B	A	•
7	I	%	#	>	@	Z	Y	X	W	V	U	T	S	R	Q	P	O	N	M	L	K	J	I	H	G	F	E	D	C	B	A
8	&	I	%	#	>	@	Z	Y	X	W	V	U	T	S	R	Q	P	O	N	M	L	K	J	I	H	G	F	E	D	C	B
9	•	&	I	%	#	>	@	Z	Y	X	W	V	U	T	S	R	Q	P	O	N	M	L	K	J	I	H	G	F	E	D	C
10	A	•	&	I	%	#	>	@	Z	Y	X	W	V	U	T	S	R	Q	P	O	N	M	L	K	J	I	H	G	F	E	D
11	B	A	•	&	I	%	#	>	@	Z	Y	X	W	V	U	T	S	R	Q	P	O	N	M	L	K	J	I	H	G	F	E
12	C	B	A	•	&	I	%	#	>	@	Z	Y	X	W	V	U	T	S	R	Q	P	O	N	M	L	K	J	I	H	G	F
13	D	C	B	A	•	&	I	%	#	>	@	Z	Y	X	W	V	U	T	S	R	Q	P	O	N	M	L	K	J	I	H	G
14	E	D	C	B	A	•	&	I	%	#	>	@	Z	Y	X	W	V	U	T	S	R	Q	P	O	N	M	L	K	J	I	H
15	F	E	D	C	B	A	•	&	I	%	#	>	@	Z	Y	X	W	V	U	T	S	R	Q	P	O	N	M	L	K	J	I
16	G	F	E	D	C	B	A	•	&	I	%	#	>	@	Z	Y	X	W	V	U	T	S	R	Q	P	O	N	M	L	K	J
17	H	G	F	E	D	C	B	A	•	&	I	%	#	>	@	Z	Y	X	W	V	U	T	S	R	Q	P	O	N	M	L	K
18	I	H	G	F	E	D	C	B	A	•	&	I	%	#	>	@	Z	Y	X	W	V	U	T	S	R	Q	P	O	N	M	L
19	J	I	H	G	F	E	D	C	B	A	•	&	I	%	#	>	@	Z	Y	X	W	V	U	T	S	R	Q	P	O	N	M
20	K	J	I	H	G	F	E	D	C	B	A	•	&	I	%	#	>	@	Z	Y	X	W	V	U	T	S	R	Q	P	O	N
21	L	K	J	I	H	G	F	E	D	C	B	A	•	&	I	%	#	>	@	Z	Y	X	W	V	U	T	S	R	Q	P	O
22	M	L	K	J	I	H	G	F	E	D	C	B	A	•	&	I	%	#	>	@	Z	Y	X	W	V	U	T	S	R	Q	P
23	N	M	L	K	J	I	H	G	F	E	D	C	B	A	•	&	I	%	#	>	@	Z	Y	X	W	V	U	T	S	R	Q
24	O	N	M	L	K	J	I	H	G	F	E	D	C	B	A	•	&	I	%	#	>	@	Z	Y	X	W	V	U	T	S	R
25	P	O	N	M	L	K	J	I	H	G	F	E	D	C	B	A	•	&	I	%	#	>	@	Z	Y	X	W	V	U	T	S
26	Q	P	O	N	M	L	K	J	I	H	G	F	E	D	C	B	A	•	&	I	%	#	>	@	Z	Y	X	W	V	U	T
27	R	Q	P	O	N	M	L	K	J	I	H	G	F	E	D	C	B	A	•	&	I	%	#	>	@	Z	Y	X	W	V	U
28	S	R	Q	P	O	N	M	L	K	J	I	H	G	F	E	D	C	B	A	•	&	I	%	#	>	@	Z	Y	X	W	V
29	T	S	R	Q	P	O	N	M	L	K	J	I	H	G	F	E	D	C	B	A	•	&	I	%	#	>	@	Z	Y	X	W
30	U	T	S	R	Q	P	O	N	M	L	K	J	I	H	G	F	E	D	C	B	A	•	&	I	%	#	>	@	Z	Y	X
31	V	U	T	S	R	Q	P	O	N	M	L	K	J	I	H	G	F	E	D	C	B	A	•	&	I	%	#	>	@	Z	Y
32	W	V	U	T	S	R	Q	P	O	N	M	L	K	J	I	H	G	F	E	D	C	B	A	•	&	I	%	#	>	@	Z
33	X	W	V	U	T	S	R	Q	P	O	N	M	L	K	J	I	H	G	F	E	D	C	B	A	•	&	I	%	#	>	@

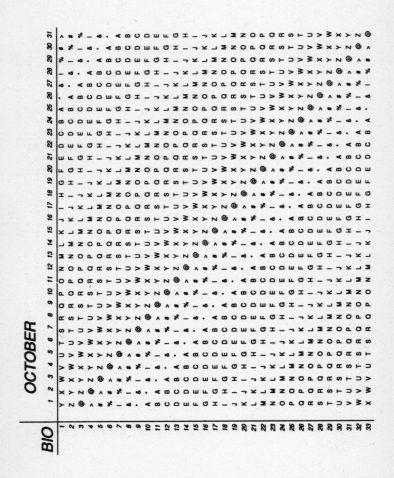

CHART B

INTELLECTUAL

NOVEMBER

BIO	1	2	3	4	5	6	7	8	9	10	11	12	13	14	15	16	17	18	19	20	21	22	23	24	25	26	27	28	29	30
1	@	Z	Y	X	W	V	U	T	S	R	Q	P	O	N	M	L	K	J	I	H	G	F	E	D	C	B	A	•	&	I
2	>	@	Z	Y	X	W	V	U	T	S	R	Q	P	O	N	M	L	K	J	I	H	G	F	E	D	C	B	A	•	&
3	#	>	@	Z	Y	X	W	V	U	T	S	R	Q	P	O	N	M	L	K	J	I	H	G	F	E	D	C	B	A	•
4	%	#	>	@	Z	Y	X	W	V	U	T	S	R	Q	P	O	N	M	L	K	J	I	H	G	F	E	D	C	B	A
5	I	%	#	>	@	Z	Y	X	W	V	U	T	S	R	Q	P	O	N	M	L	K	J	I	H	G	F	E	D	C	B
6	&	I	%	#	>	@	Z	Y	X	W	V	U	T	S	R	Q	P	O	N	M	L	K	J	I	H	G	F	E	D	C
7	•	&	I	%	#	>	@	Z	Y	X	W	V	U	T	S	R	Q	P	O	N	M	L	K	J	I	H	G	F	E	D
8	A	•	&	I	%	#	>	@	Z	Y	X	W	V	U	T	S	R	Q	P	O	N	M	L	K	J	I	H	G	F	E
9	B	A	•	&	I	%	#	>	@	Z	Y	X	W	V	U	T	S	R	Q	P	O	N	M	L	K	J	I	H	G	F
10	C	B	A	•	&	I	%	#	>	@	Z	Y	X	W	V	U	T	S	R	Q	P	O	N	M	L	K	J	I	H	G
11	D	C	B	A	•	&	I	%	#	>	@	Z	Y	X	W	V	U	T	S	R	Q	P	O	N	M	L	K	J	I	H
12	E	D	C	B	A	•	&	I	%	#	>	@	Z	Y	X	W	V	U	T	S	R	Q	P	O	N	M	L	K	J	I
13	F	E	D	C	B	A	•	&	I	%	#	>	@	Z	Y	X	W	V	U	T	S	R	Q	P	O	N	M	L	K	J
14	G	F	E	D	C	B	A	•	&	I	%	#	>	@	Z	Y	X	W	V	U	T	S	R	Q	P	O	N	M	L	K
15	H	G	F	E	D	C	B	A	•	&	I	%	#	>	@	Z	Y	X	W	V	U	T	S	R	Q	P	O	N	M	L
16	I	H	G	F	E	D	C	B	A	•	&	I	%	#	>	@	Z	Y	X	W	V	U	T	S	R	Q	P	O	N	M
17	J	I	H	G	F	E	D	C	B	A	•	&	I	%	#	>	@	Z	Y	X	W	V	U	T	S	R	Q	P	O	N
18	K	J	I	H	G	F	E	D	C	B	A	•	&	I	%	#	>	@	Z	Y	X	W	V	U	T	S	R	Q	P	O
19	L	K	J	I	H	G	F	E	D	C	B	A	•	&	I	%	#	>	@	Z	Y	X	W	V	U	T	S	R	Q	P
20	M	L	K	J	I	H	G	F	E	D	C	B	A	•	&	I	%	#	>	@	Z	Y	X	W	V	U	T	S	R	Q
21	N	M	L	K	J	I	H	G	F	E	D	C	B	A	•	&	I	%	#	>	@	Z	Y	X	W	V	U	T	S	R
22	O	N	M	L	K	J	I	H	G	F	E	D	C	B	A	•	&	I	%	#	>	@	Z	Y	X	W	V	U	T	S
23	P	O	N	M	L	K	J	I	H	G	F	E	D	C	B	A	•	&	I	%	#	>	@	Z	Y	X	W	V	U	T
24	Q	P	O	N	M	L	K	J	I	H	G	F	E	D	C	B	A	•	&	I	%	#	>	@	Z	Y	X	W	V	U
25	R	Q	P	O	N	M	L	K	J	I	H	G	F	E	D	C	B	A	•	&	I	%	#	>	@	Z	Y	X	W	V
26	S	R	Q	P	O	N	M	L	K	J	I	H	G	F	E	D	C	B	A	•	&	I	%	#	>	@	Z	Y	X	W
27	T	S	R	Q	P	O	N	M	L	K	J	I	H	G	F	E	D	C	B	A	•	&	I	%	#	>	@	Z	Y	X
28	U	T	S	R	Q	P	O	N	M	L	K	J	I	H	G	F	E	D	C	B	A	•	&	I	%	#	>	@	Z	Y
29	V	U	T	S	R	Q	P	O	N	M	L	K	J	I	H	G	F	E	D	C	B	A	•	&	I	%	#	>	@	Z
30	W	V	U	T	S	R	Q	P	O	N	M	L	K	J	I	H	G	F	E	D	C	B	A	•	&	I	%	#	>	@
31	X	W	V	U	T	S	R	Q	P	O	N	M	L	K	J	I	H	G	F	E	D	C	B	A	•	&	I	%	#	>
32	Y	X	W	V	U	T	S	R	Q	P	O	N	M	L	K	J	I	H	G	F	E	D	C	B	A	•	&	I	%	#
33	Z	Y	X	W	V	U	T	S	R	Q	P	O	N	M	L	K	J	I	H	G	F	E	D	C	B	A	•	&	I	%

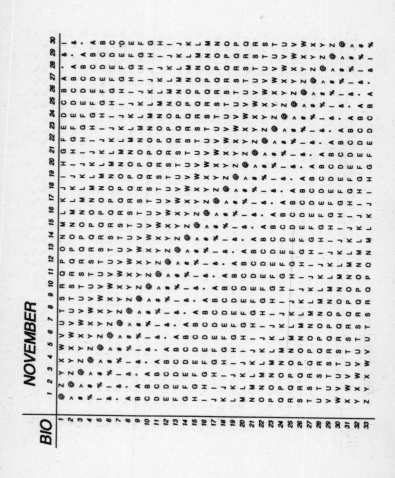

DECEMBER

BIO	1	2	3	4	5	6	7	8	9	10	11	12	13	14	15	16	17	18	19	20	21	22	23	24	25	26	27	28	29	30	31
1	%	#	>	@	Z	Y	X	W	V	U	T	S	R	Q	P	O	N	M	L	K	J	I	H	G	F	E	D	C	B	A	•
2	I	%	#	>	@	Z	Y	X	W	V	U	T	S	R	Q	P	O	N	M	L	K	J	I	H	G	F	E	D	C	B	A
3	&	I	%	#	>	@	Z	Y	X	W	V	U	T	S	R	Q	P	O	N	M	L	K	J	I	H	G	F	E	D	C	B
4	•	&	I	%	#	>	@	Z	Y	X	W	V	U	T	S	R	Q	P	O	N	M	L	K	J	I	H	G	F	E	D	C
5	A	•	&	I	%	#	>	@	Z	Y	X	W	V	U	T	S	R	Q	P	O	N	M	L	K	J	I	H	G	F	E	D
6	B	A	•	&	I	%	#	>	@	Z	Y	X	W	V	U	T	S	R	Q	P	O	N	M	L	K	J	I	H	G	F	E
7	C	B	A	•	&	I	%	#	>	@	Z	Y	X	W	V	U	T	S	R	Q	P	O	N	M	L	K	J	I	H	G	F
8	D	C	B	A	•	&	I	%	#	>	@	Z	Y	X	W	V	U	T	S	R	Q	P	O	N	M	L	K	J	I	H	G
9	E	D	C	B	A	•	&	I	%	#	>	@	Z	Y	X	W	V	U	T	S	R	Q	P	O	N	M	L	K	J	I	H
10	F	E	D	C	B	A	•	&	I	%	#	>	@	Z	Y	X	W	V	U	T	S	R	Q	P	O	N	M	L	K	J	I
11	G	F	E	D	C	B	A	•	&	I	%	#	>	@	Z	Y	X	W	V	U	T	S	R	Q	P	O	N	M	L	K	J
12	H	G	F	E	D	C	B	A	•	&	I	%	#	>	@	Z	Y	X	W	V	U	T	S	R	Q	P	O	N	M	L	K
13	I	H	G	F	E	D	C	B	A	•	&	I	%	#	>	@	Z	Y	X	W	V	U	T	S	R	Q	P	O	N	M	L
14	J	I	H	G	F	E	D	C	B	A	•	&	I	%	#	>	@	Z	Y	X	W	V	U	T	S	R	Q	P	O	N	M
15	K	J	I	H	G	F	E	D	C	B	A	•	&	I	%	#	>	@	Z	Y	X	W	V	U	T	S	R	Q	P	O	N
16	L	K	J	I	H	G	F	E	D	C	B	A	•	&	I	%	#	>	@	Z	Y	X	W	V	U	T	S	R	Q	P	O
17	M	L	K	J	I	H	G	F	E	D	C	B	A	•	&	I	%	#	>	@	Z	Y	X	W	V	U	T	S	R	Q	P
18	N	M	L	K	J	I	H	G	F	E	D	C	B	A	•	&	I	%	#	>	@	Z	Y	X	W	V	U	T	S	R	Q
19	O	N	M	L	K	J	I	H	G	F	E	D	C	B	A	•	&	I	%	#	>	@	Z	Y	X	W	V	U	T	S	R
20	P	O	N	M	L	K	J	I	H	G	F	E	D	C	B	A	•	&	I	%	#	>	@	Z	Y	X	W	V	U	T	S
21	Q	P	O	N	M	L	K	J	I	H	G	F	E	D	C	B	A	•	&	I	%	#	>	@	Z	Y	X	W	V	U	T
22	R	Q	P	O	N	M	L	K	J	I	H	G	F	E	D	C	B	A	•	&	I	%	#	>	@	Z	Y	X	W	V	U
23	S	R	Q	P	O	N	M	L	K	J	I	H	G	F	E	D	C	B	A	•	&	I	%	#	>	@	Z	Y	X	W	V
24	T	S	R	Q	P	O	N	M	L	K	J	I	H	G	F	E	D	C	B	A	•	&	I	%	#	>	@	Z	Y	X	W
25	U	T	S	R	Q	P	O	N	M	L	K	J	I	H	G	F	E	D	C	B	A	•	&	I	%	#	>	@	Z	Y	X
26	V	U	T	S	R	Q	P	O	N	M	L	K	J	I	H	G	F	E	D	C	B	A	•	&	I	%	#	>	@	Z	Y
27	W	V	U	T	S	R	Q	P	O	N	M	L	K	J	I	H	G	F	E	D	C	B	A	•	&	I	%	#	>	@	Z
28	X	W	V	U	T	S	R	Q	P	O	N	M	L	K	J	I	H	G	F	E	D	C	B	A	•	&	I	%	#	>	@
29	Y	X	W	V	U	T	S	R	Q	P	O	N	M	L	K	J	I	H	G	F	E	D	C	B	A	•	&	I	%	#	>
30	Z	Y	X	W	V	U	T	S	R	Q	P	O	N	M	L	K	J	I	H	G	F	E	D	C	B	A	•	&	I	%	#
31	@	Z	Y	X	W	V	U	T	S	R	Q	P	O	N	M	L	K	J	I	H	G	F	E	D	C	B	A	•	&	I	%
32	>	@	Z	Y	X	W	V	U	T	S	R	Q	P	O	N	M	L	K	J	I	H	G	F	E	D	C	B	A	•	&	I
33	#	>	@	Z	Y	X	W	V	U	T	S	R	Q	P	O	N	M	L	K	J	I	H	G	F	E	D	C	B	A	•	&

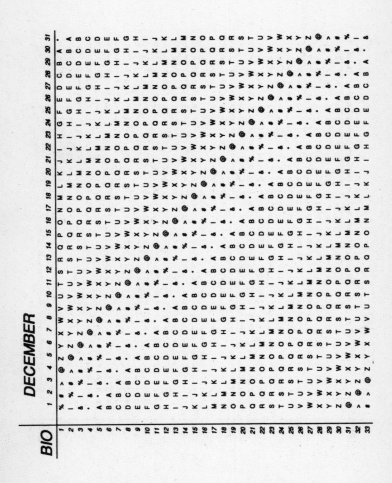